T0319850

Regulatory Failure and the Global Financial Crisis

Regulatory Failure and the Global Financial Crisis

An Australian Perspective

Edited by

Mohamed Ariff

Bond University, Australia

John Farrar

Bond University, Australia

Ahmed M. Khalid

Bond University, Australia

Edward Elgar

Cheltenham, UK • Northampton, MA, USA

Published by
Edward Elgar Publishing Limited
The Lypiatts
15 Lansdown Road
Cheltenham
Glos GL50 2JA
UK

Edward Elgar Publishing, Inc.
William Pratt House
9 Dewey Court
Northampton
Massachusetts 01060
USA

A catalogue record for this book
is available from the British Library

Library of Congress Control Number: 2011932939

ISBN 978 0 85793 532 8 (cased)

Typeset by Servis Filmsetting Ltd, Stockport, Cheshire
Printed and bound by MPG Books Group, UK

Contents

List of contributors   vii
Preface   xii

1   Timeline of crisis and introduction   1
    Mohamed Ariff and John Farrar

PART I   ORIGINS OF THE CRISIS AND IMPACT ON
           BANKING AND FINANCE

2   The origin of the global financial crisis: an alternative view   15
    Mohamed Ariff

3   Exchange rate changes and global trade imbalances: China as
    a major creditor country   36
    Ronald I. MacKinnon

4   Bank capital adequacy: where to now?   44
    Kevin Davis

PART II   CRISIS IMPACT ON ECONOMIC ACTIVITIES
            AND COSTS

5   Unemployment and the global financial crisis: who suffered
    most and why?   67
    Melisa Bond and Noel Gaston

6   The fiscal policy response to the global financial crisis: a
    critique   89
    Tony Makin

7   Cost consequences to the economy and finance   104
    Ahmed Khalid

v

PART III   GOVERNANCE AND REGULATORY ISSUES
           OF THE CRISIS

 8   Improving the governance of financial institutions   127
     John Farrar

 9   The work of IOSCO and the financial regulatory framework   139
     Jane Diplock

10   Balancing national and international interests   147
     Wayne Byres

PART IV   LESSONS FROM THE CRISIS

11   Executive remuneration in Australia   161
     Allan Fels

12   Regulatory lessons from the global financial crisis   168
     Jeffrey Carmichael

13   Should we stop the IMF from doing what it should not do? A
     radical idea   188
     Ross P. Buckley

14   When history is ignored, business black swans and the use and
     abuse of a notion   214
     Graeme Dean and Frank Clarke

Index   231

Contributors

Mohamed Ariff holds a Chair in Finance in Australia at the Bond University and a visiting endowed Chair at the University Putra Malaysia. His tertiary qualifications were from the universities of Singapore, Wisconsin-Madison and Queensland. He has held visiting professorship/fellowships in the universities of Boston, Evansville, Harvard, Melbourne, Tokyo and UCD Ireland. He worked in the industry including central banks before working at the National University of Singapore and Monash University. His McGraw-Hill book, *Investments*, by Bodie, Ariff, Rosa, Marcus and Kane is a top-selling investment book. His 104 articles in accounting, banking, economics and finance have appeared in ranked journals along with 14 research books. He served as an elected President of the prestigious Asian Finance Association during 2004–07. His main interests are in teaching and research in banking and finance. He is a series editor for Edward Elgar Publishing.

Melisa Bond is a member of staff in the Economics faculty at Bond University, Australia. Her research was concerned with estimating the effect of immigration on the labour market outcomes of Australians. She has co-authored the chapter with Noel Gaston.

Ross P. Buckley is a Professor of Law at the University of New South Wales, Australia, founding Series Editor of the *Global Trade Law Series* of Kluwer of The Hague; and Series Co-Editor of Kluwer's *International Banking and Finance Law Series*. He was the founding Executive Director of the Tim Fischer Centre for Global Trade & Finance at Bond University, and is currently a Senior Fellow of the Fischer Centre and of the Asian Institute of International Financial Law, University of Hong Kong. His principal area of interest is international financial regulation. He has authored or edited 11 books and over 90 articles and book chapters. He has consulted government departments in Australia, Indonesia, the US and Vietnam and served as an expert witness for the US Department of Justice.

Wayne Byres is Executive General Manager, Diversified Institutions Division within the Australian Prudential Regulation Authority. He is responsible for overseeing the prudential supervision of all of Australia's large and complex financial conglomerates, as well as most foreign-owned financial institutions operating in Australia. Mr Byres joined APRA at its establishment in 1998 and has held various senior supervision and policy roles within the organization. Prior to APRA, he spent 13 years with the Reserve Bank of Australia, in the supervision area, and also worked at the Bank of England. Mr Byres has also served on a number of domestic and international regulatory groups, including the Joint Forum and a number of Basel Committee on Banking Supervisions committees, task forces and working groups. He holds an Honours degree in Economics and a Master's degree in Applied Finance.

Jeffrey Carmichael is CEO of Promontory Financial Group Australasia. He was formerly Chairman of the Australian Prudential Regulation Authority, Professor of Finance at Bond University, and held senior positions with the Reserve Bank of Australia. He has served on a number of Government inquiries including the Wallis Inquiry and as Chairman of Tactical Global Management Pty Ltd, the Australian Financial Institutions Commission, the Queensland Office of Financial Supervision, and Starland Pty Ltd, and as a board member of Colly Cotton Ltd and the Queensland Treasury Corporation. Dr Carmichael has a PhD in Economics from Princeton University and holds an Officer of the Order of Australia (AO) for service to finance, education and the community.

Frank Clarke is Discipline of Accounting Emeritus Professor, University of Newcastle, Australia; he also holds a honorary professorship at The University of Sydney.

Kevin Davis has been Professor of Finance at The University of Melbourne since 1987 and is Research Director of the Australian Centre for Financial Studies. His research interests include financial markets and instruments, financial institutions management, financial regulation, financial engineering, corporate finance and valuation. He has published widely in these fields and is a regular contributor to public debate. In 2003 Kevin was appointed by the Federal Treasurer to prepare a report on 'Financial system guarantees', as background to the introduction of Australia's Financial Claims Scheme in 2008. He is a director of: SIRCA (the Securities Industry Research Centre of Asia-Pacific); Melbourne University Credit Union; Financial Management Association of Australia, and co-chair of the Australia–New Zealand Shadow Financial Regulatory Committee.

Graeme Dean is a Professor, Discipline of Accounting, Faculty of Economics and Business, at the University of Sydney, Australia.

Jane Diplock is the Chair of the Securities Commission, New Zealand

and has been Chair of the Executive Committee, IOSCO since 2001: she also chairs the Executive Committee. During her tenure, the Securities Commission has been given significant additional responsibilities and powers in enforcement, oversight and supervision. Jane holds other international roles: member of the Financial Crisis Advisory Group on financial reporting issues; member of the Steering Committee for the International Integrated Reporting Committee working to create a globally accepted accounting for sustainability. She is also a member of the Trans-Tasman Leadership Forum. Previously Jane has held various senior executive government positions in Australia and was appointed an officer of the General Division of the Order of Australia (AO) in January 2003.

John Farrar is Emeritus Professor of Law at Bond University, Australia, and Professor of Corporate Governance and Director of *The New Zealand Governance Centre*, University of Auckland. He was Dean of Law at: University of Canterbury (1985–88); Bond University (1993–96); and University of Waikato (2004–08). He earned his PhD and LLD respectively from the Universities of Bristol and London. He is the author of a number of books and papers on Company and Commercial Law and Corporate Governance. He has also been active in law reform in the United Kingdom, New Zealand and Australia, and was a member of the Legislation Advisory Committee of New Zealand (2004–08). In 2008 he was made an Honorary Life Member of the Australian Law Teachers Association for services to legal education in Australia and New Zealand.

Allan Fels AO is Dean of the Australia and New Zealand School of Government (ANZSOG) and is concurrently Professor in the Faculty of Economics and Business at Monash University, and a Professorial Fellow in Political Science at the University of Melbourne, Australia. He is a fellow of the Academy of Social Science of Australia. He is or has recently been a member of a number of advisory boards to the Australian Government. Fels was Chairman of the Australian Competition and Consumer Commission (ACCC) (1995–2003); the Trade Practices Commission (1991–95); and the Prices Surveillance Authority (1989–92). He was co-chair of the OECD Trade and Competition Committee (1996–2003). Professor Fels was Director of the Graduate School of Management, and Professor of Administration at Monash University (1984–91). He was awarded the Order of Australia, AO, in 2001.

Noel Gaston is a Professor of Economics and the Director of the Globalisation and Development Centre at Bond University, Australia. After his doctorate at Cornell University, he worked at Tulane University in the United States. He has held visiting appointments at Osaka

University, the University of Tokyo and the Cabinet Office in Japan; Seoul National University in South Korea; the University of Konstanz and the University of Göttingen in Germany; as well as the Productivity Commission, Australia. He has published more than 80 articles and has co-authored two books. The academic area in which he has achieved most recognition is for research on various aspects of globalization and labour markets.

Ahmed Khalid is Professor of Economics and Finance at the Bond University, Australia, and holds a PhD in economics from Johns Hopkins. He worked at the National University of Singapore and USAID (Pakistan). His interests are in applied macro, monetary economics, econometrics, international finance and financial sector reforms. His publications include three books, and internationally refereed articles, consultancy/project reports. He was a visitor at the Washington–Lee University, Limberg Institute of Financial Economics, World Bank, LUMS (Pakistan), and PIDE Pakistan. He has consulted for the Asian Development Bank, UNDP, SEANZA, the CitiGroup, and the Haans Seidel Foundation.

Ronald I. MacKinnon is the William D. Eberle Professor of International Economics at Stanford University, USA, where he has taught since 1961. His fields of specialization are international economics and development finance, while his recent research/consulting interest is on China. He has been awarded honorary professorships in five Chinese universities. His books have been translated into several European and Asian languages: a few examples are *Money and Capital in Economic Development* (1973), *Money in International Exchange: The Convertible-Currency System* (1979), *The Order of Economic Liberalization: Exchange Rates under the East Asian Dollar Standard: Living with Conflicted Virtue* (2005). Professor McKinnon has been a consultant to central banks and finance ministries the world over, including international agencies such as the World Bank and International Monetary Fund.

Tony Makin is Professor of Economics at the Griffith University, Australia. Before joining Griffith, he was International Consultant Economist with the International Monetary Fund, is a member of AUSPECC, and has represented Australia at meetings of the structural issues group of the Pacific Economic Co-operation Council. He has previously lectured at the University of Canberra and University of Queensland, and has served in the federal departments of Finance, Foreign Affairs and Trade, The Treasury and Prime Minister and the Cabinet. He obtained his PhD from the Australian National University, has published many journal articles and book chapters on international monetary and financial issues, and is the author of books on: *Global Imbalances, Exchange Rates, and Stabilization Policy*; *Global Finance and the Macroeconomy*; and *International Macroeconomics*.

Preface

As we entered the third year, 2010, of the Global Financial Crisis, an increasing number of books had appeared with fantastic insights on this epoch-making banking-cum-financial crisis. 'Do we need another book on this subject?' is a relevant question the authors of this book should answer. Each of the major books to date sheds light on this crisis from a personalized focus of a writer's particular perspective. For example, one of the earliest writers, Gillian Tett, did an anthropological diagnosis of a cult of invincibility among the derivative specialists in the investment banking circle, a feeling of originality that led to unfettered innovations that spawned one dangerous, yet untested, linked-financial product originally named BISTRO, which became the CDO (collateralized debt obligation). That invention is the link as to why the crisis spread to the world. Joseph Stiglitz's book (2009) examines the crisis as a failure of government to regulate the freewheeling financial markets that produced huge incomes for the major titans of the New York and London firms under a epoch of light-touch regulatory framework, engineered by lobbyists.

Our book has a different objective. It arose from a multi-profession scrutiny in Australia as to why this event emerged, how it developed into a major world crisis, and what lessons are being learned from it by the G20 nations and individual governments busy putting a work-in-progress to save the world from a repeat of the same. We had practising professionals in regulatory organizations such as central banks, prudential institutions, securities commissions used to grappling with new regulations: practising investment managers, chief economists and fair-trade people, all of whom looked at the ways the industry was impacted. We had very eminent scholars of the like of Ronald MacKinnon of Stanford University and many others from major research universities. All these contributors described their research on a common theme of the crisis to bring a multi-dimensional perspective on the event still unfolding in different forms in some economies as we enter the second decade of the new century.

This effort to make available a multi-dimensional industry-relevant book was made possible by very generous financial support from Bond University with more contributions in some forms from the following universities: Auckland, New South Wales and Sydney, as well as Stanford

(USA) and the Australian National University. The editors wish to record their gratitude to Bond University, for letting us engage in a major current issue debate of this century. Lastly, we thank all the contributors to the book for an excellent collaboration resulting in this book.

The book editors appreciate the efficient processing of the manuscript through its blind review process and pre-production process. In particular, this book benefited from the excellent editorial services of Jo Betteridge and Nicolas Wilson.

The editors record their sincere appreciation to the publisher for encouraging the project to hold a symposium on the GFC, and the subsequent production of this book.

Mohamed Ariff, John Farrar and Ahmed Khalid
Bond University, Gold Coast, Australia: November 2011

1. Timeline of crisis and introduction

Mohamed Ariff and John Farrar

1.1 INTRODUCTION

The word 'global' appeared in the Australian financial press discussions of what was then described as the *international* financial crisis in 2008. The world has since come to accept the term 'Global Financial Crisis' (GFC). It is everybody's knowledge that the GFC mutated during April 2007 and September 2008 to become the world's most virulent banking/financial crisis to occur in 80 years. The GFC has ravaged the world's economies, shaved world income by some US$800 billion in 2008, slowed growth considerably in the three years since 2008, and hollowed out or killed some of the major financial players, not just in the USA and the UK, but also around the world. A lot has been written about this crisis. Do we need another book on this topic?

This book is a prognosis of the crisis as analysed by leading scholars and professionals in accounting, banking, economics, finance, law and regulation. This book also has a contribution by Ronald MacKinnon, a world-renowned scholar associated with the influential idea of financial suppression that led to financial liberalization and sequencing policy reforms in the 1980s across the developing countries. The book examines the subject from a broad perspective to encourage lessons to be learned from many dimensions and actions to be taken to avoid the excesses of the financial/banking markets during the past 15 years to 2009.

This book traces the origins of the crisis, examines the impacts on economies, and how so many titans of the financial world collapsed, while also identifying a number of lessons for re-governing/regulating the promised new world financial framework as being fashioned by the G20 nations, still hard at work at this task as this book goes to press. This book is the product of a carefully reviewed compilation of writings of contributors who presented their ideas and analyses at a public meeting in Sydney on 9 April 2010 before revising their contributions for the present volume. The aim of the book is thus to present a convincing in-depth understanding of how the crisis originated in April 2007 in the USA – soon also in the UK – and thereafter spread to the rest of the world.

From about the year 1994, the UK and the US regulators had succumbed to powerful banking lobbies that were given credibility by the writings and speeches of prominent thinkers that fostered a false idea. This lobby helped to nurture hugely deregulated legal environments in the UK and USA, resulting in the greatest degree of financial-cum-banking deregulation in place by 2004. This idea was premised on a false notion that markets could correct themselves through self-regulation! With so much freedom, financial firms in those legal regimes made loans with little regard for credit-worthiness of borrowers in an environment of low interest rates hovering around 1 to 2 per cent per annum that deprived savers of incentives to save and importantly lowered investor vigilance on high-return investment products.

The UK's Gordon Brown espoused the same philosophy of what he called 'light-touch regulation'. His aim was to further foster and retain the recently-freed British pound as a world currency and to promote London as the world's greatest financial centre. Evidence available in 2010 suggests that the great titans of the world of finance controlling Wall Street and the City of London knew that debtors would default, after gouging unprecedented amounts of easy credits during 1994–2004, once interest rates went up, as they did in June 2004 to September 2006 with upward revisions by the US Federal Reserve. The credit splurge over 1994–2004 led to a huge liquidity build-up, fuelling bubbles in financial markets, accompanied by a bulge in mortgages that led to the sub-prime lending scandal in the USA.

Across the world, the financial sectors of several emerging new economies of the world had been deregulated by the 1990s on the urging of the World Bank and the IMF who advocated and carefully tutored the emerging economies to deregulate currency and capital controls. This global financial liberalization was justified by new ideas of the need for financial liberalization as espoused by academic thinkers (MacKinnon, Shaw, Fry) who were concerned about lack of capital for growth in emerging economies, so reforms brought about a high degree of deregulation of emerging economies. This helped knit the world's financial markets for currencies, bonds and shares of those emerging economies to those of New York and London. The world benefited from capital flows from developed nations, not from exchange rate reforms, which periodically worked to the detriment of smaller economies exposed to the vagaries of capital flows, be they from banks, portfolio investments, or as foreign direct investments.

The contagion from the crisis spread more to those economies which had (i) a high degree of financial deregulation and (ii) economic relationships with the West. The result was that the crisis spread rapidly to some

60 economies with those characteristics when the world markets for borrowing collapsed in September 2008. This pre-existing condition in emerging economies helped to spread the crisis from just a few developed economies to the rest of the world from September 2008 onward. For example, China, with 62 per cent of her trade going to USA/Mexico, while also holding huge amounts of US-dollar-based securities for servicing her world trade, felt the crisis impact. Unlike the democracies of the world, the freedom to make policy changes without any public discussion helped the leaders of China to pump the world's largest amount of stimulus package to regain and recover the growth path. Not so elsewhere, where consensus-building for resource mobilization took more time.

1.2 WHY DID THIS CRISIS OCCUR?

Why did this crisis happen? How did it spread to the rest of the world? What were the impacts and costs of the crisis? What were the failings of regulations and governance? Are there lessons to be learned from the crisis? These are the questions that the contributors to this book address in the 13 ensuing chapters. Before providing a summary of the contributions of the book, the reader is referred to a catalogue of events on how the crisis started in April 2007 and then spread to the rest of the world (Figure 1.1).

The first outward sign of trouble in the financial sector began with the mortgage firms failing in the major economies, notably in the USA and the UK. As is seen from the timeline of events in Figure 1.1, the first victims were the investors in New Century Finance, a large mortgage firm that went bankrupt in April 2007, some months *after* interest rates started to increase because Ben Bernanke of the US Federal Reserve Bank upped cash rates to cool the then high-growth US economy. The US economy had been growing due to the substantial credit splurge between 1994–2006 created by deregulation of bank-like firms, allowing them to merge freely and also to create more credit by taking mortgages off the accounting book through untested new linked-products with the false promise of high return in safe investment! When this weakness was noted by market participants, players withdrew their investments. Between April 2007 and July 2008 more financial firms, including those considered solid, started to go bust. Ordinary depositors lined up at banks to withdraw their savings across the world. It appeared then that the crisis came from sub-prime loans going bad: is this true?

With foreclosures of some 400000 properties in the USA, mortgage repayments to the banks diminished substantially. Under the US property laws, borrowers just had to abandon the property with no legal obligation

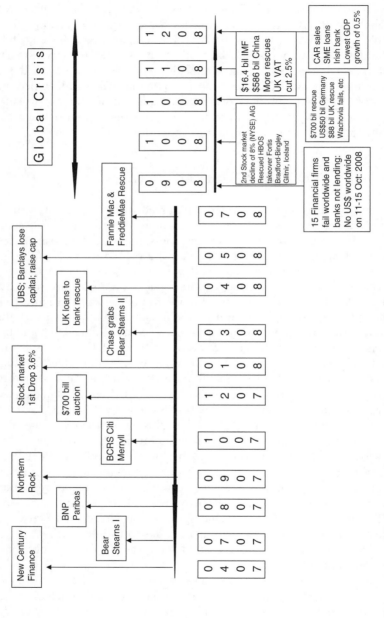

Figure 1.1   Global financial crisis: major events on a timeline

to service the loan in what is termed no-recourse loans! Ginnie Mae and Fannie Mae were broke. The insurance titan AIG insured the risk of the mortgage-backed securities that the banks had been selling since 1994, the start of the property bubble, and that great name became another victim of the crisis. Merrill-Lynch went bust when stock and bond market prices tumbled as the interest rates increased: Bank of America bought Merrill for a pittance. Bank stock prices plunged to about 20 per cent of prices in 2006.

Herein lies the actual origin and the *real* reason why financial firms went bust in spectacular fashion. All kinds of lenders and the high street banks were unable to service the customers who had bought a special form of a derivative, a linked product, the so-called CDO (collateralized debt obligations insured by the likes of AIG), which are financial instruments described by Warren Buffet as the *financial weapons of mass destruction.*

These CDOs amounting to US$12 000 billion in 2006, that is 75 per cent of the real US economy, were sold to customers around the world by the Wall Street banks with offices in New York and London. These financial firms removed chunks of mortgages from their accounting books by selling them to investors expecting high returns as if these were safe investments. The rating agencies joined in to quality-rate these instruments as safe, with an A-rating! The result was an inside job of major banks reaping huge fees in such deals while ignoring the likely fallout when interest rates would go up. At the US Senate hearing in June 2010, Goldstein of Goldman Sachs admitted that his firm made money by selling bets on such an eventuality.

About 25 per cent of these CDOs were bought back by the banks at a discount of 25 to 45 per cent in 2006–07. A simple calculation will show that this amount of discount is a loss to the banks and must have depleted the wafer-thin regulatory equity capital of US banks many times over: regulations set it at 2.5 per cent of total assets as core capital. The CDO-led hollowing of finance firms is the *real* origin of the crisis. Information that was not in the public domain before the crisis, since this market was not a public market with routine disclosures, is now forthcoming in 2010. That reveals that the real reason for creating huge capital losses of major financial firms was the return of the CDOs to the issuers after the sub-prime failure.

It appears that the top end of Wall Street knew this could happen, but felt safe in the often-proven belief, by reference to history, that the governments would rescue the banks: the bigger the banks, the higher the likelihood of such rescue. Letting the big banks go bankrupt would lead to, for example, another world depression of the kind our forefathers experienced in 1929–33 when banks were allowed to fail and money was made expensive at the time of the then financial crisis by the central banks not loosening credits.

As more and more financial firms failed across the world in the next 15 months from April 2007, the banks retreated to holding tightly on to their own cash, as well as the cash provided by central bank rescue packages, in order to preserve banking liquidity. Naturally the banks refused to lend to other banks, later also to normal non-bank firms, thus the essential *payment system* of modern economies collapsed. It is the latter action that actually led to signs of failure in the real sector: example, General Motors and Chrysler. That collective action by banks resulted in a worldwide blackout of cash in September 2008. Nobody could borrow any money! Normally about US$400 to US$800 billion could be raised easily at a time. This led to an ever greater number of financial firms (and later, real sector firms) going bankrupt from September 2008. What started as a regulatory-forgiveness-based financial crisis in developed nations metamorphosed into the Global Financial Crisis in that month.

1.3   ORGANIZATION AND CONTRIBUTIONS OF THE BOOK

To aid in the diagnosis of the crisis, the chapters of the book are grouped into four parts. The reader will find in Part I a discussion of the crisis as it unfolded and how the financial institutions responded as best as they could. Part II traces the impact on the economy. Given the serious impact on employment, we begin this part by discussing how unemployment increased around the world. The governance and regulatory framework are discussed in Part III. We focus on the failure of governance and the general lack of rules of prudence to govern financial activities, including excessive pay to top executives. In Part IV, the reader will find a set of lessons to be learned from the crisis.

1.3.1   Origin and Impact on Banking Finance

The chapters in Part I provide a clear description of how the GFC originated in two major economies, and then spread through to the rest of the world to some 60 nations. In Chapter 2 the reader is shown evidence that debunks the popular view that the origin of the crisis was sub-prime lending made worse by the sudden increases in interest rates in June 2004 onward. The contribution by Mohamed Ariff traces the origin of the crisis to the design of exotic derivatives traded in private markets, and sold to private parties across the world with promise of high returns at a time of historically depressed interest rates worldwide. This chapter argues that the crisis happened because of massive deregulation of the financial sectors that permitted (i) financial firms to merge with savings banks, which made savings banks highly risky with high-risk products and (ii) banks to experiment with new financial products with unknown system-wide impact, while (iii) investor amnesia in search for high returns resulted in the failure of investors to discipline financial firms engaging in financial alchemy.

Investors were reeling with such low incomes from their investments in financial markets that they bought the bankers' promises of high and safe returns through *linked* banking products, which promised higher returns than those that are available on savings accounts. These linked banking products would not have existed in the form of private trades with no information, if, first, they were not ranked as safe by rating companies and second, regulators had not created light-touch, deregulated financial sectors in the UK and the USA. So, it is arguable that the failure to maintain significant key regulations such as Glass–Steagall Act provisions, failure to require sufficient reserves and failure to approve highly risky bets-based banking products being sold to customers are the very reasons for the emergence of the crisis.

The eminent scholar and thinker, Ronald MacKinnon adds his contribution to this debate by dubbing China as a new major immature creditor country still learning how to act responsibly to highlight how China's massive deposit of money in the US markets is partly to blame for the credit splurge. There is a continuing discussion around the world's capitals, except in Beijing, that the imbalances created by China's method of managing its currency and the world's demand for cheap manufactured goods are not sustainable. Serious thinkers such as Krugman, Stiglitz, Buffett, King and others have spoken loudly about the harm to the world economy if significant countries create huge imbalances such as is the case of trade surpluses in favour of a few countries seeking export-led growth.

Bill Evans, a leading practising economist in Australia's banking sector, revealed in his speech in Sydney, hard facts about how the crisis has increased the cost of intermediation for average Australian banks. He provided evidence presented at the public discussion on 9 April 2010 on how the structure of pricing for money in the banking sector has changed.* The cost of borrowing in terms of spread in buy–sell has gone up threefold for Australian banks to secure funds. Reports in late 2010 indicate that banks' return on equity for that year has fallen from 18 per cent to 15 per cent due to this and the banking spread has increased modestly after the crisis.

In Chapter 4 Kevin Davis suggests that the post-crisis regulatory target will be to increase the requirements for capital adequacy of all deposit-taking institutions, a reality now with CAMEL III announced in August 2010. The big banks will have to have another class of bank capital providers who will be called upon to supply more capital when a bank is in need of liquidity, an idea under active consultation within the G20 nations. Believe it or not: for now, governments have avowed that they will not rescue insolvent banks in future crises. The Bank for International Settlement has come up with voluntary regulatory changes to be slowly eased in from 2013 to 2019 to achieve these ideals being discussed as the book goes to print.

1.3.2   Economic and Cost Impacts of the Crisis

Almost three years after the crisis, a key economic damage has been noted as the inability of major economies to create jobs for the average workers. The issue here is the impact of the crisis on employment. In a joint chapter with Melisa Bond, Noel Gaston provides a substantial discussion on the winners and losers of labour participation. While the crisis had made things worse for some countries such as the USA, some others with resources have spent money – the so-called stimulus spending – to reverse the impact on employment. Australia's new labor government had a huge pot of money as budget surplus in 2007 left by the outgoing coalition government. This money came in handy to spend as a huge stimulus to regain employment. The incoming labor treasurer took credit as a great economic magician creating some 600000 jobs on the back of the resources-boom-led demand for Australia's resources by spending the large stimulus. China spent the world's largest amount of stimulus money to regain growth and employment. We think that the ability of firms to create jobs will remain a major economic issue of the next decade long after the crisis has abated, given the unbalanced growth strategy of some major countries.

Tony Makin makes an analysis of the fiscal impacts of the crisis on how governments respond in handling the budget issues. His insightful comments, supported by sound theories and observations, predict the dilemma faced by policy-makers to address recovery. While prudent policy dictates that the long-run welfare is assured by restraining expenditure, the short-run objective of politicians used to short-term election objectives is to stimulate economic activities first to regain employment and second to reduce welfare expenditures if more people become unemployed from budget trimming. This piece is a significant contribution to the debate on policy correctness and policy rightness.

The cost to all economic agents has been substantial in this crisis and this needs to be documented. Ahmed Khalid's chapter is an excellent dialogue on this issue. While the aggregate impacts on the GDP of countries are easy to illustrate, it is difficult to examine costs at other levels of the economy. He documents such issues as decline in net repatriation of residents of countries with foreign workers. The impact on trade, on emerging economies, the costs of stimulus packages and the costs of rescue packages are important cost items on which this chapter provides facts to the reader.

1.3.3 Governance and Regulation

In a broad sense, the GFC can be characterized as a massive failure of governance of financial firms in major economies. John Farrar identifies key issues of the GFC as regulatory failures. He discusses the relevance of corporate governance, particularly the governance of financial institutions. He focuses on key government failures and then discusses the redefinition of the regulated state and how efforts in those directions can improve the governance of financial institutions.

Capital market reform is on top of the agenda of IOSCO. Jane Diplock provides some significant insights into the new regulatory processes that are needed to avoid a future repeat of crises. Her argument is that modern finance corporations are interlinked just as animal species are interrelated in a natural environment. The consequence of what the financial market players do by way of innovations and business actions may have significantly different effects on an economy from the impact on, say, the banking sector. The increased interrelationship of the economy on financial actions is little understood, and so there is a need for new thinking on how to bring in that knowledge of the system-wide impact of one actor on the whole financial sector and the economy. IOSCO has tasked itself to look at this aspect to ensure financial stability, which is studied from a broader perspective than from the narrow perspective of a single sector such as is the case when a regulatory body, for example, a prudential regulator, examines regulations on what is good for banking and its customers, ignoring the system-wide impacts.

The contribution of another senior regulator, Wayne Byrnes of the Australian Prudential Regulation Authority (APRA) is on the subject of how each country balances its own interests against those of international interests. It is a lesson on policy objective-setting as well as the thorny road to ensure international consensus on what is good for the world as a whole in financial regulations. The message that comes from these three contributors is that governance is an important issue, and that one needs to have a holistic aim of what regulations the overall economy needs while not forgetting the private interest of nations that is in conflict with regulations that will be good for the world.

1.3.4   Lessons Learned?

The last three contributions of mostly practising economists are on the subject of lessons to be learned from this opening crisis of the twenty-first century. One key governance issue is executive compensation as in financial and real sector firms, which have been excessively high, often irrespective of performance. Allan Fels brings his in-depth knowledge of this topic to the readers. He examines the steps, sometimes hesitant ones, taken by governments to control this behaviour. The progress being made on this front is addressed by him.

Jeffrey Carmichael discusses the major lessons learned for regulatory reforms from this crisis. He is ably qualified as a noted academic, senior regulator and now CEO of an investment firm to draw key lessons from this crisis. At a narrower level, the inadequacy of international institutions to perform their required tasks is highlighted by Ross Buckley. He takes on a radical idea of closing down international institutions that are failing to deliver outcomes enshrined in their constitutions. According to him, the IMF should be closed down.

In a joint chapter on how the rules of accounting have been changing with pressure groups demanding certain directions, Graham Dean and Frank Clarke provide a critical exposé of what has gone wrong on this regulation-setting front. This chapter provides insights on how regulatory capture can also occur in professions, in this case accounting-rule-setting professions. Wrong-footed standards are often the result of special interests pushing for specific standards, which has serious deterimental long-run consequences.

1.4   COMMENT

The ideas expressed in this book are from careful observations of what has transpired during the period April 2007 to April 2010. Many more discussions on how to reform – a better word is refine or re-govern – the rules of actions for the financial sectors of the world are still ongoing, and are unfinished business at the time this book goes to print. What emerges as a clear fact is that the GFC happened because US- and UK-based lobbies persuaded governments to allow financial institutions to have a much freer hand in their business activities based on the fallacy that self-regulation would suffice, so existing safety-first regulations were taken off. Second, new untested ideas hoisted on to the financial sectors could have unintended effects if the system-wide impact is not taken into account. If the public are enticed to place bank deposits with a bet on something else (linked products) – and the prudential regulators do not see this as wrong-footed – as the only way to obtain decent returns on life savings, then this would, and actually did, have a disastrous impact on the system when the bets came off from April 2007!

As Jane Diplock, an internationally-savvy regulator, has persuasively argued, the system-wide impact of how the financial market players' actions in a self-regulated environment affect the world economies in a *symbiotic* manner was still little understood in the 1990s as much as in 2010. A challenge to the G20 nations is to come up with what is good for the world, not just for some countries. This must be similar in spirit to how the Bretton Woods agreement was fashioned in 1946 with the aim to build a better world. Of course, after 30 years of excellent progress, the Bretton Woods institutions have become mammoths unable to achieve what they set out to do because of regulatory capture. The G20 nations and the advisors to that body have to set aside narrow interests of some countries and work for a better financial world than what we have come to witness since the breakdown of the Bretton Woods in August 1973.

While the old adage that regulators know how to fight the previous fire may be true, it would be wise to move regulations forward to fashion rules that at least prevent similar aspects of the current crisis from reoccurring. The world is awaiting the completion of the work-in-progress on this front from the lessons learned.

NOTE

*   Note from editors: The paper presented by Bill Evans is not included in this book. This is entirely due to the decision of the editors not to await for Bill to come back from his involvement in another project, which got in the way of timely submission of his contribution to this book. However, his comment, summarised briefly here, is valid, and policy changes are taking place in Australia in line with the hard facts as pointed out by him on how the GFC affected the industry.

PART I

Origins of the crisis and impact on banking
and finance

2. The origin of the global financial crisis: an alternative view

Mohamed Ariff

> I will do my utmost to spur the risk takers to do more . . .
> Gordon Brown, Chancellor of the Exchequer, 2001, Chatham House Lecture

2.1 INTRODUCTION

Massive risk-taking behaviour on the part of financial market participants was squarely behind this century's opening financial crisis and the ensuing economic turmoil that reduced the 2007–08 world GDP with predictable consequences. With massive interventions of central banks' lending money, the liquidity trap that occurred in August–September 2008, when no money was available for borrowing, was eased so that the world could stabilize credit availability soon afterwards to meet consumption and production demands for funds. With government treasuries no-holds-barred free (stimulus) spending amounting to some 6 per cent of domestic income in 60 countries or US$3600 billion, the world economy has crawled along since 2009 to grow at an anaemic rate of about 2.2 per cent after having fallen from the growth trend of 4.6 per cent before the crisis started in 2007.

The asset bubble that built in many countries over 1994 and 2006 has been burst, with real estate and security prices having corrected to levels far below what these were at the height of the bubbles grown on the back of the freewheeling liquidity splurge over several years. At the time of writing, the verdict is still not out as to whether the worst of the fears for sufficiently rapid economic recovery to reverse record unemployment and sovereign debt could be reversed in 2011. The future holds a lot of uncertainty for the orderly development of the world's developed and developing countries.

While these general facts are well known to informed readers, what is less clear is what caused the crisis (Global Financial Crisis, GFC). The mass media have a view squarely in line with what the triumvirate of politicians, bankers and financial market players are promoting. That view is:

the Alan Greenspan era made returns on money very low; banks enticed worthless borrowers to buy properties and other assets; when Bernanke, the incoming Fed chairman, upped interest rates during a short span of two years, these asset holders disgorged or abandoned the assets, which led to losses to the banks; banks were about to go down, and the central banks rescued them! A simple, plausible explanation, but that is not how it happened. As this view of sub-prime lending as the origin of the crisis is widely promoted, so it seems to have sunk into the public mind-set. However, the analyses of the crisis as reported in more serious studies suggest a more complex origin of the crisis. This chapter examines this alternative, less reported sequence of events that led to the most calamitous loss of income, employment and the greatest debt burden in history.

The rest of the chapter is organized as follows. Section 2.2 is a brief but essential statement about what we know, and what we do not know about financial system stability so as to provide the less publicized aspects of the banking sector, the central actor in this crisis. In section 2.3 we provide three sets of factors that have been observed during the pre-crisis years. These are termed the precursor conditions as *facilitating* the crisis to erupt. The consequences of the crisis are well-known, but section 2.4 records a short summary on this topic to highlight the natural consequences predictable as the financial sector went into siege mode and then shut funds off to consumers and producers, the ordinary people and corporations. The consequences of the crisis are discussed in the final section.

2.2   WHAT WE KNOW AND DO NOT KNOW ABOUT THE FINANCIAL SECTOR

Financial crises have been a very recurrent event in human societies. The famous works of the late Kindleberger (2005 [1978]) documented how panics and manias developed so frequently over the previous three centuries. Another famous study by Minsky (1974) postulates that all financial crises originate from easy credit or too much liquidity created as credits by easy bank credit policy and/or monetary policy, which help to secure the participation of the masses in high-risk financial activities. This is exactly what happened during the GFC, as will be described in a later section. The crisis is portrayed in Figure 2.1 (see details in Figure 1.1, in Chapter 1).

The four phases of the crisis can be described as the result of investor panic that resulted in a large number of financial firms going bankrupt over a six-month period from April 2007 starting from the US, then Holland, then the UK, then Germany, France and then in the rest of the world. The financial systems of major economies came to a standstill,

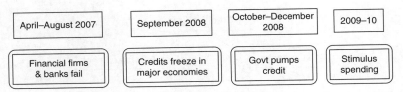

Figure 2.1   The sequence of events in the global financial crisis

unable to provide credits; that is, the financial sector's intermediation function failed! To protect the investing public, the governments of major countries propped up some financial firms and banks by providing (a) liquidity credits and (b) capital later. Finally, as contagion spread to the real sector when banks could not provide credits for production, output of the real economy declined fast in 2008. On the advice of the IMF, governments spent an equivalent of 6 per cent of GDP to stimulate economic activities.

While a crisis can be analysed *ex post*, its advent is always unforeseen because it is not possible to identify the new force(s) – Minsky calls it *displacement* – at work in each subsequent crisis nor how *panics* build up, which derails the financial system. While Holland's Tulip Mania of 1637 was driven by investors buying the false promise of huge profits of a tulip-selling firm, the new displacement factor in that event was the lack of corporate laws to prevent speculators promoting outlandish claims of profits and selling it to the public, so the masses believed that untold riches could be earned by selling Dutch tulips to the world.[1] The GFC had a Dutch tulip called the collateralized debt obligation (CDO), about US$12 trillion of which were sold around the world with a promise of high returns. The 1885 corporate monopoly build-up in the US real sector to control prices was the result of a lack of laws on anti-competitive behaviour of corporations using combinations to increase profits of basic goods. Thus, each crisis occurs because, prior to the crisis, there is a build-up of behaviour that is new, *and* often there is no regulation to guide or control or prevent that risky behaviour.

In this case, the good regulations that were around were eased off in favour of self-regulation. The literature on the prognosis of crisis appears to suggest the following behaviour of financial firms and investors in a typical financial crisis: see Figure 2.2. Most financial crises start with a period of *credit splurge* created mostly by banks (other financial firms such as parallel banks also create credits). Minsky is adamant that all crises start with banks creating too much credit, which leads to too much leverage being taken by the financial sector, households, firms and governments. An event occurs that displaces the tranquillity of the all-is-well

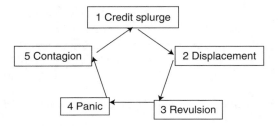

Figure 2.2   The behaviour of corporations and investors in a crisis

feeling with assets already priced too high and organizations with too much leverage: he calls this *displacement*. Very quickly, as happened between April and August 2007, *revulsion* sets in among investors, which leads to panic selling of assets, which constitutes the crisis. In most cases, other writers have observed a *contagion* spreading from the source of the crisis to others, as happened from five major economies to some 55 other economies in 2008–09. We like to call this behaviour the Pentagon of Financial Crisis to describe the behaviour that constitutes the crisis time and again. Some writers, (Calomiris, 2007) for example, suggest that a weakening of fundamentals can become the displacement factor, rather than just a liquidity build-up in an economy.

Some crises are thus caused by what are termed fundamental shocks. A number of scholars (Chen et al., 2007; Rochet and Vives, 2002; Carlsson and van Damme, 1993; Diamond and Dybvig, 1983) have studied crises, and propose two other reasons for crises: fundamentals and panics. The nineteenth-century US economy had frequent crises, which were caused by episodes of fundamental failures. For example, a huge build-up of failed liabilities of failed businesses remaining in banks weakened the banking sector, which led to a shortage of funds for corporations to function. Note that these were the days when the US had no meaningful banking laws. This is a case of a fundamental factor: credit weakening leading to crisis. The four crises around the 1930s were caused mostly by one fundamental factor, namely that the central banking action not to provide liquidity to the economy led to soaring prices for funds, which affected the fundamentals of production and consumption for years.

Another reason proposed in the literature is panic. It is not always possible to identify why panics occur. As a reason for the origin of crises as amply documented by scholars, it is caused by two conditions. If the contracting parties to a financial contract have a binding contract, then both parties are bound to honour it. An insurance firm lending money to a firm has a binding contract, so that the insurer is unlikely in most cases to panic if the firm's earnings go down in one particular year of a 10-year loan contract. On the other hand, US$43 billion in the hands of private individuals in the case of WorldCom meant that the private individuals could sell off the bonds very quickly when the news of the accounting scam in that corporation became public in 2001. The public investors panicked on the news of the scam, and precipitated the demise of the company within 9 months by panic selling. The bond prices went to under US$200 for each $1000 redeemable value.

Panic-led crises happen all the time in publicly traded markets when a corporation has funding contracts that can be liquidated very fast by holders. Banks have an incomplete contract with depositors, as depositors can take their money out of the banks, as they did over March 2007 to December 2008. When the international investors holding the collateralized debt obligations did not receive their promised returns, about half of them returned the contracts to the originators in Wall Street and London, and thus began the unwinding of the investment companies during the GFC. The change in the fundamental, namely the Federal Reserve's six rounds of interest rate increases, led to a severe shock, which led to the collapse of mortgage payments, and consequently the promised payments to the CDO holders dried up. So the banks were forced to buy them back at 45 per cent discount, which depleted the wafer-thin capital of the Wall Street and London banks and traders! Thus, fundamental shocks can happen as a consequence of panic on the part of investors.

2.2.1   Is there a Theory to Explain Crisis?

Is there a theory or framework that can foretell when crises are coming? There is none. The famous Harrod–Domar financial market equilibrium or the quadrilateral exchange-rate relationship in the theories of Cassel and Fisher for currency do not provide a means of judging the stability of the financial sector nor the banking sector. These are not theories of financial sector equilibrium. Attempts are being made recently to build a theory of equilibrium (Allen and Gale, 2007; Calomiris, 2007) in financial markets, which could provide some beginning in this direction. Thus, one could suggest that three forces are at work behind the origin of crises: (a) new behaviour of market participants for which there is no regulatory norm could endanger stability; (b) panics of those who hold incomplete contracts by their pre-emptive action to withdraw funding can lead to fundamental shocks; and (c) weakening of fundamentals can build to a level when a crisis could occur.

What about regulation or the structure of the markets? The financial sector that developed after World War II was based on (i) fixed exchange rate of major currencies; (ii) opening the world to both trade in goods *and* free flow of capital; (iii) central banks tasked with orderly economic and financial activities based on market signals under active promotion of regulations to promote competition. These were to be achieved by international institutions working with domestic institutions, with all parties participating to make decisions. These are not bad things, and the world has benefited from these laudable visions, which produced remarkable progress of human welfare in the second half of the twentieth century (despite massive deprivation building in poorer countries, since the birth of unconstrained capitalism in the 1990s).

With the breakdown of (i) above in the 1970s, when exchange rates began to be floated, trade in money has become a worldwide activity, yielding for those who trade in money (Paul Krugman, the 2009 Nobel Laureate and adviser to President Obama, calls them the paper-shufflers) an increasingly larger share of GDP than ever before. Press reports state that the share of the income for the paper-shufflers was 8 per cent of GDP in 1969 in the US and it was 34 per cent of GDP in 2006. This is starkly visible in those places where money is changing hands (London, New York, Zurich, Tokyo, Chicago, Frankfurt, Sydney, Hong Kong, Singapore, Cayman Islands, etc.) where the culture of high-risk-taking behaviour has been encouraged, taught to graduates going to those places for work, and high-risk behaviour is being brewed worldwide even in the banks used by ordinary people.

The activities of these traders, while essential for the orderly flow of funds across the world (that is why they exist) have created a class of traders who take massive risks in bets on short moves of the financial markets and earn huge profits. These profits enrich the parties taking huge risks, but it is a zero sum game where what one loses becomes a gain for another player. The important consequence of this activity is that the middlemen who do the trading amass untold riches. These middlemen – the Lehman Brothers, the readers can add more names – become addicted to taking more and more risks, thus adding to the build-up of massive risk-taking behaviour in the whole financial system. That is the reason, observers say, why Wall Street is opposed to regulating their trading or even making the trade public by requiring the over-the-counter (OTC) markets to reveal information on the risk of their trades.

The first thing we know now after the crisis, is a sober realization that high-risk-taking behaviour is intrinsically destabilizing to the financial system with the potential for building expectations based on unrealistic assumptions, just as in the days of the Tulip Mania in 1637! In the absence of meaningful regulations to retard/fence-in high-risk-taking behaviour, we know now that a bilateral game of profit-making can degenerate so badly that third party losses occur because the high-risk behaviour leads to bad consequences for economic and consumption activities. We will return to this theme on pages 29–31.

The second thing we know is this. By regulating the banking system tightly, it is possible to banish crises, whereas allowing the banking system to be lightly regulated can enable economies to get more resources for growth. There were no banking crises during 1945–70 when banks were mostly owned by states or wealthy families in many countries, and industries and the public were heavily dependent on banks for their funds. With the deregulation starting in 1971 – and also coinciding with the abandoning of the fixed exchange rate system in that year – the frequency of banking crises picked up. History shows evidence that economies go through these phases of regulatory tightening after a crisis and regulatory loosening as things improve, when banking lobbies gain favour with the rule-makers (the Clinton–Bush era in the US and Brown–Blair era in the UK). Most of the banking regulations such as investor protection laws, anti-monopoly laws, deposit insurance, and so on were passed after major crises such as the 1876 financial meltdown, the Great Depression of the 1930s, the Brazilian crisis in 1971 and the Asian financial crisis of 1997, to mention a few events.

Banking regulations are driven by a desire to prevent future crises by removing the *last-known causes* of the last crisis. Since there is no theory of how a crisis occurs, every society learns to regulate in this incremental fashion by addressing the known causes, each episode at a time. Regulation could not foresee what will happen when newer forces build up in the economy such as the appetite for risk-taking via the inventions of so-called derivative trades mushrooming to a size tens of times bigger than the real sector on which these derivative bets are made. For example, the latest crisis was built on the heightened taste for high-risk financial action becoming institutionally built into the system on the backs of poor rating signals, poor choice of who should get mortgage loans, poor choice of CDOs to reduce bank core capital, and so on, as we will see on pages 29–31.

Hence, what we know repeatedly is that crisis prevention is not possible, since newer forces at work in the financial system begin to emerge that could not be foreseen as being likely to prompt a crisis until it is too late. Bernanke did not foresee how the Fed's interest rate hikes would unravel the banking sector's massive risky investments in sub-prime loans nor how the US$12 trillion worth of loan-based derivatives would come home to Wall Street and London at half the value, for example from Iceland. The result was that the high-risk activities of these two new behaviour patterns burst (a) the banks and (b) the investment houses and hedge funds within

18 months of the rate rises. Within a year, 60 interlinked economies suffered around the world. This is the origin of the crisis.

2.3   THE GENESIS OF THE CRISIS

There is wide agreement in the research circles (see the writings of Paul Krugman in *The New York Times*) that the GFC started in April 2007 in the United States when a credit corporation, New Century Finance, failed. Within five months the trouble spread to other credit corporations, then to the UK with Northern Rock in trouble, then to Germany's Dresdner Bank, to Japan's Mitzuho Bank. By August 2008, 16 months from the start of the crisis, key financial firms were seriously affected, and the central banks of key nations started to pour in money to rescue merchant banks, credit companies and banks (see Figure 1.1 in Chapter 1 for a simple timeline of the crisis).

Meanwhile the stock markets of the world started in August of that year to register the woes of the real sector firms that were in danger of not being able to get funding for production. Stage 2 started in September 2008, when banks did not have enough capital to lend or even balance their books: for a week during 8–15 September, no one could borrow in the market! A record number of 15 large financial firms went bankrupt in that month alone. This was the eye of the storm; the banks were all broke and ceased trading in the overnight markets which they usually do to balance their books. What had been up to August a financial crisis of major economies now became global in nature when no one could borrow US dollars in September. During normal times, typically about US$400 to 800 billion can be borrowed easily.

The spread in cash markets, normally about 10–20 basis points (0.2 per cent), jumped to six times that because borrowers were bidding up on the demand side and supply was not there. From about June 2007, the major central banks started to prop up the banking system by providing liquidity and later capital so that banks could get out of the siege they had got into. It was later, when the credit crunch led to real sector weakening, that the governments of some 60 countries started to pump in money to stimulate economic activities. The IMF gave a pointed directive for stimulus spending of up to 6 per cent of GDP by the affected countries. Australia, which had a new labour government, China and Singapore, all dependent on exports, spent more than that to revive their economies.

The crisis thus had four phases: (I) April 2007–August 2008 (Financial Panic); (II) September–December 2008 (Siege); (III) January–June 2009 (Financial Rescue); (IV) July–December 2009 (Liquidity Provision and

Figure 2.3   Popular view of the origin of the global financial crisis

Stimulus Spending). Thus, what started as a panic of investors (in real estate and derivative positions in exotic financial instruments) in search of high returns in the major economies where the interest rates were very low by historical comparison, spread to the rest of the world as the contagion reached the international financial system because 60 countries had much more open current and capital accounts. The inability of the banking systems in those 60 countries to fund consumption and production led to the shrinkage of the real sector in 2008 by 1.1 per cent, or about US$700 billion.

We propose to call this genesis of the crisis the proximate events of the crisis: investor panic; financial siege; financial rescue; and stimulus spending, in that order. This is simply the chronology of the four events that constitute the crisis. What is needed is to investigate the origin of the crisis. The suggestion that the investors failed to monitor closely or even relaxed their guard on the profligate financial firms engaging in high-risk behaviour does not help us understand why and how the crisis happened. Thus, we need to investigate the preconditions that existed over a longer period of time that promoted the build-up of high-risk-taking behaviour by financial firms and the investors whom they serve.

To do that effectively, let us examine the popular view about the crisis (see Figure 2.3). The first firm to go bankrupt in the US was a credit corporation providing credits to real estate borrowers: it went bankrupt in April 2007.

Northern Rock, another mortgage firm, which borrowed in the short-term markets where funds were cheap given worldwide low interest rates, could not find money in the cash market to back up its long-term loans, and so it went sour in the UK. The US mortgage loan was 50 per cent of GDP in 1998, and rose to 75 per cent by 2007/8. Household credits doubled to 130 per cent of GDP in 2006.

The US housing foreclosures rose to 400 per cent during 2007–08. Of these foreclosures, sub-prime loan cases were 25 per cent of the total foreclosures although the sub-prime cases represented less than 5 per cent of housing stock. The real estate values in major economies kept going up, with real estate purchases on the back of the worldwide low interest rates.

The real estate prices started going up in 1995 when interest rates had moderated substantially. After the interest rate fell below 2 per cent in 2001, real estate investment surged, with the prices going up by anywhere between 10 and 20 per cent every year, from 2002 right up to the first half of 2006. For the second half of that year, the increase slowed to 7.6 per cent. Then it declined steadily, losing up to 18 per cent in the second quarter of 2008 alone. The cumulative decline in just 18 months to 2008 was 54 per cent. Thus, all real estate credits suffered, not just sub-prime credits.

A case can be made that the real-sector collapse was the beginning of the crisis, given the massive effect that foreclosures in the real estate sector would have had on banks' (a) income, (b) dividends, (c) capital adequacy and (d) charges for bad and doubtful loans. To attribute the crisis to sub-prime borrowers, as promoted by the media, is to exonerate the bad investment decisions of the majority of other than the real-estate-based borrowers from contributing to the crisis. Sub-prime lending was only a small part of the 400 per cent increased foreclosures: in fact only half of all the sub-prime loans were foreclosed. Thus, it is the real estate speculation that doubled the housing credits, of which the sub-prime lending did not contribute a major portion. It is the slow build-up of a taste for high-risk–high-return play that started when interest rates steadied and then declined below 2 per cent from 2002. The source for the creation of the sub-prime loan market as well as the bandwagon effect of real estate speculation lies elsewhere in the monetary policy pursuits of Alan Greenspan during the Clinton–Bush era. Thus, we reject the idea that the origin of the financial crisis was the sub-prime loans leading to housing foreclosures and banking crisis.

2.4   THE PRECONDITIONS FOR THE CRISIS

Another thread of the Bush–Clinton era was the increasing dependence of the US economy on funds from foreign sources. Nixon–Bush Sr administrations revved up the flight of production to foreign locations because it was in line with their favoured nation status given to China and, more importantly, to increase the then already low returns to US capital providers. The last three decades of outsourcing production has been the main catalyst for improving returns to shareholders, and the capital owners are now lobbying against bringing even high-tech production back to the US economy. From about the end of the 1970s, the economy had stagnated with the high cost of production, and the average returns to shareholders during the Reagan era were just about 10–12 per cent of capital. With massive production shifts to low-cost production sites such as Mexico and later China, and re-importing the goods produced by US firms to the US, the US firms started to double and, in some cases, quadruple return to capital. The net result was that the US was running a trade deficit which would, left to the trade alone, weaken the economy, but it was saved by a flow of funds to the dollar, being the trading currency of the world.

The extra foreign currency in the trade surplus of nations such as China was kept in the US financial markets to service the trade. Mexico and the US accounted for 62 per cent of China's exports in 2006, so China kept the money in US dollars. This provided a stimulus to prevent the interest rate from going up in the bill markets that finance trade. Importantly, the gains in the capital account of the US from these foreign sources offset the deficits in the merchandise account. This led to US residents living on the credit of other countries, so the interest rates did not go up, were further kept down by the monetary policy of Alan Greenspan, and US households lost the taste for savings as returns were minimal except in asset investments.

A second thread that was building up to facilitate higher risk-taking behaviour by financial firms (so these firms could promise higher returns to investors) was a 10-year period of financial firms in the US nibbling at strong regulations, which had been built over 70 years to make the banking system safer. This started in 1992, when the WTO negotiations had promised to open up the financial sectors so that entry barriers in the financial sectors of most countries would be lifted in the future. Wall Street and the City of London were hoping to build giant financial corporations to take over the financial sectors of the 54 countries that signed the WTO deal to open the banking sectors in 2003.

The first of this nibbling was to remove statutory reserves, which was accomplished earlier than 1992 by some countries. With the huge flow of funds to the cash market in the US financial system, the removal of the reserve ratio, the first line of banking safety, had been lifted by abolishing the 3.5 per cent statutory reserves for banks. With a reduced regulatory requirement, banks could now provide more credit than before, because of the higher money multiplier that creates more credit money, so more bank profits resulted. In 1999, Clinton signed the Gramm–Leach–Bliley Act, which softened the anti-monopoly provisions of the Glass–Steagall Act. With commercial banks having very low returns during the low-to-moderate interest rate period then prevailing, those two changes paved the way for banks to take in the investment and security trading firms as subsidiaries, and to make more profits and report higher profits; this was good for shareholders, but the plight of savers was that their deposit rates were very low. This (the mergers of investment banks and insurance firms with commercial banks) the banking sector achieved in two stages. Banking conglomeration started across states. From over 15 000 banks in a highly competitive dual licensing regime, the number of banks shrunk to about 7000 when holding companies cut across state barriers.

Banks could now own commercial banking operations used by the general public, requiring low-risk operations, while also owning the high-risk operations of investment banks and securities trading houses. The taste for high risks was beginning to build in the banking sector. Parallel banking firms with no supervision of the Fed were licensed (imagine Bear Stearns or Lehman Brothers lending money to banks) adding US$5.2 trillion credit lines. Regulatory changes permitted the birth of parallel banking companies as did also the Securities and Exchange Commission (SEC), by softening the net capital rule for lending: banks set up Special Vehicle Companies (SVC) off the balance sheet to do this. There was this new factor that was at work from 1992 to 2006, which we call regulatory forgiveness, or weakening, to enable more risks to be taken by the financial market players.

The next two regulatory changes prompted the financial sectors to take more risks. The first, in 1999, involved the temporary powers given by Clinton, urged by Alan Greenspan, under which the four largest banks were given permission to acquire investment banks and securities trading. Then the repeal of the Glass–Steagall Act in 2004 removed the safety wall erected between commercial banking and more risky other banking. The stage was now set for experimentation with more risky financial activities. Hedge funds cropped up around this time to service the wealthy investors who also had a taste for high-risk investments: about half the hedge funds went bust during the GFC. While this was going on, the low interest rate in major economies persisted (see *The Economist*, 1996, on the death of inflation), and after increasing their profits by merging with investment/ insurance firms the commercial banks were looking for other ways of making money.

This was the start of the dangerous invention of the exotic securitization process under which all kinds of fancy derivatives crept in to banking product offers, adding to the risk of financial transactions in commercial banks. Imagine Barclays Bank offering to give a higher return if a depositor would only agree to make a bet on the FTSE going above 5000 points in the next 12 months after a deposit was made? This kind of bet-based deposit was offered across the world to the general public who could not get much interest income on their savings unless they took up such bets, when the offered interest rates were 4–6 per cent compared with the 1–2 per cent without the bet. The ordinary depositors were asked to take greater risks in an environment of rock-bottom deposit rates, and they

did. Even a humble bank in Singapore offered depositors with more than
$100 000 to take a bet on overnight cash rates remaining below a certain
point over seven years! When overnight rates went up, there was no
return, and the capital would have been eroded if the investors wanted to
withdraw their deposits. Ordinary citizens who would otherwise not have
taken part in high-risk activities were slowly schooled to take more risks,
and they agreed to do so as there were such poor returns on deposits for
savers and the retired.

With banks having dispensed with (a) the safety first reserve ratio and
(b) merging the savings bank with more risky other banks, the stage was
set for more risky activities. Securitization and derivative securities crept
in to banking. The enigmatic JP Morgan devised a new derivative, the
BISTRO, which had two potential impacts favourable to the banks. First,
this product would take part of the loan out of the loan book, and therefore, secondly, with the same capital, the bank could lend more money, so
shareholders could increase their returns. This is possible given the rule
on capital requirement: 20 per cent of 8 cents (1.6 cents) for a $derivative-
based loan instrument compared with the 8 cents for a $loan remaining in
the book. If only parts of the loan book could be securitized, then banks
would save 6.4 cents in capital and lend more money! In addition, there is
a new source of income from the sale of the new product. A single derivative contract would give a fee income of US$400 000 to the bank in addi-
tion to improving capital adequacy.

This invention in 1994 made some US$64 billion for JP Morgan and
the buyers were ready for high risk across the world. This instrument later
became the financial weapon of mass destruction of the major financial
markets in 2007. By end-2006, this product had generated US$12 trillion,
permitting more profits from more loans to be made with released capital,
and for banks to earn huge profits as fees for the derivatives sold in New
York, Germany and London, even Iceland. One commentator called it the
'fool's gold', as will be discussed later.

So, over a much longer period than the debut of sub-prime lending
in 2002, there was a slow build-up of high-risk activities in the financial
sectors. These were the result of regulatory weakening or forgiveness
coupled with poor risk assessment of new products by both the sellers and
buyers as to how these new products would fare if interest rate were to go
up suddenly. The rating agencies, which were the gods of the industry to
rate the risk of such new products, did a very poor job of risk assessment:
some commentators called the rating process 'voodoo science'. Part of the
reason was the moral hazard of telling the big conglomerate banks that
the new products they invented were very risky, when the same big banks
were responsible for how much the rating companies earned. Ratings by

Standard & Poor's (S&P) became unreliable, and there were no valuation models of how these new securities should be valued, other than what the investors were willing to pay during the euphoric years of easy credits. SEC investigated this, and pointed to bad ratings. In June 2007, at the worst time of the crisis, about US$2 trillion of securities traded were downgraded as a result, adding to more confusion.

A final factor that was at the root of the origin of the crisis was investor vigilance. A mood took hold in the minds of shareholders that bank CEOs of corporations *alone* were creating value, not the workers or the luck factor of trends in markets. This became embedded with the campaign by top management to demand and get exorbitant compensation for CEOs: like film stars, the CEOs had agents negotiating contracts. Staggering multiples of average pay for workers were paid to CEOs: the US number was 50 times average pay; in the UK it was 21; in Singapore, according to a press report, it was 151 compared to a multiple of just 8 in Japan. So, investors equated the executives' high pay as a signal of prediction of high performance. The investors hardly chastised the CEOs for their greed, but accepted this top compensation as a signal of potential high performance.

Major fraudulent behaviour started as far back as 1991 with the UK Maxwell Corporation pension scandal. More cases came to light in major economies, the cases of Enron, WorldCom, Pharmalat, HIH Insurance and so on. Yet the actions taken in most regulatory regimes were to create a code of good conduct with no hard regulations to threaten the well-being of the fraudsters. Anyway, the investors were reaping good returns in the early 2000s, so that they were happy to look away and not be vigilant about the performance of the top executives. The feeling was like in the ANZ Bank: if the bank makes 45 per cent profits and gives me a large share, why do I care about the large pay packet of the executives! Thus, the spirit of performance forgiveness pervaded the financial markets: hedge funds provide the best example of this.

Thus, we can now trace the origin of the crisis much more intelligently: see Figure 2.4.

As is evident from the figure, the financial crisis was building up for a long while, and did not just happen in 2007, nor was it due to the fraudulent lending to sub-prime customers over 2002–2006, which caused the banks to go bust. Far from it, the chain of events goes back a long way. The origin of the crisis can now be traced to the monetary and political regime targeting low interest rates that led to low earnings of the banking sector, which induced lobbying for deregulation to conserve capital and take more risks through fraudulent lending and untested financial innovations, which weakened important prudential fences.

The CEO's taste for high pay led to a duplicitous claim to superior

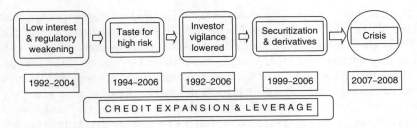

Figure 2.4   The origin of the Global Financial Crisis: a different view

performance, in the face of which new products were invented to provide promised high returns to investors, who in turn were willing to lower their vigilance on the financial firms. That is the complex network of the behaviour that led to the crisis. The important role that the CDO played as the originator of the crisis can now be traced. Strangely, the greed to secure high returns promised by dubious groups of actors in the financial markets led to the tulip-like mania for high profits that is at the root of the crisis.

2.4.1   The Collateralized Debt Obligation, CDO: Alchemy for High Returns

The invention of the CDO by JP Morgan Bank is documented in a very carefully-done study by Tett (2009). The financial press has reported how the buyers of these innovative products started to return them to the banks during 2006–07 at prices much lower than the price at which they bought. None the less there has been not much discussion on how the return of these instruments badly affected the capital base of financial firms, as no document is available on that count. The innovation was made as far back as 1994 by banks wanting to reduce their credit risk and conserve capital by selling the better-rated loans by repackaging the income streams as CDOs and selling them around the world. By 2006 the nominal value of this market was US$12 trillion.

Each time a dollar is taken off the loan book by creating this derivative, the bank has to back that loan book by 1.6 cents capital instead of 8 cents, thus releasing 6.4 cents of capital for further lending. By the same token, when the same bank has to buy back the CDO, the bank needs to top up 6.4 cents as new capital for every dollar of buy-back of the CDO. After Bernanke increased interest rates during 2004–06 on the back of the collapsing real-estate sector which was having foreclosure problems, banks were unable to provide the income streams promised to the buyers of these instruments. Thus, according to various reports in the financial press in 2007–09, CDOs were bought at a higher and higher discount, so that by

2008 the discount was 45 per cent of the original sale value. The insurance cost of the CDO, which was 2 cents per $100, escalated to 22 cents per $100, which is the main reason why AIG (the main insurer of banks with this instrument) went bust, apart from the impact of real-estate insurance.

It is therefore possible to see how the repurchase of these instruments at such heavy discount would lead to the worsening of capital adequacy of banks. First, the repurchase would mean a loss, plus the bank would have to top up 6.4 cents for every dollar of the repurchased instrument. About 25 per cent of the CDOs were bought back, which means that a huge amount of capital needed to be increased to meet the 8 cents in a dollar of loan requirement. This had a severe impact on major banks which were holding the issues. This is the reason for many top financial firms losing their capital base, and then scrambling in the market to balance the books during the first half of 2008. This is in addition to the bleeding of capital in the form of non-performing loans (the number went up from 1.5 per cent in 1998 to about 7.6 per cent in 2008) and charges for doubtful loans.

Thus the origin of the crisis is this new innovation, which made the promise of reducing capital requirement when loans are repackaged as derivatives and sold to a market with a taste for high risk in a low interest rate period. Once the interest rate went up, and the real-estate foreclosures occurred speedily as US housing prices declined by 54 per cent over 18 months, the ability of the banks to provide the returns to CDO holders worsened; in addition, the banks could not fulfil the capital adequacy provision as they had no money. Especially during 2006 and 2007, the CDOs started to come back to the issuers or holders, and that further eroded the capital base of the major players. This is why central banks in the USA and the UK provided credit for liquidity problems. Later they also provided capital injections to shore up the core capital of banks so that they could meet capital adequacy requirements, and be solvent.

Summing up the discussion to this point, the reader is likely to realize that the system-wide effect of the untested innovations (CDOs and other forms of credit derivatives offered by commercial banks) unbundled when the interest rate started to go up, thus creating buyback of CDOs at discounted prices, resulting in waves of foreclosures. What can be concluded? The origin of the crisis is not simply the sub-prime loan. The proximate origin was the collapse of the real-estate market faced with higher interest rates. The origin of the crisis can be traced to (a) the low interest rates prompting banks to lobby for (b) regulatory weakening, which fostered (c) appetite for high-risk untested innovations.

If the interest rate had not increased as it did during 2004–06, the credit splurge would have continued for a while. There would have been no incentive to abandon housing mortgages nor would investors have abandoned the high-yielding CDOs for a while. It is now clear that the prevalence of very low interest rates for a long period of time deprived adequate returns to savers, which created the taste for high-risk instruments and easy credits embedded in new derivative instruments. When interest rates increased, the resulting investor panic led to abandoning real-estate units *and* also customers across the world abandoning derivative contracts. The wafer-thin capital of the deposit-taking financial firms evaporated fast, precipitating the banking crisis. The banking crisis then led to economic crisis.

2.5 CONSEQUENCES AND LESSONS OF THE CRISIS

The consequence for the financial sector will be discussed here. The consequences for trade, monetary policy, growth, fiscal policy and the labour sector are discussed in separate chapters of the book. Let us summarize the factors at work and the sequence of events leading to the crisis (see Figure 2.5).

As the theory predicts, the credit expansion was made possible by a series of regulatory forgiveness that was happening from 1992 to 2004, which set the stage for the birth of super banks and super financial firms in Wall Street and the City of London. The success of Alan Greenspan in taming inflation to very low levels reduced returns to savers and to bondholders alike. Financial innovation aimed at conserving regulatory capital led to the creation of new financial products aimed at increasing banking income sold as high-return derivatives to innocent masses. Assets were sought after to increase returns to savers, and that led to real-estate and stock price bubbles well ahead of the prices indicated by corporate income increases. This fits well with the common observation that all financial crises are preceded by a build-up of excess liquidity on the false promise of high returns.

The *displacement* factor that cut short the euphoria was the sudden increases in interest rates by Ben Bernanke in June 2004, which led to five more increases. The asset markets (share and real estate) collapsed, leading to a 54 per cent decline in house prices over 2006–08 and a stock market decline of 36 per cent. This is the consequence of the *panic* behaviour of the market participants as the *revulsion* set in after seeing the famous icons of banks going under. The contagion then spread to 60 economies, leading to an overall loss of GDP by 1.1 per cent in 2008, and a subsequent fall in the growth of most economies in 2009. Figure 2.5 depicts the factors and the sequence of events that led to the crisis.

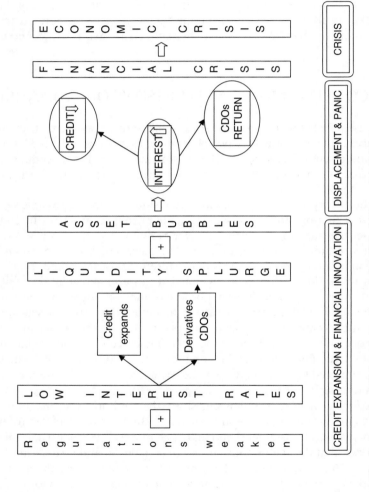

Figure 2.5 *The factors identified as the causes of the Global Financial Crisis*

32

So, what needs to be done, given the analysis of the factors at work in this opening crisis of the twenty first century? The financial sector in any economy is a handmaiden for the following: (a) ensuring timely lowest cost payments to all actors in the system; (b) banks taking the savings in the economy, and, by transforming the savings as new financial products, being able to earn and thus also produce better returns to savers; and (c) in the process of achieving (b), the financial system should not risk destabilizing the financial sector. Given these mandates for the financial sector, the different players are regulated carefully to ensure that these functions are carried out effectively, hence the necessity for balanced regulation of financial transactions.

The first failure we note in this crisis is the weak regulatory structure, which permitted high-risk financial firms with low-risk commercial banking. Next was regulation creating non-supervised entities that provided parallel finance as shadow banking. This was a slow disaster in the making in so far as the following safeguards had already been removed: the first defence of reserve ratio; the second defence of separation of high-risk financial activities from savings banks; the third defence of insulating ordinary savers – the mums and dads as well as the pensioners – ensuring them a decent return on their savings from the interest rate on deposits of ordinary investment banks. The need to conserve capital, when the interest rate is too low to yield adequate returns to capital providers to bankers, and the need of savers to earn a decent rate on funds, both prompted the banks to innovate untested new derivative securities, which required bets, thus increasing the risk needed to be taken to earn a decent return by ordinary bank depositors. This risk was bearable, so thought the depositors, but for that assumption to hold, the low interest rate must continue to sustain the huge leverage in the financial sector, the private sector, households and governments (recall what happened to the euro during 2010, when government debt became excessive and sovereign debt rose from 4 to 6.8 per cent during 2011).

The lobbying of the banks to achieve leaner capital requirement fostering weak regulations led to the ballooning of credits in a number of economies since, with derivatives, the same capital base led to more loans. Household saving was 11 per cent in good times of the US economy, but it was a minus figure in the recent period around the crisis! Apart from household debt doubling to 130 per cent of GDP in the US, private debt of 123 per cent of GDP in 1981 increased to 300 per cent in 2008. The leverage of banks shot up even faster: off-balance sheet loans formed 37 per cent of GDP or US$5.2 trillion; the leverage of 65 per cent of GDP of the top five financial institutions doubled by the time of the crisis.

Many non-banks cropped up as parallel banks (an example is Bear

Stearns); these institutions provided money, and were not supervised by the Fed. The financial press reports that the overall impact of all these increases in credits made leverage unsustainable in the whole economy. When interest rates went up in the USA and in the UK, the players would attempt to reduce their loans, and that is what happened. This is the same story as the origin of the Asian financial crisis (it cost US$94 billion to extinguish that crisis), when countries such as Korea and Thailand had debt measured at 300 to 400 per cent of equity values. Much of the money came as short-term portfolio funds (no different from what China and Mexico is providing to the US, except that these two do not withdraw). On the slightest news of the overreliance on foreign cash inflows, the foreign portfolio investors withdrew their money – about US$215 billion over 18 months during the Asian crisis: investors came to know the high leverage of the producing sector (see Ariff and Khalid, 2005).

The role of derivatives in destabilizing the banking sector, and in particular the powerful financial houses such as Bear Sterns and Lehman Brothers (credit-derivatives were their main products) and others are very evident. Calls have been made to bring all derivative trades to a platform so that the extent of the risk of these instruments for the financial sector can be judged by the market instead of the private parties to the contract under the current arrangement to keep the trade as private trades. While the exchange-traded derivatives is about US$44 trillion (2.5 times the US economy) with features such as public trade and clearing houses, there are 10 times more trades done by the financial firms as private trades between them and customers. For instance, the US$12 trillion CDO market began to erode capital of large finance firms and there was no information known at that time as to how this would add risk to the stability of the financial sector.

The far-reaching consequence for the financial sector is the urgent need to restructure the financial system such that the banking system serves the depositors with safe practices under a set of regulations to rein in the bankers, preventing them from engaging in high-risk banking that would again destabilize the effective intermediation function of banks between savers and borrowers *without creating too much risk* regarding destabilizing the sector. Finally the financial markets that trade whatever type of products to investors should do so in a *transparent manner with risks revealed ahead of time*, and the returns should not be based on superlative risk-taking investment instruments.

The G20 group is labouring hard to draw up regulations and to restructure the financial system with these two objectives. This work is still in progress, so we are unable to make an assessment of this new structure. Some basic beginnings appear to have come about: the Basel Accord III to increase core capital but by too little; the US Dodd–Frank Act to make big banks provide more capital; some moves in the UK to limit executive pay. The G20 meeting in November 2010 has not come up with any major agreements on further badly-needed reforms. So the lessons learned have not led to the passing of new laws to protect the financial system from a repeat of the same.

NOTE

1. As discussed on pages 29–31, a new product called the BISTRO was designed in 1994 by the JP Morgan people in London and New York, and later metamorphosed as the collateralized debt obligation CDO. This product promised to give huge returns, and the nominal value of this market grew to US$12 trillion by 2006, or two-thirds the size of the US economy. The disenchantment of the customers in 2007 of this new product's (call it the tulip bomb of GFC) failure to yield high returns broke the banks in London, Frankfurt, Tokyo and Wall Street.

REFERENCES

Allen, F. and R. Gale (2007), *Understanding Financial Crises*, Oxford: Oxford University Press.

Ariff, M. and A. Khalid (2005), *Financial Liberalisation and the Asian Financial Crisis*, Cheltenham, UK, and Northampton, MA, USA: Edward Elgar Publishing.

Calomiris, Charles W. (2007), 'Bank failures in theory and history: the Great Depression and other "contagious" events', NBER Working Papers 13597, National Bureau of Economic Research, Inc.

Carlsson, Hans and Eric van Damme (1993), 'Global games and equilibrium selection', *Econometrica*, **61**(5), 989–1018.

Chen, Q., I. Goldstein and W. Jiang (2007), 'Payoff complementarities and financial fragility: evidence from mutual fund outflows', *Journal of Financial Economics*, **89**(2), 339–56.

Diamond, D.W. and P.H. Dybvig (1983), 'Bank runs, deposit insurance, and liquidity', *Journal of Political Economy*, **91**(3), 401–19.

Economist, The (1996), 'Is inflation dead?', 13 April US edition.

Kindleberger, C.P. (2005), *Manias, Panics, and Crashes: A History of Financial Crises*, (5th edition), first published in 1978, New York: Wiley.

Minsky, Hyman P. (1974), 'The modeling of financial instability: an introduction', in *Modeling and Simulation*, proceedings of the Fifth Annual Pittsburgh Conference.

Rochet, Jean-Charles and Vives, Xavier (2002), 'Coordination failures and the lender of last resort: was Bagehot right after all?', Discussion Paper Series 26264, Hamburg Institute of International Economics.

Tett, G. (2009), *Fool's Gold: How Unrestricted Greed Corrupted a Dream*, London: Little, Brown.

Note: Other newspapers referred to were: *Financial Times*; *Wall Street Journal*; *International Herald Tribune* for data and statistics quoted in the body of the chapter.

3. Exchange rate changes and global trade imbalances: China as a major creditor country

Ronald I. MacKinnon

3.1 PRELUDE

In the decade of 2000–2010, the US dollar experienced a volatile period. Up to mid-2008, the dollar depreciated significantly against most major currencies while the renminbi (RMB) or the yuan was fixed at 8.28 yuan per dollar: it has been fixed since 1995. Nevertheless, after 2000, net saving in China began to increase while net saving, both private and government, in the US declined sharply. Unsurprisingly, this led to a large bilateral trade surplus of China (and with many other countries) trading with the United States.

In the United States, this saving imbalance between the two countries was misinterpreted by many economists and politicians to be the result of a misaligned exchange rate. The rhetoric was that the renminbi was *undervalued* and led to what was popularly called China-bashing in order to prompt Congress action to appreciate the RMB. Eventually the People's Bank of China (PBC) gave in to American protectionist threats to impose tariffs on imports from China. In July 2005, China began to slowly appreciate the currency against the dollar at about 6 per cent per year. This one-way bet, following this policy change that the RMB will be higher in the future, led to a deluge of hot money inflows and an explosion in Chinese foreign exchange reserves resulting in inflation and a threatened loss of internal monetary control. China's trade surplus also kept increasing at about US$800 billion a year, which added to the perception that the two issues were related.

In the worldwide credit crunch during the last half of 2008, an unexpected upsurge in the global demand for dollars (McKinnon et al., 2010) caused the dollar to appreciate sharply against most other major currencies while carrying the RMB also with it. The PBC then took the opportunity of a strong dollar to stop the one-way bet on RMB appreciation against the dollar. The exchange rate was reset at 6.83 RMB per dollar in July 2008, where it more or less remains today as at September 2010. Hot money inflows stopped at least temporarily, enabling the PBC to mount a vigorous program of domestic credit expansion in 2008–10 that pulled China and much of the rest of Asia out of the global downturn with positive echo effects in Europe (mainly Germany) and the United States.

So the first objective of this chapter is to show analytically that pressure on saving-surplus countries, such as China, to appreciate their government-controlled exchange rates is counter-productive. The expectation of such appreciation creates financial chaos with hot money inflows, and the aftermath of any discrete appreciation will not clear the surplus in net saving in any predictable way. Indeed, the trade surplus of a creditor country could actually increase with currency appreciation, as I argue here.

The second objective is to show that floating the exchange rate of a *still-learning* major creditor country with a large trade net saving surplus such as China is simply not viable financially. I define a still-learning creditor country, call it immature creditor, as one whose own currency is not used for international lending but must resort to building up claims on foreigners denominated in some major international money: the US dollar in China's case (the yen in the case of Japan in the early 1970s).

3.2 FLOATING THE CURRENCY AS A CHOICE

If, in trying to float the RMB, the Chinese government were to withdraw completely from the foreign exchange market, then China's private financial institutions such as the banks, insurance companies, pension funds, and so on could not stand the risk of building up dollar claims on the asset sides of their balance sheets since all their liabilities would revert to RMB. This currency mismatch would so inhibit private financial institutions from acquiring the dollar assets thrown out by the trade surplus that the RMB would just spiral upward indefinitely, instead of downwards as the popular press analysis claims. The yuan-dollar rate would become indeterminate.

3.2.1 Trade Relations between the USA and China: a Historical Perspective

Nobody disputes that almost three decades of US trade (net saving) deficits have made the global system of finance and trade more accident-prone, especially with the recovery of China's economy after China spent a large amount of money to stimulate the economy following the 2007 global financial crisis. Outstanding dollar debts have become huge, and actually threaten America's own financial future. Insofar as the principal creditor countries in Asia (Japan in the 1980s and 1990s, China since 2000) are industrial countries relying heavily on exports of manufactures, the transfer of their surplus savings to the saving-deficient US requires that they collectively run large trade surpluses in manufactures. The resulting large American trade deficits have worsened the *natural* decline in the relative size of the American manufacturing sector, and eroded her industrial base.

One unfortunate consequence of this industrial decline has been an outbreak of protectionism in the United States, which is exacerbated by the conviction that foreigners have somehow been cheating with their exchange rate and other commercial policies. The most prominent of these have been associated with New York Senator Charles Schumer. In March 2005 he co-sponsored a bill to impose a 27.5 per cent tariff on all US imports from China until the RMB was appreciated. His bill was withdrawn in October 2006, when shown to be obviously incompatible with America's obligations under the World Trade Organization. But Schumer threatens to craft a new China bill for 2010 that is WTO compatible. So, the new bill received majority support in the Senate with overwhelming votes in October 2010, but is awaiting further moves even to become law.

Furthermore, Congress legislation requires the Secretary of the Treasury to investigate any country that runs a trade surplus with the United States and to pronounce on whether or not the surplus country is manipulating its exchange rate. So far in 2010, the current Secretary Timothy Geithner has been narrowly avoiding having to label China a currency manipulator, which, if done, would involve as yet unspecified sanctions that could lead to a trade war.

However, the prevailing idea that a country's exchange rate could, and indeed should, be used to bring its external trade into better balance is often wrong. Unfortunately, this conventional wisdom is based on faulty economic theorizing. It need not apply in a globalized financial system where capital flows freely internationally. Under financial globalization, forcing a creditor country such as China to appreciate its currency is neither necessary nor sufficient, and need not be even helpful for reducing its trade surplus. What are the issues involved?

3.3   THE EXCHANGE RATE AND THE TRADE BALANCE: THE DEBATE

For a home country, consider the identity from the national income accounts:

$$X - M = S - I = \text{Trade (Saving) Surplus}$$

where X is exports and M is imports (both broadly defined), and S is gross national saving and I is gross domestic investment.

Most economists and commentators focus just on the left-hand side of this accounting identity. It suggests that a depreciation of the home currency will make exports cheaper in world markets, and so exports will expand. Similarly, the home country's imports will become more expensive in domestic currency, so these should contract. Thus conventional wisdom has it that the overall trade balance should improve if the underlying price elasticities for exporting and importing are even moderately high. This seemingly plausible result is very intuitive, so even journalists can understand and perpetuate it.

But this elasticities approach is basically microeconomic and quite deceptive. The export function X is looked at on its own and the demand for imports M is looked at on its own even by supposedly sophisticated econometricians who purport to measure separately the price elasticities of exports, and of imports, to exchange rate changes. Thus, it is called the elasticities approach to the trade balance.

However, if you analyze the right-hand side $(S - I)$ of the identity, the emphasis is macroeconomic. For the trade balance to improve with exchange depreciation, overall domestic expenditures must fall relative to aggregate output. This is the same as saying that domestic saving must rise relative to domestic investment. Looked at this way, one cannot presume that the US net saving will rise when the dollar is devalued.

Indeed, the presumption may go the other way when domestic investment (fueled in part by multinational firms) is sensitive to the exchange rate. Suppose the RMB were to appreciate sharply against the dollar. Potential investors, either foreign or domestic, would now see China as a more expensive place in which to invest, and the US less expensive. This might set off a minor investment boom in the United States, where investment expenditures rise from a relatively small base, and a major slump results in China's huge investment sector which is currently about 45 per cent of her GNP. Overall, investment-led expenditures in China would fall, the economy would contract, and Chinese imports could fall.

This is what happened to Japan from the 1980s into the mid-1990s when the yen went ever higher. Japan became a higher-cost place in which to invest, so that large Japanese firms decamped to invest in lower-cost Asian countries, *and* in the US itself. Even though yen appreciation slowed Japan's export growth, the trade surplus of the slumping economy increased. (In 2010, about 36 per cent of GDP comes from outside investments. This could very well happen if China were to revalue RMB and move her investments outside.)

No wonder China is reluctant to appreciate its currency! Like Japan in the 1980s and 1990s, its trade (saving) surplus would likely not diminish because domestic saving is relatively insensitive to the exchange rate even though investment in a globalized financial–industrial world is sensitive. However, foreign critics in the US and Europe with the misleading elasticities model (which does not take international investment choices into account) in their analyses would come back and say 'you just didn't appreciate enough'.

With this adverse expectation of continual RMB appreciation, the upshot would be further hot money inflows. The People's Bank of China would be, as it has been, forced to intervene to buy dollars on a grand scale to prevent an indefinite upward spiral in the RMB. But the accumulation of dollar foreign exchange reserves threatens a loss of internal monetary control as base money in China's banking system expands at an equal rate, and somehow has to be sterilized.[1]

3.4   CURRENCY MISMATCHES AND CHINA AS AN IMMATURE INTERNATIONAL CREDITOR

3.4.1   The Impossibility of a Free Yuan/Dollar Float

While a discrete appreciation of the RMB by moving the government-controlled peg for the yuan–dollar rate would be deleterious, is there not an alternative market-based solution for determining the exchange rate? 'It is China's decision about what to do with the exchange rate – they're a sovereign country', Secretary for Treasury Timothy Geithner said. 'But I think it is enormously in their interest to move, over time, to let the exchange rate reflect market forces, and I am confident that they will do what is in their interest', he said while visiting Boeing and other exporters in Washington State (Geithner, 2010).

Secretary Timothy Geithner's tone here is much more measured and careful than in previous episodes of American China-bashing where various congressmen, journalists, industrialists, union officials and economists, who are intellectually trapped by the elasticities model, have called for a large appreciation of the RMB against the dollar. But would Secretary Geithner's more moderate and seemingly reasonable approach to let the yuan–dollar rate reflect market forces, that is, by floating, work?

China has a large ongoing net saving (trade) surplus that somehow has to be financed by lending to foreigners. But the RMB is not (yet) an internationally accepted currency. Thus the build-up of financial claims on foreigners is largely denominated in dollars (some in euros, yen and sterling), not RMB. Moreover, under the threat that the RMB might appreciate in the future, foreigners become even more loath to borrow in RMB. So we have the making of a severe currency mismatch if the PBC were to withdraw from the foreign exchange market, that is, to stop buying the dollars necessary to stabilize the yuan–dollar rate.[2] Under such a free float, Chinese private (non-state) financial institutions such as banks, insurance companies and pension funds, would become responsible for financing the trade surplus. So they would have to build up dollar claims on the asset side of their balance sheets even though their liabilities (domestic bank deposits, annuity and pension obligations) would be denominated in RMB. Because of this mismatch, they would face the threat of bankruptcy should the dollar depreciate. If the dollar appreciates, they will have bumper returns.

China's current account surpluses have been so large, between US$200 billion and US$300 billion per year, having ballooned to US$ 800 in 2010, that when cumulated they would quickly dwarf the net worth of China's private financial institutions. Thus, except for transitory transacting, these private institutions would refuse to accumulate the dollar claims being thrown off by the current account surplus once the PBC left the market. Under such a free float with no willing buyers of dollars, the renminbi would just spiral upward indefinitely with no well-defined upper bound for its dollar exchange rate. And remember that the appreciated RMB need not reduce China's trade surplus.

Of course the PBC could not just stand idly while a continually appreciating RMB caused both exports and domestic investment to slump. So it would revoke its free float and re-enter the foreign exchange market to buy dollars to re-stabilize the yuan–dollar rate. But this adventure in floating would have further undermined expectations, and make it more difficult to re-establish a credible yuan–dollar rate from which hot money inflows were absent. The PBC and State Administration of Foreign Exchange (SAFE) could well find themselves with much larger dollar exchange reserves than the current incredibly high $2.5 trillion, and with the economy knocked off its high growth path.

What is the more general lesson here? Suppose an immature creditor country like China continues with high net saving ($S - I$) leading to a large build-up of foreign currency claims. The resulting currency mismatch within its domestic financial system will cause a free float to break down. Unlike what Secretary Geithner suggests, *there is no market solution*. So the best that the country can do is to stabilize its exchange rate through official intervention sufficiently credibly that hot money flows are minimized. And this is the strategy that China has been trying to follow, but which is continually knocked off course by American and European China-bashing to appreciate the RMB.[3]

3.5   THE WAY OUT

In the short term (and forever?) foreigners should stop bashing China on the exchange rate. A credibly stable exchange rate would eliminate hot money inflows into China and make it much easier for the PBC to continue with its huge domestic credit expansion, which has made China the leading force in global economic recovery;

In the medium term, the net saving in the US and China needs to be better balanced. The US should cut back on its huge fiscal deficits and constrain private consumption while China continues stimulating private consumption. With trade better balanced, American manufacturing could recover and protectionist pressures would lessen; and

In the long term, China should continue to encourage the *internationalization* of the RMB. With a stable yuan–dollar rate, foreigners would be more willing to borrow in RMB from Chinese banks and even be willing to issue RMB-denominated bonds in Shanghai. By gradually escaping from its internal currency mismatch, China would be well on the road to becoming a 'mature' international creditor with lessons learned from this approach.

NOTES

1.   See Lee (2009) and Qiao (2007) for details.
2.   Readers can also refer to Mundell (1963).
3.   See Geithner (2010), McKinnon (2010a), McKinnon (2010b), and McKinnon and Schnabl (2009) for more details on this issue.

REFERENCES

Geithner, Timothy (2010), Associated Press statement, 23 May.
Lee, Brian (2009), 'Carry trades and global financial instability', Stanford University, 30 April.
McKinnon, Ronald (2010a), 'Rehabilitating the unloved dollar standard', Stanford University April.
McKinnon, Ronald (2010b), 'A stable yuan/dollar rate forever?', posted in the *Financial Times* Economic forum, 22 March.

McKinnon, Ronald and Gunther Schnabl (2009), 'The case for stabilizing China's exchange rate: setting the stage for fiscal expansion', *China & World Economy*, **17** (1), 1–32.

McKinnon, Ronald, Brian Lee and David Wang (2010), 'The global credit crisis and China's exchange rate', *The Singapore Economic Review*, **55** (2), 53–272.

Mundell, Robert (1963), 'Capital mobility and stabilization policy under fixed and flexible exchange rates', *Canadian Journal of Economics and Political Science*, **29**, 475–85.

Qiao, Hong (Helen) (2007), 'Exchange rates and trade balances under the dollar standard', *Journal of Policy* Modeling, **29**, 765–82.

4. Bank capital adequacy: where to now?

Kevin Davis

4.1 INTRODUCTION

The use of minimum (risk weighted) capital requirements has been an important plank in banking regulation for the last two decades, following the release of the first Basel Capital Accord in 1988. Since that time, there have been various modifications to the Basel framework, and a comprehensive revision (Basel II) was produced in 2006 with many countries, such as Australia, commencing introduction one or two years later. Coincidentally, the introduction of the Basel II framework came very close to the time of the onset of the Global Financial Crisis in mid-2007, with numerous banking failures and difficulties globally. Even though Basel II was yet to have a significant effect,[1] the GFC experience has led to a rethinking of approaches to capital regulation and numerous proposals for changes to that framework (as well as more wide-ranging questioning of the appropriate degree and scope of financial sector regulation).

Among those proposals are suggestions for: the use of a (non-risk-weighted) leverage ratio as an adjunct to the Basel II risk-weighted capital requirement; contingent capital requirements; countercyclical capital buffers; higher quality capital; a higher quantity of capital; capital maintenance (dividend restriction) requirements; and changes to regulatory risk weights. To assess the merits of these proposals, and possible effects, it is important to clarify the concept of bank capital, and that is done in section 4.2 below. It is also useful to trace briefly the history of capital requirements and bank capital experiences during the GFC. Thus section 4.3 reviews the history of capital requirements and bank capital ratios and discusses some of the difficulties in measuring capital appropriately – and thus in relying upon it as a regulatory tool. Section 4.4 examines the capital experiences of banks during the GFC and section 4.5 draws out issues arising from those experiences. Section 4.6 provides an overview and analysis of the various proposals which have been advanced for changes to bank capital regulation. Section 4.7 concludes.

4.2 THE CONCEPT OF BANK CAPITAL

Bank capital is a residual item in bank balance sheets calculated as the difference between assets and those other liabilities which have more senior (prior) claims on the bank's revenue stream and (in the case of failure) assets. It represents the claim of the bank's owners on the net assets of the firm and acts as a buffer to absorb fluctuations in the value of assets (such as those due to loan defaults or variations in securities prices) and liabilities. It is this latter characteristic which gives rise to its role in prudential regulation, with minimum capital requirements being seen as a way of protecting other stakeholders – particularly depositors (or a deposit insurance fund standing in their stead).

In principle, capital corresponds to shareholder equity and is associated with control (voting) rights over the organization. Regulatory practice, however, has broadened the definition of capital to include some other liability items (such as some forms of debt and hybrid securities) which rank below deposit liabilities and which therefore also serve as a buffer to protect depositors from loss. And since the riskiness of the banks' activities is an important determinant of the adequacy of the capital buffer, minimum required regulatory capital since the Basel I Accord has been calculated by applying risk weights to assets (and off-balance sheet items).

Because it is calculated as a residual item, the measured quantity of bank capital depends crucially on the methods of valuation of assets and other liabilities. If, for example, a loan recorded as an asset worth $100 is actually worthless, or the market value of a security which the bank has purchased has fallen by $100, the true quantity of capital will be overstated by that same amount. This has led to a long-standing debate on appropriate accounting practices for banks – most specifically relating to the use of historical cost versus mark-to-market accounting. But also relevant has been the question of provisioning for loan losses, because the creation of such provisions involves a corresponding reduction in shareholder equity.[2] Recent accounting standards had overturned previously long-standing banking practice of creating provisions on the basis of forward-looking expected losses, in favour of provisions based on realized or identified potential losses. In 'boom' periods, when loan defaults are below long-term averages, this practice can be argued to overstate capital available for dealing with credit losses in a downturn.

Discussion of bank capital is also complicated by another perspective – that of the market value of the bank's equity. This may vary substantially from accounting values, because it reflects investors' expectations of the value of future profits of the bank (adjusted for the perceived riskiness of the bank's activities). This will differ from the 'book' (accounting) value because of differences between the mark-to-market value of bank assets (and liabilities) and their accounting values, as well as the 'franchise' value of the bank. Bank owners will prefer management (who, in principle, they control) to operate the bank in such a way that the stock market value is maximized while their exposure to loss is minimized. Where their share investment provides limited liability, there is an incentive to minimize the amount of contributed capital. Using the terminology of option pricing, the owner's stake in the bank has a pay-off which resembles that of a call option on the value of the bank's assets – unlimited upside and limited downside – with the value of that pay-off increasing with the volatility of the bank's assets and leverage. These incentives to increased risk-taking and higher leverage should, in principle, be moderated by other claimants on the bank recognizing the adverse consequences for their own claims, and demanding appropriately higher compensation for the increased risk. But in practice, the ability of other claimants to recognize the level of risk-taking is limited, while explicit or implicit guarantees of bank deposits (or other liabilities) by government as part of a broader 'safety net' also weaken the extent of discipline exercised by those other stakeholders.[3]

4.3   A BRIEF HISTORY OF BANK CAPITAL

Bank capital arrangements have changed substantially over time. For example, some historical examples (including Australia, Scotland, UK, USA) involved bank shareholders having double or unlimited liability. Government-owned banks were once more common (although government ownership has re-emerged reluctantly during the GFC), in which situations the relevance of an explicit capital base, rather than a government promise of repayment, can be questioned. Mutual banks (or other similar depository–lending institutions) were also more common, and in such institutions there is no distinction between owners and depositor customers, although the accumulated reserves constitute a form of 'communal' capital able to absorb losses and protect individual deposits.

Over the long term, bank capital relative to assets has fallen substantially. Kaufman (1992, Figure 1) shows that the ratio of equity to assets for US banks fell from over 50 per cent in the mid-1880s to the mid-teens in the period between the formation of the Federal Reserve in 1914 and the establishment of the Federal Deposit Insurance Corporation in 1933, and subsequently declined to the 6–8 per cent range. Lewis and Davis (1987, Table 5.1) present equivalent data for UK banks, showing that in 1880 the ratio of equity capital to assets was 16.8 per cent, then falling consistently to 2.7 per cent in 1950 before recovering to around 5 per cent in subsequent decades. In the case of Australia, Butlin et al. (1971), Table 2i) provide data indicating that shareholders' equity as a ratio to total assets for Australian trading banks was 19.6 per cent in 1876 and 15.4 per cent in 1901, but had fallen to 6.7 per cent in 1945.

The Basel I Capital Accord of 1988 (together with prior introduction of minimum capital requirements in some countries such as the UK and USA) led to a global stabilization of risk-weighted capital ratios Indeed, Jackson (1999) indicates that the average ratio of capital to risk-weighted assets in the G10 countries increased from 9.3 per cent at the Accord's introduction (which prescribed a minimum 8 per cent risk-weighted ratio) to 11.2 per cent in 1996. There is, however, some evidence that equity/asset ratios continued to decline, although interpretation is clouded by bank use of preference stock and valuations of intangible assets.[4] In the US, for example, '[t]angible total assets rose from 16 times tangible common equity in 1993 to a multiple of 25 in 2007' (Hoenig, 2010).

Why 8 per cent was chosen as an appropriate quantity of capital for the minimum requirement has never been justified on a prudential or systemic risk basis. Rather, it appears that it was a figure capable of being met by banks in all the G10 nations without too much stress, and not too distant from existing national averages (although differences in national accounting practices made cross-country comparisons tenuous). The Basel Accord also introduced a distinction between capital items based on a 'quality' characteristic. The 4 per cent minimum Tier 1 capital requirement, comprising shareholders' funds and some other securities, was essentially seen as capital available to absorb losses on a going concern basis, and for which an absence of mandatory distribution payout requirements would enable conservation of capital in a period of stress. Tier 2 capital was perceived as other securities, with some degree of longevity, subordinate to, and thus providing a buffer for, deposits in the event of a winding up.

The original Capital Accord focused on capital required to meet counterparty default (credit) risk, and incorporated credit risk associated with off-balance sheet activities into the framework. Since that time, various amendments have been made to the Basel Capital framework. Recognition that banks face more than one type of risk was reflected in the 1996 amendment to the Accord, which incorporated market risk from trading activities.

The most fundamental changes have been those incorporated in 2006 in Basel II. These changes involved:

- Introduction of a distinction between a *standardized* approach and an *internal ratings based* approach, with the latter enabling large banks, approved by their regulator, to use their own internal models in the determination of risk-weighted assets and regulatory capital requirements;

- changes to the risk weights in the standardized approach, including use of credit rating agency gradings to assign risk weights;
- more attention to securitization and other off-balance sheet items;
- introduction of a capital requirement for operational risk;
- provision for national regulators to impose capital requirements for interest rate risk in the banking book; and
- calibration of overall requirements which may involve some possible reduction in regulatory capital requirements for large internal rating based (IRB) banks, but with no planned change in aggregate capital requirements for the banking sector as a whole.

The absence in the original Basel II proposal of any intention of increasing the aggregate capital position of the banking sector is particularly worth noting for two reasons. First, bank leverage has been dramatically lower than that in other sectors of the economy. Financial sector regulation and supervision, particularly the existence of a 'financial sector safety net' providing some degree of protection for bank creditors, is a major reason for this situation. Second, the GFC has led to substantial reassessment of the nature of that regulation and the appropriateness of banks operating with such low capital ratios, particularly following the decline in equity to assets ratios observed in the first decade of the twenty-first century.

4.4   BANK CAPITAL EXPERIENCES DURING THE GFC

While the GFC affected all nations to some degree, it could reasonably be argued that the banking sector problems were primarily a transatlantic phenomenon, with the USA and Europe experiencing the greatest difficulties. That can be seen in two ways. One is by examining the estimates of bank write-downs of asset values (and thus balance sheet equity) as shown in Table 4.1. The US and UK banks have the greatest estimated write-downs with cumulative loss rates over twice that of banks in the euro area and over three times that of the Asian area. This is also reflected in a second indicator of the behaviour of bank share prices, with March 2010 bank share prices in the US and Europe having recovered to only around half of their mid-2007 level. In contrast, the bank share price recovery in Australia and Asia (excluding Japan) has been to around 80 per cent (see RBA, 2010, Graph 1).

The consequences for both banks and banking systems have been

Table 4.1   *Banking sector losses: estimated global bank write-downs by domicile (2007–10), US$billion*

	Estimated Holdings	Estimated Write downs	Implied Cumulative Loss Rate (percent)
US banks			
Total for loans	8059	588	7.3
Total for securities	4502	296	6.6
Total for loans and securities	12561	885	7.0
UK banks			
Total for loans	6744	398	5.9
Total for securities	1625	57	3.5
Total for loans and securities	8369	455	5.4
Euro area banks			
Total for loans	15994	442	2.8
Total for securities	6907	224	3.2
Total for loans and securities	22901	665	2.9
Other mature Europe banks			
Total for loans	3241	134	4.1
Total for securities	729	22	3.0
Total for loans and securities	3970	156	3.9
Asia banks			
Total for loans	6150	84	1.4
Total for securities	1728	30	1.8
Total for loans and securities	7879	115	1.5
Total for all bank loans	40189	1647	4.1
Total for all bank securities	15491	629	4.1
Total for loans and securities	55680	2276	4.1

Source: http://www.imf.org/external/pubs/ft/gfsr/2010/01/c1/table1_2.csv

dramatic. Figure 4.1 shows the dramatic decline in market capitalization during the GFC for some of the world's largest banks and also shows the rise to prominence of the Chinese banks.[5] Figure 4.2 shows the experience of the major Australian banks over the same period.

The consequences have been dramatic at the national level, as shown over a longer-term horizon (1999–2009) in Figure 4.3, with the US and UK banking sectors suffering dramatically. While the Australian banking sector appears to have had a significant increase in market capitalization over the decade, this is partly due to the effect of exchange rate changes on the US$ figures used.

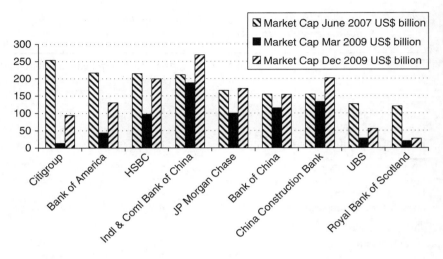

Source: Financial Times.

Figure 4.1   Changes in bank market capitalization

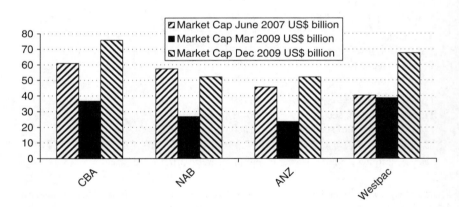

Source: Financial Times.

Figure 4.2   Changes in Australian bank market capitalization

While the headlines have focused upon large bank failures and problems, the economic problems associated with the GFC have transmitted
problems with delayed effects to smaller banks. In the USA, for example,
the Federal Deposit Insurance Corporation (FDIC) has closed 41 banks

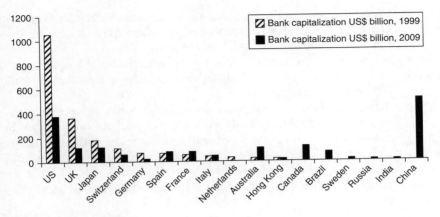

Source: Financial Times.

Figure 4.3   *Bank capitalization changes by country*

in the first three months of 2010 and 140 banks during 2009, compared to 25 in 2008 and only 23 in total for the years 2001–2007.[6]

4.5   CAPITAL LESSONS FROM THE GFC

Stevens (2009) identifies five lessons from the GFC including: inadequate bank capital and mis-measurement of risk; inadequate attention to liquidity risk; growth of systemically important shadow banking institutions (often linked to banks); complexities in national regulators dealing with multinational banks facing difficulties; the tendency for the financial sector to impart procyclicality. Within the first of those categories, a number of lessons about deficiencies in the capital adequacy regime have emerged from the GFC:

- Inadequacy of Value at Risk (VAR) for determining capital requirements;
- risk weights based on historical experience over a relatively benign period are inadequate for risk exposures in downturns;
- excessive liquidity risks (such as commitments to off-balance sheet entities) were partly a result of financing techniques which avoided capital requirements;
- valuations of complex financial assets can be problematic, particularly when markets are disrupted, with adverse consequences for reliable measurement of capital;
- collateralized financing created risks;

- bilateral exposures through over-the-counter markets in derivatives created complex risk interdependencies which may be avoided by the use of Central Clearing Counterparties;
- banks were unwilling to reduce cash distributions to equity and other investors for fear of signalling weakness – even though this reduced their capital bases;
- the current Basel capital framework allows banks to operate with very low shareholders' funds. (For example, a bank with a Tier 1 risk-weighted ratio at the 4 per cent minimum, and with assets with a 50 per cent risk weighting, could have an equity/assets ratio as low as 2 per cent); and
- ratings provided by credit ratings agencies were not good signals of default risk.

4.6   PROPOSALS FOR BANK CAPITAL REQUIREMENTS

There have been a large number of proposals suggested by individuals, private and official sector working groups, and regulatory agencies for changes to bank capital requirements.

4.6.1   Increased Capital Levels

As noted earlier, the setting of capital requirements at 8 per cent of risk-weighted assets has never been fully justified in terms of its adequacy regarding either prudential requirements for individual banks or systemic risk issues. Following the GFC there has been much discussion about whether higher capital levels are desirable, with most commentary arguing for substantial increases.

Greenspan (2010), for example, points to the behaviour of credit default swap (CDS) spreads for US banks since the onset of the GFC. In early 2007, prior to the crisis, 5-year CDS spreads for six major US banks averaged around 17 basis points – with this figure indicating that investors in bank debt had to pay very little (17 basis points per annum) to insure against default by the bank. At that time, the equity/assets ratios for those banks were around 10 per cent. The CDS spreads had jumped to over 400 basis points following the Lehman failure, and on the basis of subsequent declines in the spread in response to equity injections under the TARP programme, Greenspan derives a ball-park estimate of an equity/assets ratio of 14 per cent as necessary to reduce spreads back to their previous low implied default risk levels.

Other analysis (e.g. Brunnermeier et al., 2009) has focused on the fact that a minimum requirement should only be a part of a regulatory capital supervision process. If there is to be some critical capital level at which regulators act to resolve a bank, there needs to be a 'ladder' of capital ratios – each lower rung of which involves some increasingly stringent regulatory position being taken. In this perspective, it is the potential for regulatory forbearance which needs to be minimized, a view which finds its strongest support in the prompt corrective action (PCA) requirements of US legislation.

4.6.2 Additional Capital Requirements for Systemically Important Institutions

There are a number of proposals suggesting that large, systemically important financial institutions should face higher capital requirements than smaller institutions with similar underlying risk of failure – which may be described as a 'bigness tax'. Two separate arguments can be advanced for such additional capital requirements.

The pervasiveness of the 'too big to fail' (TBTF) perception underpins one argument. If it is widely believed that large, systemically important, institutions will not be allowed to fail by regulators, they are in effect receiving an implicit government subsidy enabling them to raise funds more cheaply than otherwise. This has adverse competitive consequences as well as being an implicit cost to taxpayers – for which ideally compensation should be received. Higher capital requirements reduce both the implicit benefit accruing to the bank's owners, and the risk of failure, and thus the extent of the subsidy.

An alternative argument advanced, for example, by the Squam Lake group of economists (Squam Lake, 2009a) is based upon the externalities which such large financial institutions create for the economy. These externalities take several forms reflecting the effect of aggregation of risks in a large institution rather than in a number of smaller ones. First, the consequences of a large institution facing failure are more significant because the impact of any forced asset sales on financial market prices is larger. Second, failure will impact on many more counterparties, simultaneously creating problems for their own solvency.

How to adjust capital requirements for systemically important institutions to incorporate macro-prudential risk effects remains to be determined. The Geneva Report (Brunnermeier et al., 2009) suggests augmenting the capital requirement by a multiplicative factor which would reflect such signals of macro prudential risk as leverage, maturity mismatch and rate of expansion. These factors do not, however, take into account the 'interconnectedness' of individual large financial institutions or the key role they play in the financial system network, which is crucial to understanding the extent of externalities associated with their failure (or actions to avert such an outcome).

In its Financial Stability Report, the IMF (2010) reviews a number of proposals which focus on interconnectedness. One approach would be to link systemic capital charges to interbank correlations of equity returns. While easy to implement, this is, at best, a rough and ready measure of interconnectedness which may have limited relevance in periods of market stress. Another is to utilize the concept of co-value-at-risk (covar) which estimates how the value at risk of other financial institutions behaves when a specified institution is experiencing negative outcomes. Yet another (although suggested in the form of a tax rather than a capital charge) would be based upon positions in the OTC derivatives markets. (This is consistent with the regulatory desire to encourage exchange traded or centrally cleared derivatives in order to reduce bilateral interdependencies and consequent spillovers).

The IMF itself (IMF, 2010) suggests two possible approaches. One, using network analysis and simulation, estimates the level of impairment that a particular institution's failure would impose on capital positions of other institutions. The second, based on the covar concept, would relate systemic risk capital charges to an institution's probability of failure and the effect it would have on system-wide credit VAR.

4.6.3   Contingent Capital

A number of proposals have been put forward for the introduction of *contingent capital* which generally involve banks being required to issue hybrid debt securities which convert automatically into equity if certain trigger conditions (such as reaching a low pre-specified equity/assets ratio) are met. The objectives of such proposals are that bank capital would be automatically augmented by the conversion in conditions where this is desirable, and it may also be argued that investors in such securities would closely monitor bank performance and thus enhance market discipline.

One of the earliest proposals for requiring contingent capital was made by Flannery (2005) who argued for a requirement for banks to have on issue some minimum ratio of 'reverse convertible debentures' (RCDs) to assets. Should the bank's capital ratio, measured using the market value of equity, fall below some specified level, RCDs would convert automatically into a fixed value of bank equity (that is, the number of shares received would be inversely related to the share price). This fixed-value conversion arrangement is the same as that found in the converting preference shares popular during the 1990s with Australian banks (Davis, 1996) although the trigger conversion mechanism is novel. The RCDs would not prevent bank failure (if bank asset values fell by more than the total of equity and RCDs on issue) but would provide an automatic 'top up' to equity for smaller declines in bank asset values (as reflected in equity prices). To the extent that the conversion value was specified to be some larger amount than the face value of the securities, shareholders would suffer a dilution in the event of a conversion.

Another version of the contingent capital proposal emanates from the Squam Lake group of economists (Squam Lake, 2009b). It involves two necessary conditions being met in order for conversion to occur. One condition is that regulators declare that a systemic crisis exists, with this condition being aimed at limiting risk of investors to conversion only occurring in a crisis, and not being simply due to poor performance of the bank involved. This imposes discipline on bank managers who might otherwise regard such securities as a form of 'reserve' equity which can be called upon if excessive risk-taking has unfortunate outcomes. The second necessary condition is that the bank has hit some minimum equity/ assets ratio or other such covenant requirement, protecting investors in well-capitalized banks from risk of conversion, and altering the political lobbying process for regulators to declare a systemic crisis which is likely to occur.

Another approach is suggested by Kashyap et al. (2009), and involves requiring banks to buy insurance policies that will pay out if a crisis state of the world occurs, thus augmenting equity capital. To ensure that the provider of the insurance policy is able to meet the payoff required, they propose that the insurer be required to invest an amount equal to the sum insured in Treasury (risk-free) securities in some form of trust fund. From the insurer's perspective this investment can be viewed as akin to invest-ing in a form of 'catastrophe bond', in which catastrophe involves loss of principal, but for which the return is otherwise high (involving both the interest earned and insurance premiums received).

Another approach is suggested by Hart and Zingales (2009) who view banks as being equivalent to levered investors, borrowing from depositors and other fund providers to invest in a risky portfolio of assets. They use the analogy of margin calls to suggest that bank creditors should be able to demand injections of equity into the bank when the risk of the bank being unable to meet its obligations to creditors reaches some undesirable level. They suggest that CDS spreads may provide an appropriate signal, with spreads above some level triggering a 'margin' call in the form of a regulatory requirement for the bank to issue new equity. They prefer use of this market-based mechanism to regulatory discretion to require banks to recapitalize. How such a requirement would affect bank stock price dynamics, whether it might create opportunities for strategic manipulative behaviour, and what type of equity injection is appropriate are questions requiring further elaboration.

The Hart and Zingales approach could, if the equity injection were required from existing shareholders, be seen as a form of 'less than limited liability' structure for bank shareholders – akin to cases of double or unlimited liability found in long distant banking systems. But it is only applicable (and intended) for large financial institutions for whom there are CDS markets. Implementing such an approach more generally could be achieved if bank equity took the form of partly paid shares, where a call for the unpaid amount would correspond more closely to the margin call concept. But in modern financial markets where bank shares turn over rapidly, requiring that bank equity took the form of an investment with a contingent liability could create significant problems for investor understanding.

A form of contingent capital has already been issued by (among others) Lloyds Bank in November 2009 as contingent capital notes (popularly referred to as 'CoCos') which are debt securities which convert automatically into equity if the bank's capital ratio falls below 5 per cent. There are many who are sceptical about the merits of such securities, arguing that conversion would induce adverse market reaction to the bank, and that hedging of risk by holders of CoCos involving increased shorting of the bank's shares as the conversion point was neared would depress the share price, leading some to describe such securities as 'death spiral convertibles' (Aldrick, 2010).

These proposals can be viewed as attempts to ensure that the public sector (taxpayer) does not become the provider of contingent capital such as happened during the GFC. Those actions included direct government equity injections into stricken banks, but also included the government provision of guarantees of bank deposits and debt. Although no explicit equity injection is made in that latter case, the actions should be viewed as essentially equivalent – in that the government budget provided the buffer to absorb bank losses. While fees were generally charged for those guarantees, it is arguable whether a fair return for the risk taken on was received by governments (and taxpayers).

4.6.4 Changes to Regulatory Risk Weights

One consequence of the GFC experience has been a recognition that the Basel II Accord needed revision, even though it had not been in operation in the lead-up to the GFC. In July 2009, the Basel Committee announced a number of changes including higher capital charges (and outlining other required operational requirements) for some securitization assets (including re-securitizations such as CDOs) and for liquidity facilities provided by banks to off-balance sheet conduits. This recognizes the role which these activities played in the crisis. These changes also involved requirements for banks to undertake an appropriate Internal Capital Adequacy Assessment Program (ICAAP) and for discrepancies between that and regulatory capital assessments to form the basis of a dialogue with supervisors. Changes to international accounting standards for the valuation of financial assets were also supported.

In December 2009, a consultative document was released outlining proposed changes to capital requirements as follows:

- an increase in the quality of the capital base, such that Tier 1 is to be predominantly shareholders' funds, with other Tier 1 instruments to be subordinated, with discretionary non-cumulative dividends or coupons, no maturity nor incentives to redeem;
- an increase in the relative counterparty risk weights for financial institutions versus corporates, to reflect the greater correlation of risks in the case of the former;
- increased capital requirements for counterparty risk on derivatives, repo and securitization transactions;
- lower relative risk weights for counterparty derivatives exposures to central clearing counterparties versus bilateral exposures;
- use of 'downturn' probability of default estimates to accompany 'downturn' loss given default estimates;
- use of 'stressed' VAR figures in determining capital requirements;
- reduced reliance on ratings agency assessments in the standardized approach; and
- expected loss provisioning.

4.6.5 A Leverage Ratio

There is strong support internationally for the introduction of a non-risk-weighted minimum leverage ratio as a supplement to the Basel risk-weighted capital requirement. Indeed, in some countries such as the USA, a minimum leverage ratio (equity/assets) existed prior to the introduction of Basel I and has remained in place, at 3 per cent for 'strong' banks and 4 per cent for other banks (World Bank, 2008), as a complement to the Basel risk-weighted requirement, often being the more binding constraint on bank activities.

The main argument behind supplementing the Basel requirement with a leverage ratio requirement is argued to involve the problems of adequately measuring bank risk-taking in a world of imperfect information. Because risk weights may involve errors, and because banks have incentives for increased leverage, there is the potential for them to engage in activities which are more risky than assumed in the Basel framework. A leverage ratio is simple to operate, and may contain additional information about potential bank failure than can be derived from the risk-weighted ratio. Bordeleau, et al. (2009) conclude from a study of Canadian bank capital management that a leverage ratio may be a useful complement, with banks experiencing shocks which reduce capital buffers close to required leverage ratios above the point for taking rapid action to remedy that position.

But on the downside there are problems.[7] These include incorporating off-balance sheet activities into such a simple measure, and pro-cyclicality arising from banks' losses in economic downturns reducing capital and requiring contraction of lending (and vice versa in upturns). To the extent that a leverage ratio is binding and requires banks to increase shareholder equity, it also can have adverse effects on bank profitability (if equity is a more expensive source of funds). Whether that latter effect should be a cause for concern depends on to what degree capital requirements offset the benefits banks receive from the existence of the financial safety net.

Australian banks and their regulators do not appear favourably disposed towards introduction of a leverage ratio requirement. As well as the implied downgrading of the importance of risk in capital allocation (RBA, 2010, p. 54), another reason is that, because of the preponderance of low-risk weight housing mortgages in bank portfolios, it is likely that the leverage ratio would be binding and require banks to increase their capital positions. This is reflected in Figure 4.4, which shows the relationship between risk-weighted capital and leverage ratios at the onset of the GFC in 2007. While there are many important caveats to be observed in comparing such figures across nations (including different capital measures, risk weights, consolidation etc.), it would appear that Australian banks are towards the lower end of the scale in terms of leverage ratios. But in assessing that situation, it is also the case that Australian banks have focused on housing loans partly because of the low associated capital requirements under the Basel Accord. This may reflect housing loan risk weights being too low, and a leverage ratio may induce a shift of bank activities towards other forms of lending and improve the competitive position of other forms of mortgage financing such as securitization.

The ratings agencies have also focused upon alternative measures of capital adequacy for the purposes of providing ratings. S&P (2009a, 2009b), for example, argue that neither the Basel risk-weighted capital

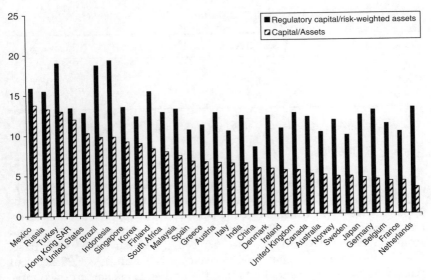

Source: IMF Global Financial Stability Report October 2009, Tables 22, 23, available at http://www.imf.org/external/pubs/ft/gfsr/2009/02.

Figure 4.4 Risk-weighted capital and leverage ratios: 2007

ratio nor the leverage ratio provide a good signal of capital strength, and that national differences in risk weightings and capital measures inhibit global comparisons of banking strength. In calculating their Risk Adjusted Capital (RAC) ratio, they opt to use industry-based risk weights, essentially assuming that all banks have the same underwriting standards for credit risk, rather than relying on the risk assessment implied in each bank's own internal models. Their risk-adjusted capital ratio estimates also include adjustments for the effects of diversification and concentration on risk.

Table 4.2 provides a comparison of the relationship between S&P calculations, the Basel risk-weighted capital ratio and leverage ratio for three of the major Australian banks (available from S&P, 2009b). The low correlation between the measures observed there is apparent when a larger sample of international banks is considered. For the 29 banks listed in S&P (2009b) with the largest RAC ratios, the correlation between the Basel Tier 1 and Leverage ratios is 0.36, and while that between the Basel and S&P ratios is 0.37, the correlation between the leverage ratio and the S&P ratio is 0.03.

Brewer et al. (2008) note that there are significant differences across

Table 4.2   Alternative capital ratios: major Australian banks 2009[a]

Bank	S&P RAC	Basel II Tier 1	Leverage
NAB	6.9	8.3	4.5
CBA	6.3	8.1	3.3
ANZ	6.1	8.2	4.8

Note: (a) Figures for CBA are June 2009, and for NAB and ANZ are March 2009

Source: S&P (2009b).

nations in capital ratios of large banks, whether measured on a risk-adjusted or unlevered basis, despite all those banks being subject to the Basel Accord requirements. For the period 1992–2005, the average leverage ratio for the largest 55 banks in 12 countries, leverage ratios ranged from 8.4 per cent (USA) to 3.01 per cent (Germany) and with Basel Tier 1 ratios ranging from 10.04 per cent (Switzerland) to 6.27 per cent (Germany). Notably, and illustrating the problems in such cross-country comparisons, their data have Australian banks having the second highest leverage ratio! They find that higher capital ratios are associated with countries in which prompt corrective action is applied, where there is good corporate governance, while they are lower in bank dominated financial markets and for larger banks.

4.6.6   Improving the Quality of Capital

Under the current Basel Accord, banks are able to meet capital requirements by including the value of various hybrid securities issued in the calculation of their capital base. The rationale has been that such securities rank behind depositors and thus are part of the buffer to absorb and protect depositors from loss. However, such securities may be of limited term and redeemable by the holders, which can see the bank 'losing' such capital in situations where its performance is weak, reducing its capital position on a 'going concern' basis. For this reason, 'core' capital represented by shareholder funds may be a preferred measure. Hybrid securities, intensively used by banks as part of Tier 1 capital since the October 1998 BIS 'Sydney' press release (*The Banker*, 2009) have tended to be disregarded by analysts in assessing bank capital strength, and government rescues of banks in the GFC have made their status as 'wind-up' capital less relevant. The Basel Committee's December 2009 proposals imply a move in this direction, with the calibration of new requirements to be determined after an impact assessment study is conducted.

4.6.7   Procyclical Capital Requirements

Because bank capital management tends to aggravate economic cycles (attempting to build up capital and reducing loans in periods of downturns etc.), there are various proposals for the introduction of procyclical minimum capital requirements. Higher minimum requirements in an economic upswing would both inhibit excessive credit creation and create a capital buffer which could be used to offset effects of a downturn, when the minimum requirement would decline. Implementing such an arrangement is complicated for several reasons. One is whether changes in the requirement would be automatically linked to certain economic indicators or at the discretion of bank regulators. Another problem lies in identifying the appropriate sensitivity of minimum requirements to economic indicators, as well as understanding how bank behaviour might change under such a regulatory approach.

4.7   CONCLUSION

The range and severity of the capital adequacy changes currently under consideration internationally could be interpreted as suggesting that the Basel capital adequacy regime was a failed experiment. Indeed, many of the proposals have elements of historical approaches to capital adequacy operating before the introduction of the Basel Accord in 1988. Higher capital ratios, identifying 'high quality' capital with shareholders' funds, contingent capital requirements imposing equity contribution requirements on some stakeholders of troubled institutions, and use of a leverage ratio requirement all have antecedents in the history of banking.

While inadequacies of the regime were exposed by the GFC, it is more appropriate to view the current proposals for change as part of an evolutionary process involving adaptation of regulation to ongoing financial sector development and innovation – itself partly the result of attempts to avoid the constraints imposed by regulation. But it is also appropriate to note that there appears to have been a widespread shift in attitudes towards the appropriate balance between government regulation and market freedom in the case of financial markets.

How many of these proposed capital adequacy changes will be implemented remains to be seen. But an implication of higher capital adequacy standards arising from any of these measures is an increase in the cost of bank intermediation. Whether that is ultimately borne by bank customers or their shareholders is an empirical question, but it seems likely (unless the scope of prudential regulation is expanded significantly beyond banks) that some decline in the relative share of banks in the financial intermediation process will result.

To the extent that bank intermediation was artificially favoured in the pre-GFC environment by the existence of the financial safety net (including such things as 'too big to fail' policies, implicit or underpriced government guarantees and insurance, Central Bank liquidity support facilities), this outcome is not necessarily undesirable. An efficient financial system should facilitate financing activities along the whole spectrum of risk-taking. To the extent that bank executives were able to exploit regulatory distortions which facilitated or encouraged high-risk activities being conducted by supposedly low-risk, prudentially regulated banks, this situation needs to be reversed.

Finding the appropriate regulatory balance is a difficult task. What increase in the private cost of bank financial intermediation counterbalances the social benefits from the (hopefully) lower risk of further financial crises such as the GFC? If intermediation outside of the prudentially regulated sector is encouraged, will that help or hinder financial stability? What changes in securities and market regulation might be required? These and other questions need to be included in the cost–benefit analysis process by which the various capital adequacy proposals should be judged and an appropriate package of changes selected. Whether the political processes (both national and international) through which an outcome will be decided will reflect such analysis is another question.

NOTES

1. Although see Blundell-Wignall and Atkinson (2008), who argue that proposed reductions in housing mortgage loan risk weights influenced bank strategies and contributed to the growth of sub-prime lending in the USA. Brown and Davis (2004) also note the significant influence of banks' Basel II planning on development of internal risk management systems.
2. In some nations, accounting presentation of balance sheets involves subtracting provisions from loans to display a 'net' loan figure, while in others 'gross' loans are shown and a separate liability item of provisions also shown.
3. In principle, risk-based deposit insurance premiums should, if appropriately calibrated, counteract this effect.
4. The significant decline in leverage ratios of UK Banks since 2000 is shown in World Bank (2008, Figure 1).
5. Note that these figures reflect a mix of share price changes and equity injections and, in the case of non-US banks, valuation changes due to exchange rate changes.
6. Data from http://www.fdic.gov/bank/individual/failed/banklist.csv.
7. See World Bank (2008) for more information on strengths and weaknesses of a regulatory leverage ratio.

REFERENCES

Aldrick, Philip (2010), 'Mervyn King's plan for bank capital "will backfire"', *The Telegraph*, 11 February.

Banker, The (2009), 'The capital conundrum' *The Banker*, 1 December.

Blundell-Wignall, Adrian and Paul Atkinson (2008), 'The sub-prime crisis: causal distortions and regulatory reform', in P. Bloxham and C. Kent (eds), *Lessons from the Financial Turmoil of 2007 and 2008*, Sydney: Reserve Bank of Australia.

Bordeleau, Etienne, Allan Crawford and Christopher Graham (2009), 'Regulatory constraints on bank leverage: issues and lessons from the Canadian experience', *Discussion Paper 2009-15*, Bank of Canada, available at http://www.bankof-canada.ca/en/res/dp/2009/dp09-15.pdf.

Brewer III, Elijah, George Kaufman and Larry Wall (2008), 'Bank capital ratios across countries: why do they vary?', *Journal of Financial Services Research*, **34**, 177–201.

Brown, Christine and Kevin Davis (2004), 'The new Basel Accord and advanced IRB approaches: is there a case for capital incentives?' in Benton Gup (ed.), *The New Basel Accord*, New York: Thomson, pp. 125–49.

Brunnermeier, M., A. Crockett, C. Goodhart, A.D. Persaud and H. Shin (2009), 'The fundamental principles of financial regulation', in *Geneva Reports on the World Economy*, Geneva: ICMB International Center for Monetary and Banking Studies.

Butlin, S.J., A.R. Hall and R.C. White (1971), 'Australian banking and monetary statistics 1817–1945', *Occasional Paper No. 4A*, Reserve Bank of Australia.

Davis, Kevin (1996), 'Converting preference shares: an Australian capital structure innovation', *Accounting and Finance*, **36**(2), November, 213–28.

Flannery, Mark J. (2005), 'No pain, no gain? Effecting market discipline via reverse convertible debentures', in Hal S. Scott (ed.), *Capital Adequacy Beyond Basel: Banking Securities and Insurance*, Oxford: Oxford University Press.

Greenspan, Alan (2010), 'The crisis', Greenspan Associates LLC, 9 March, available at http://documents.propublica.org/docs/draft-of-former-fed-chairman-alan-greenspan-s-paper-on-the-financial-crisis/original.pdf.

Hart, Oliver and Luis Zingales (2009), 'To regulate finance, try the market', *Foreign Policy*, 25 March, available at http://experts.foreignpolicy.com/posts/2009/03/30/to_regulate_finance_try_the_market.

Hoenig, T.M. (2010), 'Written statement by Mr Thomas M. Hoenig: President and Chief Executive Officer of the Federal Reserve Bank of Kansas City, before the House Financial Services Oversight and Investigations Subcommittee, United States House of Representatives, Kansas City, 6 May 2010', available at http://www.bis.org/review/r100511e.pdf.

IMF (2010), *Global Financial Stability Report: Meeting New Challenges to Stability and Building a Safer System*, IMF, April, available at http://www.imf.org/external/pubs/ft/gfsr/2010/01/index.htm.

Jackson, Patricia (1999), 'Capital requirements and bank behaviour: the impact of the Basle Accord', Report by a working group led by Patricia Jackson, Basle Committee On Banking Supervision Working Papers No. 1, April.

Kashyap, Anil, Raghuram Rajan, and Jeremy Stein (2009), 'Rethinking capital regulation', available at www.kc.frb.org/publicat/sympos/2008/KashyapRajanStein.03.12.09.pdf.

Kaufman, George (1992), 'Capital in banking: past, present and future', *Journal of Financial Services Research*, **5**(4) / April, 385–402.

Lewis, Mervyn and Kevin Davis (1987), *Domestic and International Banking*, Cambridge, MA: MIT Press.

RBA (2010), 'Developments in the financial system architecture', *Financial Stability Report*, March.

S&P (2009a), *Methodology and Assumptions: Risk-Adjusted Capital Framework for Financial Institutions*, Standard & Poor's Ratings Direct, 21 April , available at http://www2.standardandpoors.com/spf/pdf/media/20090421_Methodology_ And_Assumptions_FI_RACF_04_21_09.pdf.

S&P (2009b), *S&P Ratio Highlights Disparate Capital Strength Among The World's Biggest Banks*, Standard & Poor's Ratings Direct, 30 November.

Squam Lake Working Group (2009a), 'Reforming capital requirements for financial institutions', Working Paper 2, Squam Lake Working Group on Financial Regulation, Council on Foreign Relations, April, available at http://www.squamlakeworkinggroup.org/.

Squam Lake Working Group (2009b), 'An expedited resolution mechanism for distressed financial firms: regulatory hybrid securities', Working Paper 3, Squam Lake Working Group on Financial Regulation, Council on Foreign Relations, April, available at http://www.squamlakeworkinggroup.org/.

Stevens, Glenn (2009), 'Developments in financial regulation', *Reserve Bank Bulletin*, December, pp. 28–34, available at http://www.rba.gov.au/publications/ bulletin/2009/dec/pdf/bu-1209-4.pdf.

World Bank (2008), 'Background note: banking and the leverage ratio', Financial Systems Department World Bank, available at http://crisistalk.worldbank.org/ files/Banking%20and%20the%20Leverage%20Ratio.pdf.

PART II

Crisis impact on economic activities and costs

5. Unemployment and the global financial crisis: who suffered most and why?

Melisa Bond and Noel Gaston

5.1 INTRODUCTION

This chapter examines the relationship between the deterioration of the labour market and the Global Financial Crisis (GFC). Specifically, we examine the labour market performance in 29 countries as measured by the unemployment rate. Changes in the unemployment rate are an indicator of the economic hardship experienced by workers over the business cycle. In addition to being considered a key macroeconomic indicator, this measure is a political barometer for governments.

Of course, labour markets respond to cyclical and other shocks in a number of ways. In particular, there are both quantity and price responses in labour markets: real wages might fall to insulate workers from unemployment; non-pecuniary benefits may be reduced or eliminated; workers could be pressed to take leave entitlements now, rather than later; there might be increased work-sharing, reduced overtime, a move to part-time work and increased casualization of the workforce. Arguably, increases in the unemployment rate are positively correlated with adverse changes in labour market outcomes for most workers. From a macroeconomic perspective, increases in the unemployment rate are a sufficient statistic for worker hardship and an indicator of the need for governments to intervene.

Are sustained movements in the unemployment rate due to sound or unsound economic management? Does it matter whether the labour market is a deregulated one? Are domestic labour market outcomes driven by international factors which overwhelm changes in domestic conditions? These are the principal questions posed in the present chapter.

We focus on two measures of labour market deterioration and recovery. First, we examine which countries were hardest hit by the GFC, as measured by the size of the increase in the unemployment rate. We explore the characteristics associated with these economies, and compare them to those countries which experienced the smallest change in unemployment. As a corollary, we examine the characteristics of the countries that seem to be recovering most strongly. Obviously, the latter inquiry is speculative. In response to the threat posed by the GFC, governments embarked on a combination of massive fiscal spending programmes and monetary expansion. As we shall see, some countries appear to have escaped relatively unscathed. The incumbent governments of these countries have been quick to claim credit for their fiscal stimulus spending. Those in opposition parties point to the importance of strong trading relationships with resilient Asian economies, particularly China.

The next section briefly reviews the most recent informed literature on what is known about the real effects of the GFC. Section 5.3 discusses the data on unemployment and the relative experience of the 29 countries. Section 5.4 discusses some hypotheses regarding the link between a financial crisis and labour market outcomes, at least as measured by the unemployment rate. We focus, in particular, on the initial conditions present in countries at the time the effects of the GFC started to manifest themselves. Section 5.5 concludes and provides some tentative answers to the questions posed in this chapter.

5.2   WHAT IT IS THAT WE (THINK WE) KNOW ABOUT THE REAL EFFECTS OF THE GFC

In the first instance, the GFC was propagated through international financial connections. The crisis emerged due to problems in the US market [allegedly][1] for sub-prime housing loans in the first half of 2007. Unsurprisingly, given the US origin of the crisis, countries with closer links to the US financial system or with direct exposure to asset-backed securities were the first to be affected (Claessens et al., 2010). While the timing of the onset of the crisis in most countries is relatively clear, what is less clear is which countries were most severely affected and why.

The temptation to simplify matters by arguing that the severity of labour market deterioration all boils down to the degree of exposure to the United States leads one to overlook other key factors. More specifically, those countries with domestic vulnerabilities, or what are termed 'weak initial conditions', were more likely to be among the most severely hurt. This includes countries that were poorly placed to respond to the shock with appropriate macroeconomic policies or other palliative policy measures. Those countries with more sound fiscal and monetary initial fundamentals were always the more likely to recover more easily than their counterparts.

Several recent studies have investigated whether initial conditions and global factors can explain the differential impact of the crisis across countries. For example, in two related papers, Rose and Spiegel (2009a; 2009b) find that initial conditions do a poor job in explaining the economic performance of countries during the crisis period. Rose and Spiegel (2009a) examine a range of potential causes of the crisis, covering such categories as: financial system policies and conditions; asset price appreciation in real estate and equity markets; international imbalances and foreign reserve adequacy; macroeconomic policies; and institutional and geographic features.

However, they are unable to link most of the commonly-cited causes of the crisis to its incidence across countries. In Rose and Spiegel (2009b), two major transmission channels are examined. First, the degree to which a country holding US securities that plummet in value is exposed to a US-originated crisis through a financial channel. Secondly, a country which exports to the United States is exposed to a US downturn through a real channel. They make the remarkable finding that these international linkages are *not* associated with the incidence of the crisis. In particular, countries more exposed to either US financial assets or US trade seem to behave little differently from other countries. They argue that, if anything, countries may actually have *benefited* from the US exposure!

Lane and Milesi-Ferretti (2010) show that while the crisis hit advanced economies the hardest (see also Reinhart and Rogoff, 2008), there is no evidence that higher financial integration contributed to the severity of the crisis. In fact, consistent with the findings of Rose and Spiegel (2009b), they find that more financially integrated economies actually experienced smaller output declines. On the other hand, Lane and Milesi-Ferretti (2010) do find that external vulnerabilities and openness to trade help to understand the intensity of the crisis. Specifically, they find that trade openness is correlated with the output and demand declines, consistent with the dramatic decline in international trade that occurred during the crisis.

As Claessens et al. (2010) argue, the empirical results leave much unexplained and fall far short of providing a 'one-size-fits-all' list of early warning indicators of an impending macro crisis. On the other hand, in a similar fashion to Reinhart and Rogoff (2008; 2009), they point to the accumulation of private sector debt and the failure to reduce public debt as key problems. In particular, the latter diminishes the freedom of policy-makers to respond with sufficiently large fiscal measures.

In terms of cross-country labour market impacts of the crisis, very little research has been done to date. At the theoretical level, economists have become accustomed to thinking that there is a separation between the real and financial sectors of an economy. While we are certainly far from *all* being Keynesians today, this belief has undoubtedly been shaken by recent events. Far from being an immutable constant or natural rate, the equilibrium rate of unemployment moves in response to shocks. Not only does the demand-side matter, but labour market institutions also matter for how shocks are transmitted. They do so by affecting the size and the persistence of movements in the unemployment rate in response to shocks.

Claessens et al. (2009) argue that globally synchronized recessions are longer and deeper than other recessions. Furthermore, Reinhart and Rogoff (2009) show that banking crises are associated with significant declines in output and employment; the unemployment rate rises an average of 7 percentage points over the down-phase of the cycle, which lasts on average over four years. In particular, the average duration of such synchronized recessions tends to be a quarter longer, and these financially-rooted recessions are often associated with more than two times larger cumulative output losses than other recessions. In fact, it appears that unemployment rates increase notably more in recessions with housing busts (which the present crisis is for most countries). While the effect on unemployment depends on the country in question, Furceri and Mourougane (2009) show that unemployment rates usually surge in the event of a deep financial crisis by an average of 5 percentage points in four years. By contrast, episodes of softer crises were characterized by a much smoother increase in the unemployment rates of about 1 percentage point in the four years following the start of the crisis.

Several reasons have been proposed to explain the sudden and synchronized deterioration in global macroeconomic conditions. The first was the widespread loss of consumer and investor confidence in the wake of the collapse of Lehman Brothers in September 2008 and the ensuing turmoil in global financial markets. It is possible that globalization may be a factor in this synchronization of business cycles across countries. The GFC and the deterioration in confidence, the decline in housing and equity wealth led to rapid and steep falls in personal discretionary spending. Private consumption fell sharply in the industrialized and emerging market economies in 2008. Similarly, business investment contracted in a number of countries by late 2008. Associated with these developments was the tightening of credit standards by the major lenders worldwide. This further constrained consumer and business spending. These reactions were quickly transmitted around the world through the trade channel as businesses cut back on production and employment in response to reduced demand.

While it is still early days in the post-mortem of the state of the global macroeconomy, it is still surprising how little we seem to know about the real effects and consequences of the crisis. We address this dilemma of ignorance by providing our own analysis, which we turn to in the next section. As mentioned, we focus on the unemployment rate, something which other researchers have not considered or have only tangentially considered to date.

5.3 WHAT THE DATA ON UNEMPLOYMENT REVEAL

Our analysis focuses on 29 OECD countries. As mentioned above, the developed economies were the hardest hit by the GFC. Notwithstanding, for this group of countries, the data for subsequent analysis are likely to be more reliable, so we restrict our analysis to these. The deterioration in the labour market associated with the GFC is immediately obvious in Figure 5.1. What is somewhat surprising, given that the unemployment rate is normally considered to be a lagging indicator, is that the deterioration in the labour market is evident from the first quarter of 2008. There was a run on the British bank Northern Rock in September 2007; in February 2008 it was nationalized. In the following month, US financial institution Bear Stearns was absorbed by a commercial bank following a significant US Federal Reserve subsidy. While most commentators point to the Lehman Brothers collapse as being the most noteworthy event and the day the world 'officially' took notice of the crisis, the GFC was clearly manifesting itself in the labour market well before September 2008. In the subsequent analysis, we identify the first quarter of 2008 as being the critical quarter during which things started going seriously pear-shaped.[2]

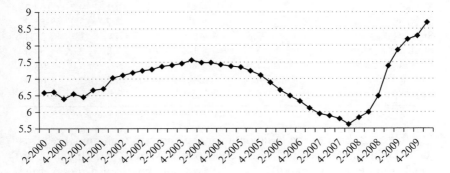

Figure 5.1   Average unemployment rate

Table 5.1   Unemployment in OECD countries

	Unemploy-ment rate (UR) 1-2008 (i)	Ave UR 10 years (ii)	Ave UR 5 years (iii)	UR Worst (iv)	UR Latest (v)	ΔUR (vi)	%ΔUR (vii)
Australia	4.0	5.7	4.9	5.8	5.3	1.8	45.0
Austria	3.8	4.3	4.6	5.1	4.9	1.3	34.2
Belgium	6.8	7.8	8.0	8.2	8.1	1.4	20.6
Canada	6.0	7.0	6.6	8.7	8.1	2.7	45.0
Czech Republic	4.4	7.5	6.9	7.9	7.9	3.5	79.5
Denmark	3.1	4.6	4.4	7.6	7.6	4.5	145.2
Finland	6.2	8.7	7.8	9.0	9.0	2.8	45.2
France	7.6	9.0	8.9	10.1	10.1	2.5	32.9
Germany	7.5	8.8	9.3	7.6	7.3	0.1	1.3
Greece	7.8	10.0	9.2	10.2	10.2	2.4	30.8
Hungary	7.5	6.6	7.0	11.1	11.0	3.6	48.0
Iceland	2.3	2.7	2.7	7.8	7.8	5.5	239.1
Ireland	5.1	4.7	4.6	13.2	13.2	8.1	158.8
Italy	6.4	8.4	7.2	8.8	8.8	2.4	37.5
Japan	3.8	4.6	4.3	5.6	5.0	1.8	47.4
Luxembourg	4.4	3.5	4.6	5.6	5.6	1.2	27.3
Mexico	3.7	3.3	3.7	6.1	5.6	2.4	64.9
Netherlands	2.8	3.4	3.9	4.1	4.1	1.3	46.4
New Zealand	3.8	5.0	3.9	7.3	7.3	3.5	92.1
Norway	2.3	3.5	3.6	3.3	3.3	1.0	43.5
Poland	7.3	15.6	14.3	9.1	9.1	1.8	24.7
Portugal	7.4	6.1	7.5	10.5	10.5	3.1	41.9
Slovakia	10.0	16.1	14.3	14.2	14.1	4.2	42.0
South Korea	3.1	4.1	3.5	4.8	3.8	1.7	54.8
Spain	9.4	10.4	9.4	19.1	19.1	9.7	103.2
Sweden	5.8	6.5	6.9	9.0	8.7	3.2	55.2
Switzerland	3.5	3.6	4.0	4.6	4.6	1.1	31.4
United Kingdom	5.2	5.2	5.1	7.8	7.8	2.6	50.0
United States	5.1	5.0	5.1	10.1	9.9	5.0	98.0
Average	5.4	6.6	6.4	8.4	8.2	3.0	61.6
Std. Dev.	2.1	3.4	2.9	3.3	3.4	2.1	48.9

Table 5.1 tabulates the basic data for the analysis. Column (i) records the unemployment rate for the 29 countries in March 2008 (the data on which Figure 5.1 are based). The next two columns record the average unemployment rate in the 10 years and 5 years immediately prior to the

first quarter of 2008 (1-2008, hereafter). The first three columns reveal considerable heterogeneity in unemployment rates across the 29 countries. In 1-2008, unemployment rates were as high as 10 per cent in Slovakia and 9.4 per cent in Spain and as low as 2.3 per cent in Norway and (interestingly enough) Iceland.

The next column of Table 5.1 records the worst (that is, highest) unemployment rate subsequent to 1-2008. Column (v) records the latest available data (in some cases for April 2010). Notable is the fact that for 17 of the 29 countries, their latest unemployment rate equals their worst unemployment following 1-2008. At the time of writing (July 2010), the crisis continues to have dire labour market consequences for some countries.

The last two columns of Table 5.1 contain two simple calculations that we focus on for the remainder of the chapter. We measure the severity of the crisis by calculating the net change in the unemployment rate experienced by each country. Column (vi), or ΔUR, is calculated as the difference in unemployment rates from 1-2008 to the worst rate recorded (that is, column (v) minus column (i)). Column (vii) expresses this figure in percentage terms, that is, %ΔUR. It is moot whether ΔUR or %ΔUR best captures the deterioration of the labour market. On the one hand, the absolute change is more readily translatable to the number of workers being thrown out of work. With the latter measure, it matters whether a country is a high or low unemployment country initially. For two countries whose unemployment rate rose by the same amount, e.g., 2.4 percentage points, there is a difference between Greece, where such a figure represents a 30 per cent worsening, and the relatively low-unemployment Mexico, where the same rise in the unemployment rate represents a 65 per cent worsening. For our main analysis below, the former measure is likely to be a cleaner measure of labour market distress, since the number of unemployed finding work during the crisis is likely to be minuscule.[3]

Sorting column (vi) from best to worst, the differential performance of the best performers and worst performers is immediately apparent. Consider Figure 5.2, paying particular attention to the stark difference in the vertical scales of both panels. The better performers have experienced moderate increases in unemployment, while the worst performers have suffered sky-rocketing unemployment. Notable is that three members of the 'P-I-I-I-G-S' group of countries (Portugal-Iceland-Ireland-Italy-Greece-Spain), which have garnered so much notoriety recently, are included in the latter group of 'worst 5' (see Figure 5.2).

Obviously, not all countries have been, and continue to be, affected to the same extent by the GFC. There is considerable cross-country heterogeneity. In the next section, we search for links between changes in the unemployment rate and a number of economic (initial) position

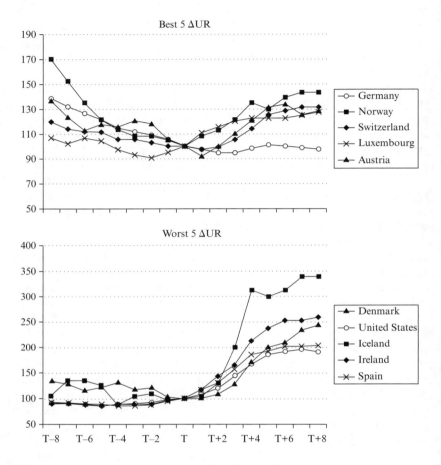

Figure 5.2   Unemployment rate index, best and worst

and performance indicators. In particular, we focus on some interesting hypotheses that have only been fleetingly examined in the recent literature.

5.4   HYPOTHESES LINKING THE GFC TO SUBSEQUENT LABOUR MARKET PERFORMANCE

In this section we return to the basic questions posed in the recent research discussed in section 5.2. Namely, how much do initial domestic conditions matter (that is, how vulnerable countries may have been or how weak institutions within countries are) versus how much global connectedness matters?

5.4.1 Exposure to Trade Matters

In recent years, there has been considerable interest in how international trade affects unemployment. For example, Moore and Ranjan (2005) and Gaston and Rajaguru (2010) incorporate equilibrium unemployment into general equilibrium trade models to show how the unemployment rate is affected by international factors, such as the terms-of-trade. Dutt et al. (2009) use cross-country panel data on unemployment and trade policy and conclude that greater openness leads to more unemployment in the short run, but to a reduction in steady-state unemployment. The common theme of models in this new literature is that there is a labour market friction generating unemployment; this means that unemployment and wages are likely to be negatively related. It also means that shocks which affect aggregate labour demand will affect unemployment.

The first hypothesis we examine is the importance of global connectedness and the strength of links to the United States in particular. Recall the Rose and Spiegel (2009b) finding that countries may have actually benefited from exposure to the United States. Without calling into question the veracity of their finding, it is so unexpected (at least by us) that it bears re-examination. In Australia, one argument that has been put forward for Australia's relative labour market buoyancy is its exposure to China. After peaking at over 10 per cent in 1993, Australia's unemployment rate steadily fell until the onset of the GFC. The drop in the unemployment rate was particularly sharp during the years of Australia's mining boom after 2002. During the 2007 election campaign, the then (Coalition) government claimed that the falling unemployment rate was due to its superior economic management and its deregulation of the labour market. The then (Labor) opposition claimed that the good numbers on the unemployment front were primarily due to the booming Chinese demand for mining resources (and certainly not to any labour market reforms). It seems that being in government changes one's perspective on such matters. In response to the threat posed by the GFC, the Labor government embarked on a massive fiscal spending programme. Unemployment increased during the GFC, but only moderately. Compared to many of its OECD counterparts, and as witnessed by Table 5.1, Australia appears to have escaped relatively unscathed. Labor was quick to claim credit for its stimulus spending. The Coalition opposition, however, now argues that the resilience of the Chinese economy has been the key.

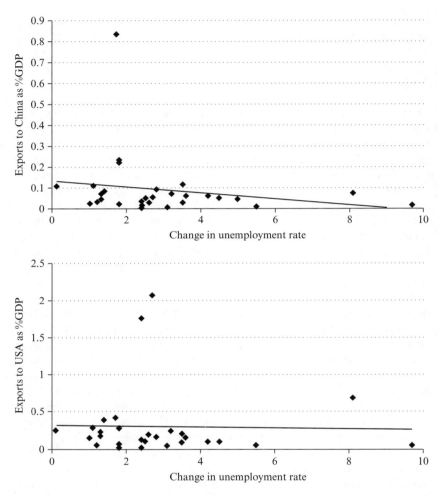

Figure 5.3   Trade and changes in unemployment

In Figure 5.3 we present plots of ΔUR and the exports to both China and the United States in 1-2008. The bottom panel is for bilateral exports, normalized by GDP, to the United States (naturally, the United States doesn't appear). The two 'northern-most' dots are for Mexico and Canada. The regression line through the cluster of points confirms Rose and Spiegel's (2009b) finding of no significant relationship (ρ = −0.01). Moreover, if we were to omit the observation for Ireland, trade exposure to the United States may be beneficial (ρ = −0.11).

Table 5.2   Components of the KOF index of economic globalization

Indices and variables		Weights
i) Actual flows		(50%)
	Trade (per cent of GDP)	(16%)
	FDI, flows (per cent of GDP)	(21%)
	FDI, stocks (per cent of GDP)	(23%)
	Portfolio investment (per cent of GDP)	(19%)
	Income payments to foreign nationals (per cent of GDP)	(22%)
ii) Restrictions		(50%)
	Hidden import barriers	(24%)
	Mean tariff rate	(28%)
	Taxes on international trade (per cent of current revenue)	(28%)
	Capital account restrictions	(20%)

Source: Dreher et al. (2008).

As for exposure to China, the story is even more clear-cut and positive. Trade with China helps buffer the labour market deterioration. (The relationship persists even if the data for South Korea are omitted.) This is consistent with the findings of Gaston and Rajaguru (2010), who find a strong inverse relationship between terms-of-trade movements and unemployment for Australia. Trade openness matters. Importantly, the openness is beneficial.

5.4.2 Globalization (Somewhat) Matters

We next examine the claim that globalization, more broadly defined, may matter. To gauge the effect of globalization on a country's labour market outcomes we employ an index that captures the extent to which countries are more (or less) globalized. When a phenomenon like globalization encompasses several aspects that, taken together, may have an effect greater than the sum of their constituent parts, it appears logical to assess these effects together. Composite indices provide an excellent way to accomplish this since they provide a single statistic on which comparisons can be based, without the confounding effects of variation at lower levels of aggregation.[4] Specifically, we use the KOF (a measure of globalization) index (see Dreher et al., 2008). It is based on a number of variables that relate to different dimensions of economic globalization (see Table 5.2). More specifically, the sub-index on actual economic flows includes data

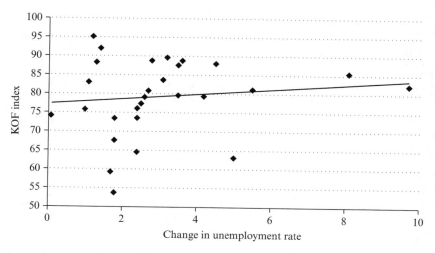

Figure 5.4   Globalization index and unemployment

on trade, foreign direct investment (FDI) and portfolio investment. Trade is the sum of a country's exports and imports and portfolio investment is the sum of a country's assets and liabilities (all standardized by GDP). The KOF index includes the sum of gross inflows and outflows of FDI and the stocks of FDI (again, both standardized by GDP). While these variables are standard measures of globalization, income payments to foreign nationals and capital are included to proxy the extent to which a country employs foreign labour and capital in its production processes. The second sub-index refers to restrictions on trade and capital using hidden import barriers, mean tariff rates, taxes on international trade (as a share of current revenue) and an index of capital controls. Given a certain level of trade, a country with higher revenues from tariffs is less globalized. To proxy restrictions on the capital account, the KOF index includes data based on the IMF's Annual Report on Exchange Arrangements and Exchange Restrictions, and includes 13 different types of capital controls. The variables are combined into two groups: actual flows of trade and investment as well as restrictions. These dimensions are then combined into an overall index of economic globalization with an objective statistical method. Table 5.2 also reports the weights of the individual components.[5]

The relationship between the KOF index and the change in unemployment is depicted in Figure 5.4. There is a weak positive relationship between the two variables ($\rho = 0.13$). This finding probably reflects at least two factors. First, since the most globalized countries tend to be the most developed, then Lane and Milesi-Ferretti's (2010) finding that the crisis hit the most advanced economies the hardest seems indisputable. Secondly, while trade to China, and by extension to the Asian region, seems to have been beneficial, economic integration with the rest of the world may have had its drawbacks. That is, which countries any given nation is integrated with still remains important, in our view. This finding is deserving of further analysis.

5.4.3   Policy Matters and 'Keeping the Powder Dry'

Next, we examine the extent to which countries were able to respond to the crisis aggressively. There are two obvious dimensions here, namely, the ability of policy-makers to use expansionary monetary and fiscal policies. The fiscal policy story has been told elsewhere and has now been annexed to the risks associated with the enormous run-up of public debt. Reinhart and Rogoff (2008; 2009; 2010) have been prominent in prosecuting this particular line of argument. It bears mentioning, however, that Wells and Krugman (2010) argue that the issue of causality is moot. Obviously, tax receipts plummet when there is a severe economic crisis.

The top panel of Figure 5.5 confirms the correlation between unemployment and fiscal status. Debt matters. Specifically, a significant and large negative correlation ($\rho = -0.38$) was found between 'General Government Net Lending–Borrowing (GGNLB)' and ΔUR, indicating that countries with a budget surplus in 2008 experienced smaller changes in the unemployment rate over the ensuing period of crisis. (Positive values of GGNLB indicate a country is a net lender or has a budget surplus, while negative values indicate net borrowers or a budget deficit.) Note that using the deficit/surplus figure in 1-2008 is partially immune to the Wells–Krugman criticism. This negative correlation remains even when Norway, a possible outlier running an enormous oil-fuelled surplus, was dropped from the sample. Not surprisingly, economies that run budget surpluses have more fiscal freedom in responding to an economic crisis and were relatively better placed to bounce back earlier and faster than their counterparts who were less fiscally disciplined. As Claessens et al. (2010, p. 289) note, countries need 'the "fiscal space" to run larger fiscal deficits when needed'.

The monetary side of the story is a more complicated one to tell. On the one hand, high growth and a lax monetary policy were key components of the boom and bubble-like conditions on the eve of the GFC. Among others, Furceri and Mourougane (2009) argue that the global saving glut and low interest rates may have encouraged excessive risk-taking by providing a vast pool of financial resources for investment. Claessens et al.

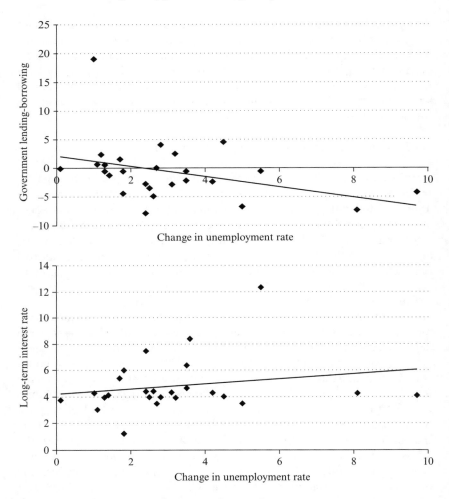

Figure 5.5   Government finance and unemployment

(2010) find that GDP growth was, on average, higher in those economies first affected by the financial crisis, suggesting that those countries experiencing booms were the first to experience downturns.

It is also the case that a low interest rate environment reflects an overly accommodative monetary policy and possibly relatively poor underlying macroeconomic fundamentals. The interest rate also includes an expectational component: *ceteris paribus* the higher the long-term interest rate, the higher the anticipated inflation and rate of economic growth. From a policy perspective, and by definition, a low interest rate means that there is less room to reduce official interest rates in response to any crisis. The lower panel of Figure 5.5 relates the long-term interest rate in 1-2008 to ΔUR. The relationship between the two variables is positive (Δ = 0.19), which belies the usual stories about monetary conditions. On the other hand, the correlation is driven by one outlier; when Iceland is dropped from the sample the correlation disappears (Δ = 0.03).

5.4.4 Labour Market Institutions and Regulation also Matter, but are not Central

Pagano and Volpin (2008) is an important contribution to the burgeoning field of how labour relations and finance interact, and in particular, on the effects of finance on labour. While financial markets allocate resources efficiently, expanding output, investment and employment and forcing inefficient firms to shut down or restructure, they also create employment risk. They note that financial crises which generate large drops in asset prices, credit crunches and waves of bankruptcies, are often associated with large negative effects on employment. Further, the GFC is an example of herding behaviour, moral hazard in financial institutions, and misconstrued regulatory policies and lax monetary policy, which all combined to eventually damage employment levels. Overall, financial integration may increase employment risk. In turn, how such integration affects labour market outcomes depends on labour market institutions. Once again, the financial and real sides of the economy cannot be divorced.

Botero et al. (2004) investigate the regulation of labour markets through employment, collective relations and social security laws. Heavier regulation of labour is associated with lower labour force participation and higher unemployment. In earlier work, Fitoussi et al. (2000) argue that anti-market labour policies sowed the seeds of high European unemployment. Among these inefficient policies are unemployment insurance benefits, which are often generous and of long duration; the high density and wide coverage of unions in wage-setting and employment protection laws that lengthen the average wait of an unemployed worker for a job. In a similar fashion, Atanassov and Kim (2009) find that strong labour laws have unintended and undesirable consequences. Highly protective employment contract laws exacerbate workers' plight by inducing more major asset sales during corporate distress. Strong union laws help underperforming managers avoid dismissal through worker–management alliances.

We use the three labour market flexibility indices that were developed by Botero et al. (2004) to evaluate how the labour environment in countries in 2008 affected post-shock labour market adjustment (See Figure 5.6). The employment laws index is a measure of the protection of labour and employment defined as an average of alternative employment contracts, cost of increasing hours worked, cost of firing workers and dismissal procedures. The collective relations laws index measures the collective relations laws using labour union power and collective disputes. The social security index measures social security benefits using old age, disability and death benefits, sickness and health benefits and unemployment benefits. The first index therefore broadly captures the notion of worker protection; the second index captures the strength of unions; and the last, the nature of the welfare state as it pertains to labour. In all cases, higher values indicate higher worker protection.

It is apparent that only the third of these indices is significantly related to unemployment adjustment. We were somewhat surprised by this (non-) finding. To check the relationship between the third index and unemployment, we also examine (in the last panel of Figure 5.6) the relationship between unemployment rates and unemployment benefit replacement rates. BRR is a direct measure of unemployment benefits generosity. The relationship here is positive, as expected, although not overwhelmingly strong ($\Delta = 0.16$).

5.4.5   Finally, How Important is Labour Productivity?

It is the mantra of economists that real GDP growth is driven by the '3Ps': population, participation and productivity. Economists are particularly concerned about changes in labour productivity and their impact on unemployment rates.[6] For our final look into matters we examine labour productivity, as measured by the increase in unit labour costs (that is, labour costs per unit of output) in the five years leading up to 1-2008. The scatter plot appears in Figure 5.7. The relationship is extremely strong. Of the variables considered thus far, the increase in unit labour costs has the strongest correlation with the rising rates of unemployment in our sample of countries. In the period leading up to 1-2008, output had been growing slower than the costs of labour for most countries. Those countries with the highest run-up in labour costs (*ipso facto*, flattest productivity growth) tended to fall the hardest and furthest when the crisis hit.

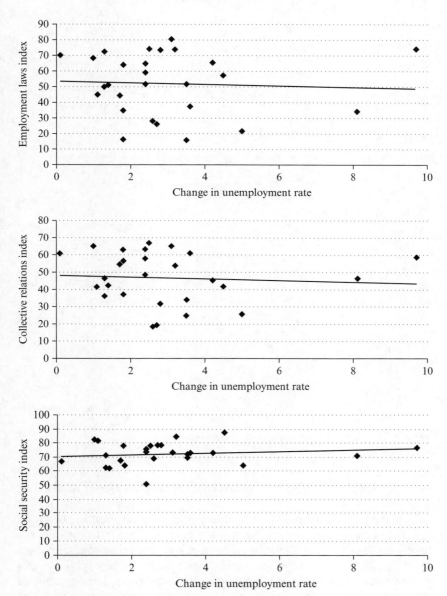

Figure 5.6   Employment regulations and unemployment

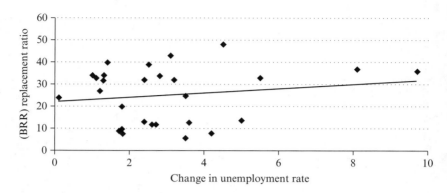

Figure 5.6   (continued)

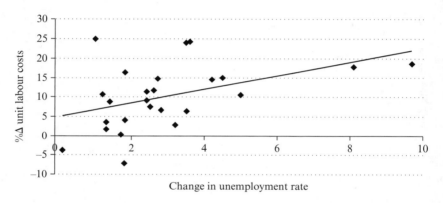

Figure 5.7   Unit labour costs and unemployment

5.5   CONCLUDING COMMENTS AND DISCUSSION

Whilst the global economy is still suffering in the aftermath of the GFC, and the consequences are still being dissected, it is nevertheless interesting to explore the characteristic differences between those countries most severely affected and those countries which seem to be experiencing a stronger economic recovery. We have addressed this issue by focusing on changes in the unemployment rate, something which other researchers have not as yet considered.

Overall, our findings are consistent with much of what is found in the recent literature, with a few notable exceptions. Economic integration does seem to be associated with higher unemployment rates post-GFC.

This general finding, although weak, is not particularly surprising given that the more developed economies, which tend to be more globally integrated, appear to have been hit the hardest in the wake of the GFC. However, the associated concern that globalization is homogenizing and exposing all countries to global shocks is an exaggerated one, in our opinion. Even within the politically integrated European Union, there is not a great deal of uniformity in social and economic policies. In fact, we see quite the opposite: each country has considerably different social expenditure programmes, labour market programmes and policies in various sectors. It is clear that greater integration is not inconsistent with diversity in economic and social policies. Fears about globalization, by contrast, stress a 'race to the bottom'. It is clear that there have been diverse labour market experiences and responses across countries in response to the crisis.

International trade is one of the more obvious channels through which the effects of the crisis are transmitted. In this regard our results are quite interesting and contrast with the general finding that greater globalization is not necessarily an unambiguous boon for countries. More specifically, we focused on trade ties with the United States as the source/epicentre of the crisis and first to enter recession as well as connectedness with high export-demanding China. Far from hurting labour market outcomes, trade with the United States was not found to have any significant effect on changes in the unemployment rate in our sample of 29 countries. Moreover, if we omit Ireland as an outlier, trade exposure to the United States may actually be beneficial. This result is in line with the conclusions of Rose and Spiegel (2009b). As for trade links with China, a strong beneficial result is found. This indicates that greater trade exposure to China has minimized the severity of labour market effects in the aftermath of the GFC. These results suggest that not only does trade openness matter, but that the diversity of trading partners is an issue that requires further examination.

To further determine the extent of an economy's vulnerability to the crisis, attention was given to the initial fiscal and monetary positions prevailing in March 2008. As rapid and massive expansionary policies were implemented in response to the GFC, the issue arises as to how much freedom governments have to absorb such a shock and the importance of having both the fiscal and monetary scope to grow out of a crisis. Economies running budget deficits experienced more severe upward movements in the unemployment rate, consistent with the view that a sound initial macroeconomic position is an important factor influencing the effectiveness of such targeted fiscal policy. The monetary story is somewhat more complicated. However, we found that countries with higher interest rates had relatively poorer labour market experiences. This result may be explained by our finding that those countries with the greatest increases in unit labour costs experienced greater increases in their rates of unemployment. Increasing labour costs without compensating productivity improvements normally encourage central bankers to raise interest rates.

Of most surprise to us is that our evidence shows little relationship between the level of labour market flexibility in an economy and labour market outcomes post-crisis. On the other hand, these findings are very much in line with Hall and Soskice's (2001) notion that national institutional architectures are distinct and tend to remain so, that is, there is no convergence to some benchmark; further, that the difference in economic performance between advanced countries with sets of economic institutions is minimal. The only significant effect of worker protection derived from our analysis was that a greater level of social security benefits available to households is associated with more severe unemployment rate changes, possibly reflecting the fact that both the generosity and ease of access to such funds creates a disincentive to negotiate with employers during times of economic hardship.

Why have some countries been hit hard in the aftermath of the GFC while others have emerged relatively unscathed? Economic integration and trade links, along with sound macroeconomic fundamentals are, in our view, important indicators of a quick economic recovery. As the amount of literature examining this issue is still small, further analysis on these findings is clearly desirable.

NOTES

1. Added by editors to acknowledge that this is the public-debate reason for the crisis, not the actual reason.
2. Claessens et al. (2009) identify the quarter during which each OECD country entered recession (defined as being one quarter of negative output growth). According to this criterion, the United States (along with Ireland and Iceland) entered recession in 1-2008. In fact, some countries' output continued growing until 1-2009 (e.g. Slovakia). While this perspective is interesting, it is orthogonal to our main query, namely, how the labour markets of various countries fared subsequent to the GFC first manifesting itself in the United States.
3. Note that the unemployment rate is defined as $UR = U/LF$, where the labour force, $LF = U+E$, with U the number of unemployed and E the number of employed. It follows that $d(U/LF) = (EdU - UdE)/(LF)^2$. Clearly, if the unemployed have difficulty finding work, then UdE is close to zero and ΔUR approximates the actual number of (formerly employed) workers laid off during the period in question, that is, EdU. Notwithstanding, the results presented in the next section are quite similar if we use the percentage change in unemployment.
4. The use of indices rather than separate variables, such as trade, FDI or immigration, addresses two well-known problems associated with investigating the effects of globalization on labour market outcomes. First is the issue of variable (mis-) measurement and interpretation. For example, it is 'usual' to find the impact of greater trade flows with

LDCs on the distribution of earnings to be small. Obviously, it requires a leap of faith to argue that globalization has similarly small effects. Second, is the issue of ignoring important variables. An issue that is neglected in much of the globalization and labour market effects literature is whether all dimensions of globalization work in the same direction on the variables of interest. This leads to obvious concerns about biased coefficient estimates. Overall, despite their shortcomings, we consider there to be distinct advantages to using composite indices of globalization.

5. To construct the indices of globalization, each variable in Table 5.2 is converted into an index with a 0 to 10 scale. Higher values denote greater globalisation. When higher values of the original variable indicate greater globalization, the formula $((V_i - V_{min})/(V_{max} - V_{min})*10)$ is used for transformation. Conversely, when higher values indicate less globalization, the formula is $((V_{max} - V_i)/(V_{max} - V_{min})*10)$. The weights for the sub-indices are calculated using principal components analysis. The base year is 2000. For this year, the analysis partitions the variance of the variables used. The weights are then determined in a way that maximizes the variation of the resulting principal component, so that it captures the variation as fully as possible. If possible, the weights determined for the base year are then used to calculate the indices for each single year back to 1970. Where no data are available, the weights are re-adjusted. See Dreher et al. (2008) for further details of the computational method.
6. See the responses by Olivier Blanchard and Christopher Sims to Fitoussi et al. (2000), for instance.

REFERENCES

Atanassov, J. and E.H. Kim (2009), 'Labor and corporate governance: international evidence from restructuring decisions', *Journal of Finance*, **64**(1), 341–74.

Botero, J.C., S. Djankov, R. La Porta, F. Lopez-de-Silanes and A. Shleifer (2004), 'The regulation of labor', *Quarterly Journal of Economics*, **119**(4), 1339–82.

Claessens, S., M.A. Kose and M.E. Terrones (2009), 'What happens during recessions, crunches and busts?', *Economic Policy*, **24**(60), 653–700.

Claessens, S., G. Dell'Ariccia, D. Igan and L. Laeven (2010), 'Cross-country experiences and policy implications from the global financial crisis', *Economic Policy*, **25**(62), 267–93.

Dreher, A., N. Gaston and P. Martens (2008), *Measuring Globalisation: Gauging its Consequences*, New York: Springer.

Dutt, P., D. Mitra and P. Ranjan (2009), 'International trade and unemployment: theory and cross-national evidence', *Journal of International Economics*, **78**(1), 32–44.

Fitoussi, J.P., D. Jestaz, E.S. Phelps and G. Zoega (2000), 'Roots of the recent recoveries: labor reforms or private sector forces?', *Brookings Papers on Economic Activity*, **1**, 237–311.

Furceri, D. and A. Mourougane (2009), 'Financial crises: past lessons and policy implications', OECD Economics Department working paper no. 668.

Gaston, N. and G. Rajaguru (2010), 'How an export boom affects unemployment', Globalisation and Development Centre working paper, Bond University.

Hall, P.A. and D. Soskice (eds) (2001), *Varieties of Capitalism: The Institutional Foundations of Comparative Advantage*, Oxford: Oxford University Press.

Lane, P.R. and G.M. Milesi-Ferretti (2010), 'The cross-country incidence of the global crisis', paper presented at the IMF/BOP/PSE Conference 'Economic linkages, spillovers and the financial crisis', Paris, 28–9 January.

Moore, M. and P. Ranjan (2005), 'Globalisation and skill-biased technological change: implications for unemployment and wage inequality', *Economic Journal*, **115**(503), 391–422.

Pagano, M. and P. Volpin (2008), 'Labor and finance', paper presented at the Korea Money and Finance Association (KMFA) on 20 June.

Reinhart, C.M. and K.S. Rogoff (2008), 'Banking crises: an equal opportunity menace', NBER working paper 14587, available at http://www.nber.org/papers/w14857.

Reinhart, C.M. and K.S. Rogoff (2009), 'The aftermath of financial crises', *American Economic Review*, **99**(2), 466–72.

Reinhart, C.M. and K.S. Rogoff (2010), 'Growth in a time of debt', *American Economic Review*, **100**(2), 573–78.

Rose, A.K. and M.M. Spiegel (2009a), 'Cross-country causes and consequences of the 2008 crisis: early warning', NBER working paper 15357, available at http://www.nber.org/papers/w15357.

Rose, A.K. and M.M. Spiegel, (2009b), 'Cross-country causes and consequences of the 2008 crisis: international linkages and American exposure', NBER working paper 15358, available at http://www.nber.org/papers/w153578.

Wells, R. and P. Krugman (2010), 'Our giant banking crisis – what to expect', *The New York Review of Books*, 13 May, available at http://www.nybooks.com/articles/archives/2010/may/13/our-giant-banking-crisis/.

6. The fiscal policy response to the global financial crisis: a critique

Tony Makin

6.1 INTRODUCTION

Since the onset of the global financial crisis in late 2008, frequent comparison has been made with the Great Depression (IMF, 2009a) which spanned the economically disastrous 1930s. However, the impact of the global financial crisis on the real sectors of economies was far less than the depths reached then, when economies such as those in Australia, Britain and the US experienced huge falls in production, deflation, and unemployment rates that ranged from 20 to 30 per cent of the workforce.

To counter the impact of the global financial crisis (GFC) on the real sector of economies, governments around the world implemented unprecedented fiscal stimulus in 2008–09, which entailed a combination of tax cuts, income transfers and public infrastructure spending. In commentary on the crisis, it has become commonplace to credit fiscal stimulus measures for subsequent recovery in many economies. Whether it was the avoidance of severe recession, higher than expected retail sales, or other miscellaneous measures of spending, we have been led to believe that things would have been much worse without the unprecedented fiscal activism.

The most recent comparable international financial crisis was the Asian financial crisis of the late 1990s. Yet Australia and many other economies coped well during that crisis, relying mainly on rapid monetary responses and shock-absorbing exchange rate adjustment, with no fiscal response at all. So whether this time around so many advanced and emerging economies needed to engage in the largest ever coordinated fiscal responses in the world remains controversial.

In an open letter to President Barack Obama published in leading US newspapers earlier this year, hundreds of US academic economists specializing in this field, including Nobel laureates James Buchanan and Edward Prescott, endorsed a statement that more government spending was not the way to improve US economic performance. Believing otherwise, they said, was 'a triumph of hope over experience'.

This chapter is divided into eight sections, and examines the macroeconomic effects of the internationally coordinated fiscal response to the recent global financial crisis and the international recession that followed. With frequent reference to Australia's experience, it evaluates which macroeconomic policies are most appropriate in response to financial crises of this kind, contrasting the effects of fiscal policy with those of monetary policy. It also highlights the legacy of recent fiscal activism in terms of the macroeconomic risks going forward.

6.2   MONETARY VERSUS FISCAL POLICY RESPONSES

Economic analysis based on standard textbook theory suggests that in Australia's case, fiscal policy has played a significantly less important role in cushioning the impact of the global financial crisis on the economy as compared with the role played by monetary policy through interest rate reductions and associated exchange rate depreciation. On the monetary side, the coordinated initial response of central banks was to dramatically lower official interest rates worldwide at the time.

In Australia's case, the monetary response to the crisis was greatly assisted by a highly flexible exchange rate that the central bank allowed to depreciate massively. By automatically boosting industry competitiveness and net exports, the exchange rate enabled the economy to absorb most of the external shock. An adaptable labour market also mitigated the impact on unemployment, way beyond official expectations.

However, while the monetary policy response has been widely applauded, the same cannot be said of the fiscal response, where no consensus is ever likely to emerge. This is because a fiscal stimulus of the nature and scale that was enacted has lasting effects that a temporary, more easily reversible, monetary stimulus does not.

The fiscal stimulus in response to the global financial crisis has been justified on intellectual grounds by the Depression economics of John Maynard Keynes (1936). The world witnessed Keynesian fiscal responses motivated by fears of a repeat of the Depression of the 1930s. Yet as the above-mentioned US economists assert: 'More government spending by Hoover and Roosevelt did not pull the US economy out of the Great Depression.' In other words, what could be called crank-handle Keynesianism, focused on government spending, did not even work when Model T Fords were around.

6.3   THE REVIVAL OF KEYNESIAN ECONOMICS

Though dormant as an influence on macroeconomic policy for years leading up to the crisis, Keynesianism has unexpectedly reappeared centre stage as the sole theoretical rationale for fiscal stimulus (see Spilimbergo et al., 2008). It should not come as a surprise that policies reflecting Keynes's ideas should provoke heated political debate. After all, Keynes in the concluding chapter of his best-known work, *The General Theory of Employment, Interest and Money*, asserted, incorrectly as it turned out, that in the post-Depression era 'somewhat comprehensive socialisation of investment will prove the only means of securing an approximation to full employment'.

The enduring appeal of Keynes's theory was that it offered a cogent explanation of the main components of the national accounts and the phenomenon of the business cycle, while simultaneously asserting that governments could easily and at little cost correct macroeconomic misbehaviour at will and as it saw fit. But this has always put Keynesianism at odds with the centuries-old tradition of economics that emphasized how prices automatically equilibrated markets and which suggested minimum government involvement in commercial exchange as the best means of allocating an economy's resources.

Such a way of thinking underpins, for instance, international trade theory and policy, which few question. By asserting the opposite – that there was a greater need for government intervention in economic activity – Keynes's theory of fiscal activism introduced a logical inconsistency to economics that his critics have always found discomforting. Keynes's central planning approach to fiscal policy was credited by his disciples in the 1940s and 1950s with saving Western capitalism from itself.

However, later critics of Keynesianism have argued that it was not fiscal expansion that ended the Depression, but that the Depression lasted much longer than it should have, especially in the US, because of a prolonged contraction of liquidity, policy-induced investment uncertainty, and large-scale retreat to international trade protectionism. The great appeal of the naive short-term Keynesianism underpinning fiscal stimulus measures is that it provides governments with a seemingly costless economic solution for addressing recession and unemployment in the here and now.

6.4   PROBLEMS WITH KEYNESIAN THEORY

As a theory, simple Keynesianism focuses exclusively on the short term, emphasizes aggregate spending as the source of economic growth, and largely ignores the future consequences of unproductive public spending and the fiscal deficits that result. This is in keeping with Keynes's own comment that 'in the long run we are all dead'.

While that comment is undeniably true, what it fails to recognize is that the vast majority of the population can in our lifetimes expect to suffer the consequences of the public debt legacy that Keynesian activism bequeaths, through higher taxes, higher interest rates, and higher inflation.

Keynes's general theory was anything but general in its original form and was premised on a special set of Depression conditions. These included interest rates at zero, ongoing deflation, and a prolonged collapse in international trade, none of which Australia suffered from during the current crisis. The theory also ignored the fact that economies could be heavily reliant on foreign capital to fund their investment.

In short, the characteristics of modern open economies like Australia are not like those Keynes sought to address. It was left to another English economist, John Hicks (1937), to make Keynes's theory more general in its application, while retaining its most useful elements such as his theory of consumption, investment and money demand.

Hicks's adaptation of Keynes's contribution, sanctioned by Keynes himself, synthesized the aggregate spending and monetary sides of an economy and for years was the mainstay of many textbooks. Yet this framework actually shows that fiscal stimulus can quickly drive up interest rates, crowding out private investment to the longer-term cost of the economy. Though Keynes is widely considered the most influential macroeconomist the United Kingdom ever produced, the United States produced a contemporary of Keynes, the much neglected Yale economist, Irving Fisher, 1867–1947.

Although Fisher's credibility during the Great Depression was damaged by his confident forecast just before the great stock market collapse of 1929 that 'stock prices have reached what looks like a permanently high plateau', he made numerous original contributions to economics and left a body of work that exhibits a clarity and consistency of thought that is lacking in the sometimes incomprehensible musings of Keynes.

While Keynes proposed a way of addressing depressions in the wake of banking crises, Fisher actually explained how banking crises can develop. However, Fisher's most notable contribution was his theory of inter-temporal choice (Fisher, 1930), which related saving, investment and interest rates through time. In a nutshell, it proposes that spending decisions made in the present are central to our economic well-being in the future and therefore that economic decision-making always has to be undertaken with the future in mind.

This theory also implies that short-term economic policies that foster consumption and unproductive public spending without regard to the future are detrimental to achieving higher long-term living standards. In a Fisherian world it's quite rational to pass on a big night out because the hangover the next day is not worth it, just as it's best not to run ill-advised budget deficits that unproductively add to public debt and prove to be a future drain on the economy.

Although Keynesianism has dominated fiscal thinking since the financial crisis began, we can catch a glimpse of Fisherian thinking in the strong emphasis that the IMF has placed on exit strategies and the need to exercise fiscal restraint into the future. Unfortunately, the application of fiscal restraint in the future to rein in budget deficits will have quite different effects from those implemented during the expansionary phase still underway.

For example, it is inevitable that in Australia, given the aversion to cutting spending, taxes will have to rise to address the debt escalation due to earlier cash handouts dispersed to favoured groups, such as students and pensioners. There were no beneficial supply-side effects in providing relief to these groups but there will be adverse supply-side effects through higher future taxes, or forgoing the option of lower marginal income tax rates that past fiscal action now prevents.

Another critical assumption of Keynes's 1936 work was that wages were inflexible downwards. While rigid wages were necessary to make Keynesian fiscal policy work in theory, this assumption is now less relevant in practice. The prime purpose of fiscal stimulus has always been to preserve jobs. Yet, ironically, greater labour market flexibility than in previous recessions did that by itself.

The major rationale for implementing fiscal stimulus is that it is supposed to counter the loss of confidence that causes a sudden spending stop. The spending that stopped most dramatically during the global financial crisis was business investment expenditure. Business investment is a key driver of the business cycle and its recovery is essential for a strong economic rebound. Yet there is a glaring contradiction in the argument that extensive fiscal stimulus is necessary for building business confidence. This is because higher government spending, and the higher than necessary long-term interest rates that result, are inimical to asset price recovery, private investment and the strength of future economic growth.

6.5 PUBLIC DEBT SUSTAINABILITY

Another factor that is usually ignored by advocates of fiscal stimulus is that the public debt incurred by governments as a percentage of GDP can take on a life of its own. Even when governments stop adding to it, public debt will grow on its own whenever the interest being paid on the debt exceeds the economy's growth rate. Even as economies recover, government debt can continue to grow as a percentage of GDP if long-term interest rates rise faster than the economic growth rate. This can occur for a number of reasons.

First, interest rates will increase as governments around the world soak up funds to cover their huge budget deficits, with the unfortunate side-effect that this lessens the availability of funds for private investment. This means that future potential national income will be lower than it would otherwise have been because the nation's productive capital stock will be lower. In other words, because the government borrowed money to spend on relatively unproductive investments, there will be relatively less investment by the private sector on productive investments.

Second, in coming years the composition of foreign debt for international borrower economies like Australia will include a bigger share of public debt relative to private debt that is not backed by productive capital accumulation, as compared with the pre-crisis situation. Before government guarantees were introduced, foreign debt was predominantly the liability of the private sector, and while global finance was more freely available, not a cause for concern. Now, as the public component of foreign debt rises, entities borrowing from abroad can expect to pay a higher interest risk premium.

Lastly, long-term interest rates will rise if expectations of higher inflation take hold, especially if financial markets think central banks are more likely to buy up (or monetize) public debt, while simultaneously expanding money supplies. In other words, the large amount of money pumped into the system by governments and central banks will fuel inflation. This occurred around the world after the Keynesian fiscal excesses of the 1970s and resulted in prolonged stagflation, which in turn exacerbated unemployment.

Given the policies of leading economies such as the US, considerably higher interest rates seem very likely, and the more they rise, the more aggressively the public debt to GDP ratio will feed on itself, requiring more drastic fiscal management than currently anticipated to bring it under control. In Australia's case, some may argue that the public debt to GDP ratio officially forecast for coming years will be relatively low by international standards, but this ignores one crucial fact: Australia is one of the world's largest international borrowers for its size.

Coupled with the fact that its fiscal turnaround has been one of the most sizeable, Australia is therefore vulnerable. Dependence on foreign capital is something Australia has in common with emerging economies, and a sudden withdrawal of foreign funding remains the greatest risk to the Australian economy.

Undergraduate textbook theory (Mankiw, 2009) of how fiscal policy operates in an open economy with a floating exchange rate tells us that a growing budget deficit due to increased government spending of the kind we have seen puts upward pressure on domestic interest rates, other things being the same.

That induces foreign capital inflow and strengthens the exchange rate, consistent with the Mundell (1963) and Fleming (1962) model of an open economy. In turn, this worsens the economy's competitiveness in relation to its trading partners, resulting in lower exports and higher imports.

Given the nature of Australia's fiscal expansion with its emphasis on direct spending rather than tax relief, as well as its relative size internationally, it should come as no surprise that this is what happened. In other words, the 'twin deficits' phenomenon returned: the consolidated budget deficit of the federal and state governments appears to have caused higher trade and current account deficits.

Another way of interpreting the widening current account deficit is that it signifies a reduction in national saving relative to national investment as shown in Makin (2009a). National saving is lower because fiscal expansion has increased household and government consumption relative to national income. Meanwhile, within the investment component of national spending, productive business investment has been displaced by less productive public investment.

Therefore international capital inflow, or net foreign borrowing, which is now required to bridge this national saving–investment gap, is funding economic activity that is not as productive as it used to be, pre-fiscal stimulus. Yet, ultimately, foreign funding of the current account deficit has to be linked to highly productive investment spending. Otherwise, foreign investors will at some stage take fright, the current account deficit will become unsustainable, and the nation's credit rating will be downgraded, leading to a further spike in interest rates.

Short-term capital inflow chasing relatively higher interest rates here than abroad has been driving the exchange rate, which for months now has hovered in the low nineties against the US dollar, way above its post-float average value in the low seventies. The upshot is that worsened international competitiveness is offsetting any possible effect fiscal stimulus may have had on employment elsewhere.

It has been oft-repeated that the Australian economy has benefited from the earlier cash handouts and additional government infrastructure outlays, including from the large federal spend on school facilities. But due to an overvalued exchange rate, these gains have come at the expense of export and import competing industries, including the labour-intensive manufacturing sector which will continue to shed jobs if competitiveness is poor.

This is not to say that fiscal expansion is the only factor influencing the exchange rate at present. So, is the stance of monetary policy – which has been in a tightening phase relative to that of trading partners, the United States – consistent with foreign investors' perceptions of risk and commodity prices? But the impact of fiscal policy on the exchange rate is certainly the most neglected.

6.6   THE RISKS OF GOVERNMENTS BORROWING ABROAD

The large trade and current account imbalances that arose around the world over the past decade played a central role in the global financial crisis and international recession that followed (Makin, 2009b). No doubt concerns about Australia's own relatively large current account deficit, and the associated additional foreign borrowing, will resurface as the deficit widens with economic recovery.

Globally, the most significant external imbalances have been those of the United States, with its external deficit and foreign borrowing on one side, and East Asia, most notably China, as well as the oil-exporting nations, with their external surpluses on the other. With a current account deficit that reached 6 per cent of its GDP in 2006, the United States was by far the world's largest international borrower, drawing in over half of traded global saving.

Given the attention these current account imbalances have received, it is worth relating in simple terms what economic theory tells us about the significance of external deficits, and when we should be wary of them. Although rarely acknowledged in regular economic commentary, current account deficits and the associated external borrowing are, in theory, economically beneficial under certain conditions. This is because allowing saving to move across borders into economies where it earns the highest rate of return can raise living standards in both lender and borrower economies.

In other words, just as free international trade in goods and services confers mutual national income gains on participating economies, so too can free international trade in saving. Viewed in this light, external imbalances benignly reflect differences in nations' saving habits and investment opportunities, rather than differences in nations' trade competitiveness, and should not normally be considered a policy concern.

However, this interpretation of the benefits of international borrowing and lending depends on some critical pre-conditions. Many of these conditions prevailed in the United States and Australia through the 1980s and 1990s, but failed to hold for the US in the years just before the crisis. In light of Australia's fiscal policy response to the financial crisis, a more circumspect view of our external deficit and foreign borrowing is now warranted as well.

A long debate ensued in academic and policy circles on this issue and two polar views about the significance of Australia's foreign debt emerged. One was that escalating foreign debt was a financial crisis-in-waiting and that policy-makers should use all instruments at their disposal, notably restrictive fiscal and monetary policy, to minimize borrowing from abroad. Foreign debt was obviously inherently 'bad'.

The other view was that external deficits and debt should not be a target of economic policy because they essentially reflected commercial decisions by private firms and financial institutions which should be expected to act in their and the economy's best interests. If not, they go into receivership, at no direct cost to taxpayers. To avoid that possibility, it was also in foreign lenders' interests to ensure that their loaned funds were used productively.

As an initiator and contributor to that debate, I long advocated the view that foreign debt incurred by the private sector was mostly 'good'. This was contrary to the other polar view whose adherents included a former employer, the Australian Treasury (where my opposing view first formed), the Reserve Bank, and both sides of politics, at different times and as circumstances suited.

Earlier research of mine (Makin, 2006) showed empirically that foreign funds overwhelmingly borrowed by the private sector contributed positively to Australia's economic growth, and by implication helped Australia achieve growth rates above the post-war long-term average of 3 per cent. Past foreign borrowing funded higher rates of productive investment than would otherwise have occurred and was also more than matched by rising domestic asset values, thereby raising national wealth.

This interpretation of current account deficits and foreign debt evidently proved persuasive, as the issue has all but disappeared from public policy debate over recent years. But in light of current and prospective global financial conditions, the view that future foreign debt increases will necessarily be benign needs qualifying.

The case for interpreting foreign debt positively was founded on several important conditions that are likely to be violated. One is that foreign borrowing is predominantly undertaken by the private sector for productive purposes. But this only follows in net terms if the federal budget is in surplus or in relatively small deficit. A second condition for interpreting foreign debt positively is that foreign funds are freely available and continue to be provided on reasonable terms.

However, in the context of a global credit crunch, this is no longer true. With governments all around the world running bigger budget deficits and borrowing more, long-term interest rates should continue to head upwards, as world recovery slowly gathers pace. This will increase servicing costs on Australia's existing foreign loans and make unviable foreign-funded projects with rates of return only marginally above the foreign debt servicing cost.

Given the economy's limited pool of domestic saving, borrowing abroad to fund future budget deficits is unavoidable. This makes comparison with public debt levels in other OECD economies, expressed as a proportion of GDP, somewhat irrelevant, for none, except for the United States and New Zealand, have been as heavily reliant on global finance over recent decades.

It used to be a tenet of Keynesian economics that public debt was not a problem because 'we owed public debt to ourselves'. Neglecting the fact that future generations have to pay it back, it meant that governments could run up public debt without worrying unduly, because its citizens and local financial institutions within the economy earned interest on it.

But this is not the case for large external borrower economies. Public debt that doubles as foreign debt precisely reduces national income by the interest payable abroad. If too much of Australia's public debt funds consumption or fails to generate a sufficient rate of return to the economy, the risk rises that foreign lenders will start to see escalating public debt, not only as bad, but ugly as well. This would have serious consequences for the nation's creditworthiness, interest rates and future economic growth.

The conditions necessary for interpreting external deficits and borrowing positively are these: first, economies engaged in international trade in saving should not unduly restrict private international capital flows and preferably have flexible exchange rates. Second, foreign borrowing in deficit economies should be primarily undertaken by the private sector, and when put to productive use, generate a rate of return in excess of the servicing costs on the debt. Third, as the Asian financial crisis of 1997–98 also demonstrated, if foreign borrowing is mainly channelled through domestic banks, as it is here, the banking system has to be very sound and not artificially distorted by government guarantees.

When examining the rise of global imbalances in the years just before the global financial crisis, it is clear that some of these pre-conditions were violated in the case of the United States. For instance, a significant component of capital inflow to the US pre-crisis came from China and other East Asian nations with heavily managed exchange rates and controls over private international capital flows.

By undervaluing their currencies against the US dollar, trade surplus economies accumulated trillions of US dollar holdings. As central banks and sovereign wealth funds were buying US government bonds and mortgage-related debt instruments that were underwritten by government agencies with these dollars, it was effectively international trade in public, not private, saving.

According to a recent IMF report on Australia (IMF, 2009b), short-term external debt held by domestic financial institutions is around half of total external debt and is a key risk to the economy in the current global environment. A more prudent fiscal response to the crisis would have provided greater insurance against such risk.

To use an analogy, if we think of foreign borrowing as a highway that allows the economy to reach the destination of a higher living standard, the highway serves its purpose well without undue risk to the economy, provided driving conditions are fine.

But if there is a crisis event like a widespread bushfire that clouds the road with smoke, making driving more hazardous, it is advisable to exercise extra caution and slow down. Yet, Australia's fiscal response to the financial crisis and the extra public sector foreign borrowing it implied was akin to hitting the accelerator under these conditions.

In other words, from Australia's perspective at least, the global financial crisis should have been treated more like a calamitous and completely unexpected natural disaster, rather than a war that had to be fought with present and future taxpayers' dollars. When natural disasters strike, the first priority is providing assistance to those most affected, whereas in wars there are also ongoing casualties and collateral damage. Unfortunately if economic history is any guide, further bad news from the front is highly likely.

6.7   FISCAL REMEDIES: THE WAY FORWARD

What has remained largely unrecognized is that fiscal consolidation that targets wasteful government programmes actually bolsters macroeconomic performance. As shown in Makin (2007), government spending can only improve national output and income if it raises the economy's productive capacity. These findings are consistent with those of conventional growth theory, but apply in the medium term, not just the long term.

Numerous empirical studies, many published by the IMF, support this and contradict the Keynesian premise that public spending of any kind is always and everywhere an effective countercyclical measure. These studies reveal that cutting wasteful public spending creates space for private investment and increases national income. This is because it increases domestic saving, reduces long-term interest rates and improves business confidence.

In short, a fiscal stimulus does not automatically generate sustained economic activity, especially following a boost in public consumption, the blunting of incentives to work and save or through poorly conceived infrastructure spending that generates a very low, or nil, rate of return. On the contrary, cutting unnecessary government spending, including middle-class welfare, is likely to be expansionary for the economy. Every dollar of spending that is cut frees up funds that are now in short supply. Preserving wasteful programmes because cutting them would be contractionary is misguided thinking.

Fiscal packages unveiled by the Australian government since the crisis were initially aimed at boosting consumption in the short term, in keeping with Treasury advice at the outset that the best fiscal response to the global financial crisis was to 'go early, go hard, go households'. However, an arguably sounder fiscal response would have been the exact opposite: go later, go easy, go firms, focusing more on the production rather than the spending side of the economy.

This does not mean that federal policy-makers should have ignored the downturn or that all aspects of fiscal stimulus packages have been unworthy. On the contrary, many infrastructure projects scheduled for future years have been overdue, therefore necessitating some businesses receiving tax relief. Business problems relating to this aspect are being addressed.

But too much faith was put in using fiscal policy to boost consumption on the demand side of the economy in the short run via tens of billions of dollars' worth of bonus payments. A different mix of measures should have recognized that the financial crisis first struck the aggregate supply side of the economy, not the demand side.

For federal fiscal policy to go later would have meant letting monetary policy go further in the first instance to pre-emptively manage the expected downturn in short-run macroeconomic activity. The Reserve Bank of Australia has had much greater scope to do this compared with central banks abroad. It also would have been advisable for federal fiscal policy to go easy in the light of the impact on budget revenue and the budget bottom line as a result of global commodity price falls and diminishing company and capital gains tax receipts.

Moreover, going easy on fiscal policy would have avoided the problem that will arise as government borrowing puts upward pressure on long-term interest rates, thereby limiting central banks' discretion to lower interest rates across the spectrum. 'Go households' meant channelling scarce federal fiscal outlays to select segments of the economy's household sector. But this ignored the fact that firms were the first victims of the crisis.

For many struggling firms, falling sales were initially less of a problem than the unavailability of credit. Paradoxically, the raft of hasty public spending initiatives implemented across the world may retard recovery if households and markets become increasingly alarmed about higher future taxation, interest rates and inflation.

Unemployment is the scourge of recessions. However, it is the business sector, not households, that ultimately employs most people, creates most of gross domestic product and invests in the economy's future. Hence, it would have been better to assist firms' bottom line directly on the cost side through rapid regulation relief and tax relief, such as payroll tax reduction, than to assist indirectly on the revenue side through trickle-down sales.

Rather than following aggregate demand-oriented approaches adopted by the US, Britain and other countries, the New Zealand government emphasized supply-side measures that will flatten marginal taxes levied on individuals, improve infrastructure and quickly lower the regulatory burden on business.

A sounder fiscal response would have included a far greater proportion of measures that bolstered private investment and production. One obvious mechanism to do that might have been to allow monetary policy and lower interest rates to have played a greater role, rather than stimulating consumption and relying on government spending that will pay a zero or negligible rate of return.

6.8 CONCLUDING COMMENTS

What matters most is the quality of fiscal stimulus, not its quantity. More productive public investment in human capital, and tax changes that improve incentives to work or induce greater private investment that creates or saves jobs, are all worthwhile. Unproductive public consumption, or measures that artificially boost private consumption as if the economy was just a giant hydraulic machine closed off from the rest of the world, are not. The benefit of pumping up total spending by any means, like digging potholes for the sake of it, is a Keynesian delusion.

For an open economy, the rate of return on government spending is critical. It should in principle at least cover the additional interest incurred, bearing in mind that because Australia spends more than it earns, the money the government borrows to fund the higher budget deficits comes from abroad. Australia remains heavily reliant on foreign credit, as always, and in these tough and highly uncertain times, the possibility of a currency crisis and risk of a downgrade to the economy's creditworthiness cannot be ignored, as instanced by the recent post-crisis experiences of Greece and Portugal.

Historically, Keynes's intellectual influence over policy-making reached its zenith overseas and here in the 1970s, which was easily the single worst decade for economic performance in the Organisation for Economic Co-operation and Development region since the Depression. That decade was characterized by Keynes's legacy of high budget deficits and high public debt, which in turn contributed to persistently high inflation, stagnant stock markets and high unemployment.

Recognizing this, former British Labour Prime Minister James Callaghan declared in 1977:

> We used to think we could spend our way out of recession. I tell you, in all candour, that that option no longer exists, and that if it ever did exist, it only worked by injecting bigger doses of inflation into the economy followed by higher levels of unemployment as the next step. That is the history of the past 20 years.

There is a strong chance that we are about to repeat that history because the global financial crisis and the consequent so-called Great Recession spawned what can only be termed a Great Fiscal Over-reaction, especially in Australia, the US and Britain, where faith in Keynes has always been strongest.

REFERENCES

Fisher, I. (1930), *The Theory of Interest*, New York: Macmillan.

Fleming, J. (1962), 'Domestic financial policy under fixed and floating exchange rates', *IMF Staff Papers*, **9**(3), 369–79.

Hicks, J. (1937), 'Mr Keynes and the "Classics": a suggested interpretation', *Econometrica*, **5**, 147–59.

International Monetary Fund (2009a), *Australia: Article IV Report*, Washington, DC: IMF.

International Monetary Fund (2009b), 'Global economic policies and prospects', Group of Twenty Meeting, March, Washington, DC: IMF.

Keynes, J. (1936), *The General Theory of Employment, Interest and Money*, Basingstoke: Macmillan.

Makin, A. (2006), 'Has foreign capital made us richer?', *Agenda*, **13**(2), 225–37.

Makin, A. (2007), 'Re-examining the effectiveness of stabilisation policy', *Australian Economic Papers*, **46**(4), 348–59.

Makin, A. (2009a), 'Fiscal "stimulus": a loanable funds critique', *Agenda*, **16**(4), 25–31.

Makin, A. (2009b), *Global Imbalances, Exchange Rates, and Stabilization Policy*, Basingstoke: Palgrave Macmillan.

Mankiw, G. (2009), *Macroeconomics*, 7th edn, New York: Worth.
Mundell, R. (1963), 'Capital mobility and stabilization policy under fixed and flexible exchange rates', *Canadian Journal of Economics and Political Science*, **29**(4), 475–85.
Spilimbergo, A., S. Symansky, O. Blanchard and C. Cottarelli (2008), 'Fiscal policy for the crisis', SPN/08/01, December, International Monetary Fund.

7. Cost consequences to the economy and finance

Ahmed Khalid

7.1 INTRODUCTION

The global financial crisis (GFC) led to a high price being paid to stabilize the economies and to serious consequences for some 60 national economies. Originating from the alleged meltdown of the real-estate sector mainly from sub-prime loans (apparently) in the United States, the crisis led to the collapse of some major financial institutions around the globe. The negative impact of the crisis was felt in the developed, emerging and developing countries although the sources of the impact varied across groups. This chapter provides a detailed analysis of the impact of the crisis on the real sector of the economy.

The precursors for the GFC may be traced back to a date as early as the 2000s, when the target rates by the Federal Reserve Bank in the US were extremely low, as low as 1 per cent, and returns for investors collapsed, prompting investors to seek higher returns in alternative markets via newer but riskier financial products. Since then, multiple factors including the housing market, changes in monetary policy and regulation of policies governing the banking and financial institutions and new technological development led to an increase in both demand for and supply of credits as well as the exposure of investors to higher risk investments. The root causes and so the origin of the GFC have been traced and explained in an earlier chapter of the book (see Chapter 2). The focus of this chapter is to understand and then analyse the *costs and consequences* of the crisis. Its focus is on developed countries, mainly the United States (US) and Europe, which were directly hit by the sub-prime loan crisis. We also analyse emerging or developing countries, which were affected as a result of a recession in output by the developed countries, which in turn affected the demand for the developing countries' exports. However, it is imperative to provide a brief on how the collapse of the real estate market allegedly initiated the crisis and then help spread the crisis to the global economy, especially in Europe.

Banks engaged heavily in credit extensions to homebuyers, and then issued mortgage-backed securities to investors and institutions within the US and across Europe. As a result, the securitized share of sub-prime mortgages increased from 54 per cent in 2001 to 75 per cent in 2006. The estimates show that, during 2008, homeowners, consumers and corporations in the US owed about $25 trillion, of which banks accounted for about $8 trillion in traditional mortgage loans; $7 trillion was provided by bondholders and other traditional lenders; while $10 trillion was generated through the securitized market, wherein lies the source of the crisis. In an earlier chapter, this has been traced to the CDO (collateralized debt obligation) markets, which was the real reason why the banks and other financial firms made heavy losses in the capital base of their operations. At the peak of the crisis, these securitized markets started closing, and almost shut down in late 2008.

Since property prices were rising, the idea was that borrowers would be able to refinance the mortgage loans since the increasing prices were a guarantee to cover defaults. Unfortunately, things did not go as planned and the US housing bubble burst in 2007 after two years of interest rate hikes that led to a breakdown of the banking and credit markets, not only in the US, but in many other countries around the globe. By October 2007, 16 per cent of the sub-prime (adjustable-rate) mortgages were either 90-day delinquent or facing foreclosure proceedings. This increased to 21 per cent by January 2008. About 936 439 US residences completed foreclosure forms between August 2007 and October 2008.[1]

While these events were unfolding, the regulators and policy-makers failed to recognize and understand the important role that investment banks and hedge funds played in the proliferation of this problem, through the use of innovative products and the risk attached to these products. The financial institutions accumulated huge debt burdens and exposed themselves to significant amounts of risk without any cover. The losses incurred, due to the collapse of the mortgage and credit markets, impacted the ability of financial institutions to lend, and hence contributed to the slowdown of the economy. The increased mortgage delinquencies were also followed by huge losses in the value of mortgage-backed securities (MBS).

By September 2008 the two largest mortgage lenders, Freddie Mac and Fannie Mae, owning 50 per cent of the $10 trillion mortgages, were placed in Federal conservatorship. Lehman Brothers, one of the largest financial services institutions in the US, was the next victim, filing for bankruptcy in mid-September 2008. Finally, shares of the large US insurance company, American International Group (AIG), dropped by about 95 per cent in value as a result of losses in mortgage insurance and insurance on MBS.

The rest of this chapter is organized as follows. Section 7.2 provides a brief overview of the global impact of the GFC. Section 7.3 discusses in some detail the cost of the GFC for developed, emerging and developing countries. These costs are broken down into social, economic and financial costs and their consequences are compared among these groups. This section also looks at the stimulus packages provided by different countries. Finally, some policy recommendations for emerging and developing economies are made to reduce their vulnerability to similar crises in the future.

7.2   GLOBAL IMPACT OF THE GFC

US wealth holders lost more than 25 per cent of their net worth between June 2007 and November 2008. The S&P 500 dropped by about 45 per cent, housing prices declined by about 48 per cent over 2004–08, total home equity fell from a peak of $13 trillion (2006) to $8.8 trillion (2008), total retirement assets plummeted by 22 per cent, saving and investment assets lost $1.2 trillion, and pension funds lost $1.3 trillion. All this added to a total loss of $8.3 trillion in the US alone. There is a rich body of literature documenting the impact of the GFC on the US economy and the numbers do not need to be repeated here.[2]

The crisis also had severe effects on the European markets, especially on investors and institutions in Europe who invested in the mortgage-backed securities issued by US banks and financial institutions. Owners of stocks in US corporations suffered losses amounting to around $8 trillion between 1 January and 11 October 2008. Their holdings declined in value by about 40 per cent, from $20 trillion to $12 trillion. In Europe, a number of financial institutions failed. Iceland was the main victim of the crisis, which spread from the US to Europe.[3]

It is widely believed that Australia was not directly affected by the crisis in the US, at least in the same way as experienced by some European countries. Edwards (2008) shows that the interest rate spread in Australia did not increase as much as in some other countries. Australian banks experienced some problems, but not to the extent felt by the US banking system. The main problem faced by Australian banks was on the liability side of the balance sheet. This was due to some banks taking some home mortgage assets off their balance sheet and placing them in vehicles financed with short-term paper (securitized). Offshore borrowing has an important role in the banking system, although Australian banks raise most of their liabilities onshore. The immediate impact of the crisis was closure (or almost closure) of the asset-backed market; offshore borrowing became extremely difficult for banks in Australia. This happened at a time when banks were experiencing an increase in demand for lending from house-holds and big business. However, it is important to note here that these changes in the assets and liabilities side of the balance sheet in the banking system did occur without any change of the default rate for bank assets or the provision for bad and doubtful debts. The relatively meagre effect on the banking system was due to the fact that the financial institutions owned only a very small fraction of the US sub-prime mortgage paper.[4]

7.2.1 Impact on Emerging Economies

Emerging economies in Asia and Africa, with relatively less developed financial markets (due to weak integration with the US financial market) were not directly affected by the financial crisis. However, Latin America, which is trade dependent on the US, was highly affected by the crisis.

The GFC did not have a direct financial effect on emerging and developing economies as these economies did not hold the innovative (or toxic) assets such as MBS. This led many analysts to believe that the impact on these economies would be negligible. However, a lagged impact in the emerging and developing economies was felt through indirect channels. Emerging economies had accumulated high levels of reserves (China being on the top) and had low levels of external debt at the time of crisis, as in East Asian economies, which provided a shield and helped to protect these countries from the direct impact of the crisis. However, the contraction and increased cost of credit and declining portfolio investment severely impacted the capital flows as both foreign direct investment and portfolio investment to emerging economies.

Portfolio investment in emerging African economies reversed from an inflow of US$18.7 billion in 2006 to an outflow of US$16.7 billion in 2008 (Arieff et al., 2009). The International Policy Centre for Inclusive Growth reports in its April 2009 edition that 'bank lending in emerging economies fell from a peak of US$410 billion in 2007 to US$167 billion in 2008' (Alarcon and Ocampo, 2009). This resulted in a severe economic downturn for some countries. For instance, South Africa, a promising emerging economy, experienced a recession for the first time in almost two decades.

Countries heavily dependent on commodity exports experienced a significant decline in export demand due to recessions in the developed countries. For instance, a fall in oil prices significantly reduced the revenues of Nigeria and Angola (Arieff et al., 2009). The recession and economic contraction in developed countries and the fall in export demand in emerging markets resulted in lay-offs of a large number of foreign workers. This impacted the developing countries in two ways.[5] First, a large inflow of residents returning home added to the already high unemployment in the country of origin. Second, a significant decline in remittances contributed to a fall in national income.[6] In the next section we discuss these costs in detail.

7.3   COST OF THE GFC

The global financial crisis caused a huge impact on affected countries and their citizens in the form of social, economic and financial costs. Here we present an analysis of these different costs across a sample of developed countries and emerging economies. For analytical purposes we include Australia, Canada, France, Germany, Japan, the United Kingdom and the United States in the sample for developed countries. The sample for emerging economies includes: China, Indonesia, South Korea, Malaysia, Mexico, Singapore and Thailand. A general discussion on some developing countries is also included.

7.3.1   Social Cost of the GFC

Widespread collapse of financial institutions resulted in a record level of job losses. The impact was an unprecedented increase in the unemployment rate in the United States and other advanced economies. The spillover effect of the loss of income in industrialized countries was felt through a sharp decline in export demand, forcing businesses to cut their production and resulting in increased unemployment. The IEG World Bank Evaluation Brief (2009) projected a sharp increase in the unemployment rate in many countries leading to significant employment losses. The same report also estimated that the crisis would result in an additional 89 million people added to extreme poverty by 2010 (those earning less than $1.25 a day).

Figure 7.1a shows that unemployment in the US increased from around 5 per cent in 2007 to above 9 per cent in 2009. This led to massive pressure on unemployment benefits and social security payments: even as 2010 is coming to an end, US congress is legislating changes to the law to continue social security to the unemployed. A similar pattern could be seen in almost all developed countries with the exception of Germany, which has gained growth. Interestingly, Figure 7.1b shows that the picture for emerging economies was not so bleak, and almost none of the emerging economies in our sample experienced any noticeable effect in this regard. Surprisingly, the unemployment rate in Indonesia declined from around 11 per cent in 2005 to below 8 per cent in 2009.

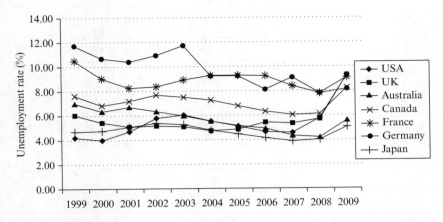

Source: IMF-IFS.

Figure 7.1a   Unemployment rates: developed countries

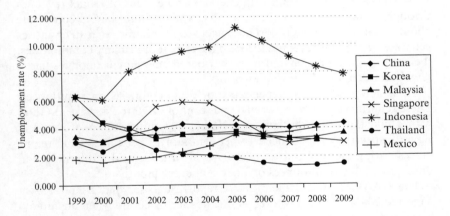

Source: IMF-IFS.

Figure 7.1b   Unemployment rates: emerging economies

As stated in section 7.2 above, the loss of output in developed countries significantly reduced the export revenues and remittances for developing countries. There are two ways to assess the actual and potential impact on migrant workers. The first method is to examine changes in employment and migration opportunities available to migrant workers due to changes in demand for foreign workers as well as the return of workers to their

Table 7.1   Highest recipients of remittances

Country	per cent of GDP
Tajikistan	45
Moldova	38
Tonga	35
Lesotho	29
Honduras	25
Lebanon	24
Guyana	24

Source: Adapted from One Pager (2009).

country of origin. The second source for this is the fall in remittances, which in some cases are major contributors to the national economy. The two issues are interrelated and could have a major impact on economic growth and could worsen the poverty situation in the developing countries. Tajikistan is a good example: it generates 25 per cent of its tax revenues through cotton and aluminium exports, whereas remittances contribute about 45 per cent to its GDP (One Pager, 2009).[7] Some African countries generate 50 per cent revenues through the export of primary commodities; the decline in export demand in export-based emerging economies had a severe effect for developing countries.

Table 7.1 presents the dependence of some countries on remittances. These remittances range between 45 per cent of GDP to 24 per cent GDP, with Tajikistan being the highest recipient of remittances. Morocco and Egypt respectively experienced 11 per cent and 15 per cent falls in remittances during the first quarter of 2009, while the Central Bank of Jordan observed a fall in remittances of 3 per cent every month.

The CARAM Asia Paper (2009) report suggests that South Korea deported 200 000 foreign workers in the post-crisis period when unemployment in the country rose to a high level of 10 per cent. Thailand did the same by deporting about 600 000 foreign workers mostly from Cambodia, Laos and Myanmar. Malaysia decided not to renew the permits of around 850 000 foreign workers. The same estimates show that migrant workers in the six Gulf States account for 40 per cent of the total workforce, or around 20 million migrant workers. South Asia (India, Bangladesh and Pakistan) is the origin for a majority of these migrant workers. The crisis was expected to impact one-third of this migrant workforce. Bangladesh and Pakistan, being the ninth and tenth largest recipients of global remittances, would lose an income of 63 per cent and 52 per cent of all remittances. Remittances in the two countries are generated in the Gulf States (CARAM Asia Paper, 2009).

Table 7.2   *Growth in remittances received by developing countries (per cent)*

Countries	2007	2008	2009 (estimate)
All developing	22.7	8.8	−5.0
Low-income	29.1	13.0	−5.4
Middle-income	21.7	8.1	−4.9
East Asia and Pacific	23.2	6.6	−4.2
Europe and Central Asia	31.5	5.4	−10.0
Latin America and Caribbean	6.6	0.2	−4.4
Middle East and North Africa	21.6	7.6	−1.4
South Asia	31.5	27.0	−4.2

Source: Awad (2009).

Table 7.2 shows the global trend of a decline in remittances since 2008. It is evident from the table that growth rates of remittances in most of the regions changed from above 20 per cent in 2007 to being negative in 2009. Obviously, this significant decline is expected to create economic and social problems for affected countries due to both loss of income and the challenge to absorb the returning nationals in the domestic economy. These problems are further aggravated by a lack of social security in developing countries. As of October 2010, there was no evidence of any emergency plan in the most affected countries to address this problem. Without appropriate policies, these countries may face severe economic problems in the years to come.

7.3.2   Economic Cost of the GFC

To evaluate the economic cost of the crisis, it may be important to understand the impact on the business cycles in emerging economies. Frankel and Rose (1998) show that trade and economic integration lead to higher synchronization of business cycles among countries. Using China and India in their case study, Fidrmuc and Korhonen (2009) found that the crisis brought 'Chinese and Indian business cycles closer to the OECD cycles'. In view of these findings, episodes of recessions in developed countries are expected to have a negative impact on the economic performance of developing countries, especially the ones having close trade and financial links with the developed markets. Here, we investigate the issue of loss of output as a result.

We follow Bordo et al., (2001) in measuring output loss. Accordingly, output loss is calculated by taking a 5-year average of trend growth before

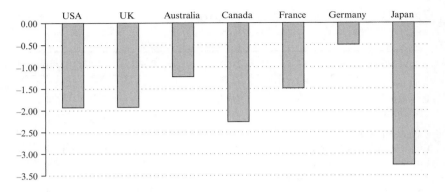

Source: IMF-IFS.

Figure 7.2a   Output losses, developed countries

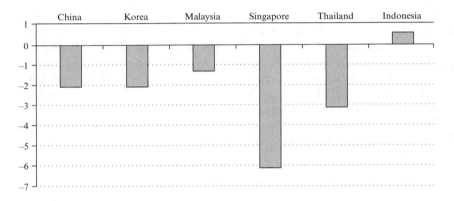

Source: IMF-IFS.

Figure 7.2b   Output losses, emerging economies

the crisis (2002–07) and comparing it with the actual growth at the beginning of the crisis (2008). Figure 7.2a shows that within the developed countries sample, Japan suffered the highest output loss of 3.25 per cent, followed by Canada (2.25 per cent), while the US and UK experienced an output loss of about 2 per cent.

Based on this measure Germany seems to be the least affected by the crisis, losing only 0.5 per cent of output compared to the pre-crisis period. Output losses in emerging economies are plotted in Figure 7.2b. Singapore shows the highest output loss of 6 per cent followed by Thailand (around

3 per cent), while output in China and South Korea was affected by 2 per cent and Malaysia by 1.25 per cent. Surprisingly, Indonesian data show no loss; rather output increased by about 0.5 per cent from its pre-crisis level.

These figures are consistent with the plots of real GDP (Figures 7.3a and 7.3b), with the declining trend more or less continuing into 2009. It is noteworthy that every single country in the sample of developed countries moved into negative growth territory, including Australia, which recorded the highest pre-crisis growth of above 4 per cent amongst the developed countries sample. By 2009, real growth for all developed countries within the sample dropped between -2 per cent (Australia) to -8.5 per cent (Canada). Among emerging economies, only Malaysia and Thailand experienced recession in the post-GFC period, with real GDP growth declining around -2 per cent. China enjoyed a high growth of 12.5 per cent in 2007, which declined to around 8.5 per cent in 2009. Singapore suffered the most, where growth declined from about 8 per cent in 2007 to around 1 per cent in 2008 and remained there in 2009 (almost zero growth) but escaped a recession.

Besides the loss of GDP and decline in growth, a number of macroeconomic variables showed large changes during the crisis period. The crisis required huge transfers on social security and a reduction in a variety of taxes; this exerted pressure on fiscal expenditure and resulted in a significant decline in fiscal balances as well as an increase in government borrowings. Deficits of the G20 increased from 1.1 per cent of GDP in 2007 to 8.1 per cent in 2009, while the deficits for advanced economies increased from 1.9 per cent of GDP to 10.2 per cent. For emerging economies, a surplus of 0.2 per cent of GDP turned into a deficit of 4.9 per cent during the same period. The developed Europe is experiencing street fights as austerity measures to save banks and to meet budgets require huge cuts to expenditure.

During the same period, advanced G20 countries experienced an increase in debt, rising from 78.8 per cent of GDP to 100.6 per cent, while emerging G20 economies had a marginal increase (37.7 per cent to 38.8 per cent).[8] Adequate time-series data on budget deficits are not available. However, a sharp increase in the US budget deficit from less than 2 per cent in 2007 to above 10 per cent in 2009 is a major impact. We do not observe a similar pattern in emerging economies. Singapore's budget shows a decline, but remained in positive territory, moving from about 13 per cent surplus in 2007 to about 6 per cent surplus in 2008.

The real estate market bubble that started increasing housing prices steadily from 2002 also impacted the prices of other consumables, resulting in high inflation in many countries. The Consumer Price Index (CPI) continued to increase rapidly from 2005 and 2008 in developed countries

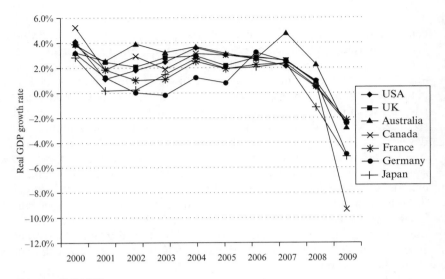

Source: IMF-IFS.

Figure 7.3a   Real GDP growth rates: developed countries

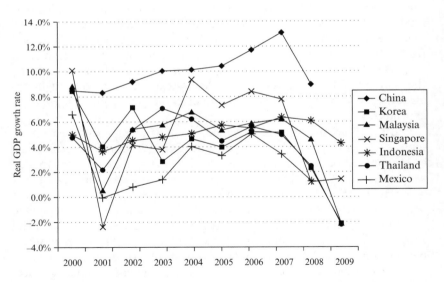

Source: IMF-IFS.

Figure 7.3b   Real GDP growth rates: emerging economies

until the bubble burst and CPI started to decline. We do not observe the same sharp increase in CPI for emerging economies. The changes in money supply as a percentage of GDP went up in both samples. Data from the UK and Japan show the highest increase in money supply in the post-crisis period. Among emerging economies, Singapore and Malaysia experienced significant increases in money supply starting from 2008.

Regarding current accounts, Canada shows a significant decline, moving from around 2 per cent surplus in 2007 to about a 3 per cent deficit in 2009. China also shows a decline of around 6 per cent, from 11 per cent surplus to 5 per cent surplus during the same period. Canada also experienced a sharp decline in its trade account, moving from 4 per cent surplus in 2007 to above 1 per cent deficit in 2009. Among emerging economies, a significant decline is also observed in Singapore. Trade surplus dropped from about 28 per cent in 2007 to less than half (13 per cent) in 2009. For a small open economy completely dependent on external factors, this is a significant drop and could have major implications for the economy.

The empirical evidence provided in this sub-section using time-series plots and growth rates of a variety of macroeconomic indicators confirms our initial assertion that (i) developed countries were the direct victim of the GFC, the US being the source of the crisis through the meltdown from the sub-prime loan market; (ii) emerging economies were less affected by the crisis; (iii) the impact on emerging economies was felt through a lag effect, a kind of spillover effect from developed countries through trade and financial and labour market linkages. This analysis is also consistent with some research published earlier and cited elsewhere in this chapter.

7.3.3   Financial Cost of the GFC

One major impact of the sub-prime crisis was a sharp decline in lending rates. The UK experienced the maximum fall in lending rates, which dropped from above 5 per cent in 2007 to about 0.5 per cent in 2009 (see Figure 7.4a). The trend is no different in many other developed countries. The US experienced a drop of about 3 per cent in 2009 from a high 8 per cent in 2007. Lending rates also dropped in emerging economies but data do not show such high volatility. The rates were maintained at levels above 5 per cent in all sample countries (see Figure 7.4b).

The sub-prime crisis also increased the volume of non-performing loans (NPLs) and provisions for NPLs as well as a large number of bank defaults. Figure 7.5a shows that NPLs increased significantly in the US from 1.4 per cent of total loans in 2007 to 3.8 per cent in 2009. Almost all advanced developed economies followed the same trend. Australia witnessed a five-fold increase where NPLs moved from 0.2 per cent to 1 per

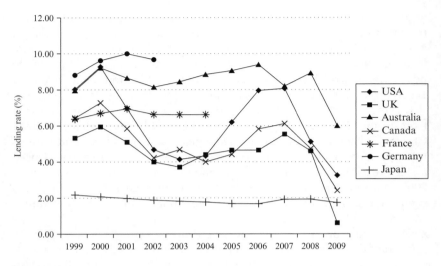

Source: IMF-IFS.

Figure 7.4a   Lending rates: developed countries

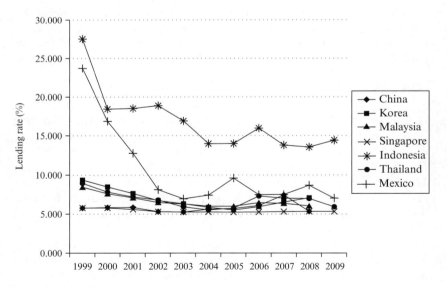

Source: IMF-IFS.

Figure 7.4b   Lending rates: emerging economies

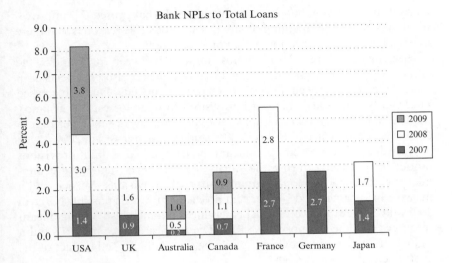

Figure 7.5a   Non-performing loans: developed countries

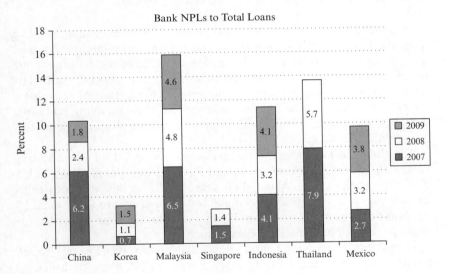

Figure 7.5b   Non-performing loans: emerging economies

cent of total loans. In comparison, most of the emerging economies show a decline in NPLs during the same period. Figure 7.5b shows that NPLs in China had a decline of 1.8 per cent in 2009 from a high level of 6.2 per cent. Malaysia and Thailand also experienced a decline in non-performing loans. It is surprising, but yet to be investigated what caused this improvement in NPLs in the emerging economies. One possible reason is that there may be lags in the realization of any problem credits.

However, in Korea, NPLs almost doubled between 2007 and 2009, rising to 1.5 per cent of total loans in 2009. Mexico also experienced an increase from 2.7 per cent in 2007 to 3.8 per cent in 2009. Due to increased uncertainty, banks also increased provisions for loan losses. For instance, the US banks increased provisions for loan losses by about 74 per cent in 2008 as a consequence of losses in 2007 and expected losses in 2009.

Australia also observed a significant increase in loan default provisions (about 76 per cent) during the same year. However, emerging economies far exceeded developed countries in such provisions. Mexico had a massive 161 per cent and 144 per cent provisions towards possible NPLs in 2008 and 2009 respectively. Other emerging economies also had significant resources allocated to possible NPLs. The modest change in NPLs but a significant increase in provisions could be due to the lagged impact of the crisis in emerging economies.

7.3.4   Stimulus Packages – Adding Burden to Expenses

A large number of bank defaults and the financial system collapses led to a significant increase in job losses and unemployment in developed as well as emerging and developing countries. Hence the main focus of economic policy during the post-crisis period is restoring confidence by stimulating economic activity. To achieve this, a number of countries extended a stimulus package to their citizens to help them in maintaining economic activities, to stimulate consumption and to help economies out of this recession see Table 7.3.[9]

The global cost of these stimulus packages accounted for about $3 trillion of the world economies or around 5 per cent of global GDP. In US dollar terms, the US had the highest amount ($787.2 billion) allocated to the stimulus package, which accounted for 5.52 per cent of GDP or 22.38 per cent of government spending. Japan's stimulus package accounted for 20.06 per cent of government expenditure.

In emerging economies, China extended a stimulus package of US$586 billion, but it accounted for 13.3 per cent of GDP, more than double what was offered by the US, although in size the Chinese economy is but 25 per cent of the US economy. Singapore is a small economy but its stimulus package exceeded all other East Asian countries. Given the significant decline in Singapore's GDP, its stimulus package accounted for about 8 per cent, though the total amount was only US$15 billion. All other emerging economies in this sample had small contributions towards

Table 7.3   Stimulus packages reported for developed and emerging economies

A: *Developed countries*

Country	Value (billions of US$)	per cent of GDP	per cent of government spending
USA	787.2	5.52	22.38
UK	30	3.24	8.04
Australia	27.4	3.34	12.46
Canada	32	2.62	16.75
France	33.1	0.21	2.53
Germany	63	1.07	4.36
Japan	100	2.11	20.06

B: *Emerging economies*

Country	Value (billions of US$)	per cent of GDP	per cent of government spending
China (2008)	586	13.30	63.90
Korea (2008)	11	1.37	5.99
Malaysia (2008)	2.09	0.95	16.34
Singapore	15	7.96	38.45
Indonesia	7.05	1.31	7.44
Thailand	3.33	1.26	5.76
Mexico (2008)	5.75	0.64	0.56

Source: Various internet sites.

stimulus packages, with Mexico at the bottom with a stimulus package of under 1 per cent of its GDP.[10]

7.4   CONCLUSION

This chapter analysed the *cost and consequences* of the global financial crisis in the developed and emerging markets. Some observations have also been made on the impact on developing countries. The crisis opened a series of challenges for academics, practitioners and policy-makers in both the developed and the developing markets. One of the challenges was to estimate the cost of the GFC to affected countries including social, economic and financial costs. Understanding these costs will help policy-makers to develop a good understanding of ways to diversify global risk in the wake of globalization and to devise strategies to promote more transparent policies, accounting practices, good governance of the banking sector and an effective regulatory structure.

There is also a need to encourage savings and investment as opposed to consumption. This raises a question on the so-called *need* for stimulus packages. Long-term measures include pro-cyclical policies, global accounting standards and regulatory norms especially for the derivatives markets. The recent financial reforms bill (passed by the US Senate in July 2010 and signed by President Obama) focuses on the regulatory restructuring of the financial system as part of these measures. It is yet to be seen if these measures will be enough to protect financial markets from similar shocks and to help achieve the above-stated objectives.[11]

The evidence in this chapter shows that developed countries were directly hit by the collapse of the US financial system. This could partly be due to the market structure where it was easy for US financial institutions to sell high-risk financial products in European markets. However, emerging economies were not directly or severely affected. A sort of delayed impact was felt through changes in international transactions, trade and capital flows and labour market changes. Developing countries were affected mainly due to declining export demand, a reduction in capital and investment flows and a significant loss in income through remittances. A number of chapters in this book have made policy recommendations for developed countries to avoid the repeat of a similar crisis or reduce its impact. Here we focus on the emerging and developing economies and suggest some policy measures which could help these countries to reduce their exposure to external shocks.[12]

First, financial sector reforms and re-regulations (not de-regulations) are important because such measures could help to restore confidence among market participants. Priority should be given to the development of money and capital markets including a secondary market for government bonds. Appropriate sequencing of reforms is an important part of the overall reform package. There are lessons to be learned from some relatively developed East Asian economies. East Asia also needs to strengthen its Regional Financial Architecture (RFA) in the light of the Chiang Mai Initiative (CMI) and accelerate steps to agree and implement suggested measures such as a move from bilateral swap agreements to a reserve pooling mechanism created from a US$80 billion regional, multilateral fund along with an agreement to provide a strong regional surveillance mechanism for this fund to function.

Second, financial reforms cannot be successful without re-regulatory restructuring – regulations to cater to the needs of a liberalized financial sector while preventing the abuses of self-regulation regimes in the UK and US. These measures will need to include, for example, more transparent policies, improved accountability of the financial institutions including the regulators themselves, a more stringent approach towards compliance, efficient monitoring and a more realistic assessment of risk valuation. These measures will create market discipline and could help to revive the financial sector.

Developing countries also need to adopt measures of macroeconomic management, for example by reducing reliance on external borrowing, and focusing on social spending such as on education and health policies that improve the living standards of the poor and reduce disparity in income distribution. Dependence on foreign aid and external borrowing distorts the capacity-building in domestic markets. Infrastructure development and the use of information technology would help build better market structures. Financial literacy is an essential element for developing countries where the pace of financial innovation is faster than the information about the risks attached to the new instrument. Lack of financial literacy is a major concern and gives rise to corrupt practices.

In the opening decade of the twenty-first century, many developing economies made use of the rapid growth of informational technology by introducing new, innovative, financial products such as debit and credit cards, loan and lease financing, and so on. However, banks and other institutions did not make any effort to educate market participants, especially the relatively less educated portion of the population. Regulators should ensure that market participants fully understand the risk of every new financial product so that, in the event of failures, the financial institutions should be liable to compensate for any increased risk-taking activities. These measures will help to restore market confidence as the world moves relentlessly towards a global financial market.

NOTES

1. Claessens et al. (2010) and Dymski (2008) provide details of these market movements.
2. See also Dymski (2008), Shah (2009) and Versi (2008) for more details on the GFC.
3. See Emerson et al. (2009) for more details of the impact of the crisis in Europe.
4. See Edwards (2008) and Ellis (2009) for information on the impact of the crisis on Australia.
5. A detailed discussion of labour market issues is provided in Chapter 5 of this book.
6. See Ali (2009), Fidrmuc and Korhonen (2009), Goldstein and Xie (2009), Griffith-Jones and Ocampo (2009), Ikome (2008), Lee and Park (2009), McCarthy (2009), Saleem (2009), Shah (2009), Versi (2008) and World Bank (2009) for detailed discussion on emerging economies in various regions.
7. A third of the labour force in Tajikistan is employed abroad, mainly in the Russian Federation and Kazakhstan (Awad, 2009, p. 34).
8. See details in IEG World Bank (2009).

9.   There is a growing debate on the role of stimulus packages in bringing recovery to the affected economies. Most agree that the United States had no option but to provide one. However, there are mixed views on whether countries such as Australia needed to have a stimulus package. This debate is based more on political reasoning than academic research. More time and sufficient data is needed to assess the effectiveness of stimulus packages for both the developed and emerging economies.
10. Whether these measures helped in stimulating the economy is a debatable issue and beyond the scope of this chapter.
11. These issues are discussed in detail elsewhere in this book (see Chapter 4).
12. Additional graphs are provided in the Appendix (p. 124) to give further results not discussed in this chapter.

REFERENCES

Alarcon Diana and José Antonio Ocampo (2009), 'How does the financial crisis affect developing countries', *One Pagers*, 81, April, International Policy Centre for Inclusive Growth.

Ali, Mohammed Mansoor (2009), 'Global financial crisis: impact of Pakistan and policy responses', paper prepared for United Nations Economic and Social Commission for Asia and the Pacific, Regional High-level Workshop on 'Strengthening the responses to the global financial crisis in Asia-Pacific: the role of monetary, fiscal and external debt policies', Dhaka, Bangladesh, 27–30 July.

Arieff, Alexis, Martin A. Weiss and Vivian C. Jones (2009), 'The global economic crisis: impact on the sub-Saharan Africa and global policy responses', Congressional Research Service, 7-5700, CRS Report to the Congress, 19 October.

Awad, Ibrahim (2009), 'The global economic crisis and migrant workers: impact and response', International Migration Programme, International Labour Office (ILO), Geneva.

Bordo, M.D., B. Eichengreen, D. Klingebiel and M.S. Martinez-Peria (2001), 'Is the crisis problem growing more severe?', *Economic Policy*, **32**, 51–82.

CARAM Asia Paper (2009), 'Financial crisis impact on migration', available at http://www.caramasia.org/presentationsper cent20&per cent20papers/Economicper cent20Crisisper cent20Report.pdf.

Claessens, Stijin, Giovanni Dell'Ariccia, Deniz Igan and Luc Laeven (2010), 'Lessons and policy implications from the global financial crisis', IMF Working Paper WP/10/44, International Monetary Fund, Washington, DC, February.

Dymski, Gary A. (2008), 'The political economy of the subprime meltdown', paper presented at the conference on Structural Change and Development Policies at the National Autonomous University, Mexico.

Edwards, John (2008), 'Australia's experience in the sub-prime crisis', Address to Finance International Expert Symposium on 'The sub-prime mortgage meltdown: origin, trajectories and regional implications', Adelaide, 16 May.

Ellis, Luci (2009), 'The global crisis: causes, consequences and countermeasures', remarks to the conference 'Australia in the global storm: a conference on the implications of the global crisis for Australia and its region', Victoria University, Melbourne, 15 April.

Emerson, Michael, Richard Youngs, Brad Setser, Fyodor Lukyanov, Lansin Xiang and Jorgen Mortensen (2009), 'The strategic consequences of the global financial and economic crisis', European Security Forum, ESP Working Paper No. 31, March.

Fidrmuc, Jarko and Likka Korhonen (2009), 'The impact of the global financial crisis on business cycles in Asian emerging economies', BOFIT Discussion Paper 11-2009, Bank of England, Institute for Economies in Transition, Helsinki, August.

Frankel, Jeffrey A. and Andrew K. Rose (1998), 'The endogeneity of the optimum currency area criteria', *Economic Journal*, **108**(449), 1009–25.

Goldstein, Morris and Daniel Xie (2009), 'The impact of the financial crisis on emerging economies', Working Paper series WP 09-11, Peterson Institute for International Economics, Washington, DC, October.

Griffith-Jones, Stephany and Jose Antonio Ocampo (2009), 'The financial crisis and its impact on developing countries', Working Paper no. 53, International Policy Centre for Inclusive Growth, April.

IEG World Bank (2009), 'The World Bank Group's response to the global crisis: update on an ongoing IEG Evaluation', Independent Evaluation Group (IEG), Evaluation Brief 8, The World Bank, Washington, DC, November.

Ikome, Francis (2008), 'The social and economic consequences of the global financial crisis on the developing countries and emerging economies: a focus on Africa', paper prepared for presentation at the 'InWent-DIE dialogue on the effects of the global financial crisis on developing countries and emerging markets', Berlin, 11 December.

International Monetary Fund (various years), *IMF Annual reports*, IMF.

Lee, Jong-Wha and Cyn-Young Park (2009), 'Global financial turmoil: impact and challenges for Asia's financial system', *Asian Economic Papers*, **8**(1), 9–40.

McCarthy, Colin (2009), 'The global financial and economic crisis and its impact on sub-Saharan economies', tralac Trade Brief 1, Trade Law Centre for Southern Africa (tralac), April.

One Pager (2009), published by the Economic Intelligence Unit, UK.

Saleem, Farrukh (2009), 'Pakistan and the global financial crisis', Centre for Research and Security Studies, January.

Shah, Anup (2009), 'Global financial crisis, global issues', available at http://www.globalissues.org/article/768/global-financial-crisis.

Versi, Anver (2008), 'Anatomy of the global financial crisis; how did the global financial crisis begin and what is the latest situation?', *African Business*, November, available at http://findarticle.com/p/articles/mi_qa5327/is_347/ai_n31058344/.

World Bank (2009), 'Swimming against the tide: how developing countries are coping with the global crisis', background paper prepared by World Bank for the G20 Finance Ministers and Central Bank Governors meeting, Horsham, UK, 13–14 March.

APPENDIX

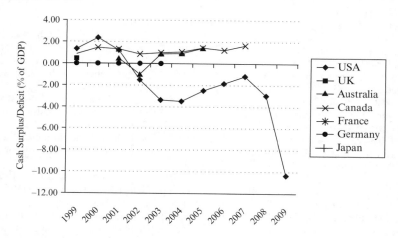

Source: IMF-IFS.

*Figure A7.1a   Budget deficit (surplus)/GDP (per cent): developed
            countries*

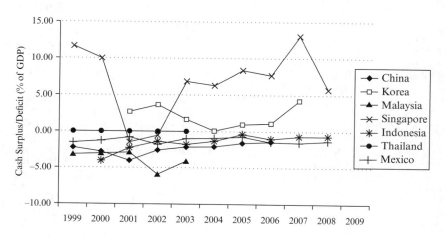

Source: IMF-IFS.

*Figure A7.1b   Budget deficit (surplus)/GDP (per cent): emerging
            economies*

PART III

Governance and regulatory issues of the crisis

8.   Improving the governance of financial institutions

John Farrar

8.1   INTRODUCTION

The global financial crisis has challenged many of our assumptions about the contemporary financial systems in place in the developed economies. In the last decade or so we have seen the re-organization and transformation of the financial services sector.[1] We assumed that in spite of market fluctuations, management of financial firms and the investors using these products basically understood their business, lines of authority were clear and followed, and adequate risk management systems and other internal controls were in place. The present crisis has shown that on the contrary this was not necessarily so. Banks have given credit to anyone who wanted it in fraudulent fashion. They have failed to handle risk effectively, with rating agencies not rating risk appropriately. Instead of expediting the flow of capital to industry they have frozen it to earn untold riches to the movers of financial contracts. As *The Economist*'s special report on international banking of 16 May 2009 said:[2]

> the costs of this failure are massive. Frantic efforts by governments to save their financial systems and buoy their economies will do long-term damage to public finances. The IMF reckons that average government debt for the richer G20 countries will exceed 100% of GDP in 2014, up from 70% in 2000 and just 40% in 1980.

The market value of capital of banks fell substantially, precipitating a significant decline in stock markets around the world, and we are still picking up the wreckage in 2011. Australian, Canadian and New Zealand banks seem in better shape but have nevertheless been swept by the storm affecting other components of the financial structures.

This discussion is organised into six sections. Section 8.2 addresses the regulatory failure, with section 8.3 specifically examining the resulting governance failure. As a contribution to debate, we discuss in section 8.4 the need for redefining the regulatory states by also setting the objectives of that state in section 8.5. Concluding remarks are provided in section 8.6.

8.2   INDUSTRY AND REGULATORY FAILURES

Why was this so?[3] The main reasons seem to be the rise of complex financial conglomerates, and the increase in complex financial transactions caused an increase in systemic risk that our risk models failed to predict or to specify how to manage. There was excessive leverage in the sector. These problems were exacerbated by the growth via licensing of a new form of shadow financial system. Perverse commission and remuneration structures encouraged irresponsible risk-taking. There was a failure in the credit rating system as well as a failure of other gatekeepers. Not only did the financial services industry fail, there were significant regulatory failures. These were unclear demarcation lines amongst regulators coupled with lack of information, monitoring and coordination. There was a failure to monitor risk, and to ensure transparency and fair dealing, the aim of a just and equitable regulatory framework.

8.3   THE IMPORTANCE OF CORPORATE GOVERNANCE

To a large extent the industry failure was a failure of corporate governance in the broadest sense.

8.3.1   Corporate Governance Matters

Corporate governance matters because:[4]

1. There is a link between corporate governance and investment growth; the quantity of investment and efficiency of allocation and monitoring matter;
2. The law influences how we mobilize capital by defining property rights and guaranteeing credible information;
3. Corporate governance is seen as a constituent element of equity risk. Bad corporate governance often signals information asymmetry and high probability of expropriation of shareholder value;
4. Investors are willing to pay a premium for companies with good corporate governance, all other things being equal;

5. The best decisions regarding allocation of capital are dependent on proper disclosure. Effective monitoring depends on sound procedures, clear lines of authority, and incentive schemes; and
6. Globalization affects this because of growing institutional investment and growing international interdependence through technology.

8.3.2 The Importance of the Corporate Governance of Banks

Corporate governance matters to banks because they are corporations themselves and it is relevant to their cost of capital and performance. Risk management is vital to financial services and affects the economy in general and the government of non-banks.

Banks are distinctive because:[5]

1. they are often part of complex financial conglomerates;
2. information is often opaque and hard to access;
3. they have more diverse stakeholders;
4. they are highly leveraged with many short-term claims;
5. they are subject to runs;
6. they are highly regulated and are subject to government monitoring;
7. they enjoy benefits of a public safety net; and
8. bank shareholder value can come from increased risk-taking.

Four important governance issues arise, from the role and composition of bank boards, the duty of care of directors; liquidity and risk management; and remuneration issues.[6]

8.3.3 The Role and Composition of the Board of Directors[7]

One of the perennial problems of corporate governance for any kind of company is the ambiguous role of the board of directors. The original role was to manage the company but the modern tendency is to refer to the role as being to manage, supervise or monitor management. The term 'monitoring' was first used in relation to financial institutions in the United States but it has been extended to companies generally. A key element in monitoring is the role of independent directors and board committees.

The definition of independent directors has tended to exclude people with specialist knowledge of companies' affairs and some argue as a consequence that they are against having a majority of independent directors on a listed company board. Recent UK research has examined the question of whether inexperienced non-executive directors facilitated bank failure and the necessity of government bailouts.

The Australian Prudential Regulation Authority's (APRA) Prudential Standard APS 510 for the governance of authorized deposit-taking institutions and Prudential Standard GPS 510 for the governance of general insurers provide detailed requirements regarding boards and senior management. The board must have a majority of independent directors at all times and the chairperson must be an independent director. A majority of directors present and eligible to vote at all board meetings must be non-executive. The chairperson must not have been Chief Executive Officer of the institution at any time during the previous three years.

Rule 7 of APS 510 and Rule 8 of GPS 510 provide that the board must ensure that directors and senior management of the regulated institution, collectively, have the full range of skills needed for the effective and prudent operation of the regulated institution, and that each director has skills that allow them to make an effective contribution to board deliberations and processes. This includes the requirement for directors, collectively, to have the necessary skills, knowledge and experience to understand the risks of the regulated institution, including its legal and prudential obligations, and to ensure that the regulated institution is managed in an appropriate way taking into account these risks. This does not preclude the board from supplementing its skills and knowledge through the use of external consultants and experts.

The UK 'Review of corporate governance in UK banks and other financial industry entities' of 16 July 2009 makes useful recommendations with regard to board size, composition and compensation. It recommends that non-executive directors should have the knowledge and understanding of the business to enable them to contribute effectively. To this end they should be provided with a personalized approach to induction, training and development which is kept under review. Non-executive directors should have access to dedicated support. It should be expected that they will give greater time commitment than has been normal in the past. The Financial Services Authority (now part of the Bank of England) has ongoing supervisory responsibilities and the review suggests that they should give closer attention to both the overall balance of the board in relation to risk strategy and the extent of training provided for board members.

Non-executive directors should be ready, able and encouraged to challenge proposals on strategy put forward by the executives. The chair should be expected to commit a substantial proportion of time, probably not less than two-thirds, to the business of the institution. The chair should have a combination of financial industry experience and a proven track record of leadership. The chair should be elected on an annual basis. The review also considers the role of the senior independent director as a sounding board for the chair. The board should undertake regular evaluation of its performance.

8.3.4 The Duty and Standard of Care[8]

From time to time there has been an argument for an increased duty and standard of care on directors of financial institutions. This kind of argument was raised in the United States in the early twentieth century, but was rejected. As long ago as 1946, Professor H. Ballantine thought that a distinction based solely on the label 'financial' as opposed to 'industrial' corporation was unjustified and anachronistic,[9] and the American Law Institute (ALI) took the same view in 1992. It said that 'in general, today banks and other financial institutions are often complex economic entities with activities far wider than the holding of deposits.[10] Industrial corporations often are, at least in part, financial institutions. Nevertheless the argument has recently been restated.

The two main arguments for stricter rules for bank directors arise first from the role of banks in providing access to credit and its importance in the economy and, second, from the special vulnerability of the banking industry and the significance of banking failure for the economy as a whole. Banks have a special role in the resetting of liquidity during times of crisis. By holding illiquid assets and issuing liquid liabilities they create liquidity for the economy and are peculiarly susceptible to a bank run. This extreme behaviour, which represents a classic prisoner's dilemma, can cause the failure of even a solvent bank. As J.M. Keynes wrote: 'Of the maxims of orthodox finance none, surely, is more antisocial than the fetish of liquidity.'[11] Added to these is a third argument that banks and other financial institutions are often elaborate financial conglomerates which are now different from industrial corporations in the Western world. The old argument is no longer true, if it ever was.

Jonathan Macey and Maureen O'Hara[12] argued in 2003 that financial institution directors should be obliged to inform themselves of whether a particular decision will: (1) impact the ability of the institution to pay its debts as they fall due; (2) materially increase the riskiness of the institution; or (3) materially reduce its capital position as measured both by a risk-based calculation and the leverage test. This links duty of care with liquidity and risk management. This is in the context of what is often a complex or opaque corporate structure. The current case law test is not that of a competent operator in financial products and is of a more general nature but taking account of the nature of the company's business and its circumstances. This falls short of the specifics of the proposed test.

8.3.5   Liquidity and Risk Management[13]

Financial institutions face financial, market, human resources and other risks. It is the role of the board and, in particular, the audit and risk management committees to monitor these risks.

It is remarkable how little attention was paid to risk management in the past. This may have been due to ownership patterns. Joint stock banks and insurance companies were subject to some system of regulation, but City of London stock brokers had no real experience of risk management prior to the Big Bang. The Council of Lloyd's also significantly failed to monitor insurance risks. Merchant banks were complacent.

Barings was undone by a rogue trader, weak management and a lax regulatory regime in the 1990s. Barings' collapse caused most City of London firms to formalize their risk management. Nevertheless it was the beginning of the end of Gentlemanly Capitalism.

The 'Final report of the Royal Commission into the Tricontinental Group of companies' in Victoria, Australia, on 31 August 1962, made strong criticism of Tricontinental's management of credit risk and the Reserve Bank's voluntary prudential supervision.

Risk management was referred to by the Cadbury Report, and in Australia it was mainly thought of in relation to the Audit Committee. It received more attention in the Australian Securities Exchange's Corporate Governance Council's 'Principles of good corporate governance and best practice recommendations', particularly in the revised version. The Australia/New Zealand risk management standard was originally adopted in 1995 and was revised in 2009 (AS/NZS ISO 31000:2009). APRA initially found it difficult to deal with its insurance responsibilities and was slow off the mark in responding to Health Insurance Holding (HIH)'s difficulties.

APRA was reformed with a full-time Executive Group in place of its previous board. In 2002 it introduced a risk-based framework with two components – a Probability and Impact Rating System (PAIRS) and a Supervisory Oversight and Response System (SOARS).[14] PAIRS deals with the riskiness of an institution, while SOARS deals with how APRA officials respond to that risk. PAIRS deals with probability and impact of failure and is based on qualitative data which results in a risk score. Some concerns have been raised about the subjective aspects of some of this process. This is where SOARS comes in, and the actual level of intervention is set by the Executive Group together with senior management. APRA now tends towards earlier and more interventionist action.

The challenge for prudential regulators such as APRA is to strike a balance between financial safety and other public policy objectives such as efficiency and competition. In the case of banking, APRA's prudential framework is based on the Basel Accords, which are currently undergoing scrutiny for adoption revision. The first Accord in 1986 was a risk-based capital adequacy regime. In 2004, Basel II introduced new and more granular capital requirements which were more sensitive to the actual risks within the bank's business. Basically the greater the risk to which the bank is exposed, the greater the amount of capital needed to safeguard solvency and economic stability. The main problem in the present crisis is to quantify exposure to derivative and credit default swap liability. As Hank Paulson has written, 'the devil was in the details – and the details were murky'.[15]

John Laker, chair of APRA, has emphasized that prudential regulators work on the fundamental premise that the primary responsibility for financial soundness and prudential risk management lies with the board of directors and senior management.[16] This involves risk identification and risk mitigation and management. The latter involves a variety of options including limiting the risks, pooling of risks, diversification, hedging divestment of risk and insurance cover. Laker discussed financial risk in terms of credit risk, traded market risk and operational risk.

An effective risk management regime must have the following characteristics:

- Clearly defined management responsibilities and accountability;
- avoidance of conflicts of interest;
- a system of approvals, limits and authorization;
- an audit committee or risk management committee to maintain internal control;
- detailed risk controls for each business line;
- an effective system of internal audit or compliance process; and
- a cushion of unencumbered high quality liquid assets to withstand high stress events, commensurate with the complexity of on- and off-balance sheet activities. This needs to be under constant review to keep pace with changes in the risk profile and the external risk landscape. This is the subject of increasing prudential regulation.

APRA adopted Prudential Standard APS 110 on Capital Adequacy in January 2009. This standard aims to ensure that authorized deposit-taking institutions maintain adequate capital on both an individual and group basis to act as a buffer against the risks involved in their activities. The key requirements are that the institution must have Internal Capital Adequacy Assessment Process; maintain minimum levels of capital; and inform APRA of any significant adverse changes in capital. In addition, Prudential Standard APS 111 deals with 'Capital adequacy: measurement of capital'. The key requirements of this standard are that authorized deposit-taking institutions must only include eligible capital as a component of capital for regulatory capital purposes; deduct certain items from capital; and meet certain limitations with regards to Tier 1 capital and Tier 2 capital. Guidance Note AGN 210.1 deals with liquidity management strategy.

These are being revised in light of enhancements to the Basel II framework in the new Basel III accord (see Chapter 4). APRA recognizes that the scope of the liquidity management strategy may vary among institutions depending on the nature and complexity of their operations. Prudential Standard APS 116, also implemented in January 2008, deals with 'Capital adequacy: market risk' and requires a framework to manage, measure and monitor market risk commensurate with the nature, scale and complexity of operations of the institutions.

In a recent IMF Working Paper, 'Basel core principles and bank risk: does compliance matter?' of March 2010, Asli Demirguc-Kunt and Enrica Detragiache consider whether compliance with Basel Core principles for effective banking supervision is associated with lower bank risk, as measured by Z-Scores. They find no evidence linking better compliance with improved bank soundness. This is a worrying finding which may reflect the difficulty of capturing bank risk using accounting measures.

Keynes distinguished between risk, to which numerical probability can be assigned, and uncertainty. Uncertainty is the risk which cannot be calculated with any degree of confidence. This relationship is less a dichotomy than a spectrum.

US banks mispriced and misjudged risk, effectively outsourcing risk assessment to credit rating agencies and gambling on a government bailout. The regulators stood back and let it happen. It has been argued that Australian banks have been better regulated. Certainly the sector has been subject to a lot of regulation, but the fact that it has emerged from the current financial crisis relatively unscathed may be due at least in part to timing and the fact that Australian banks were less of an international player at the time than their US, UK and European counterparts. This is a matter which needs further detailed research before the above claim can be sustained. One must guard against the fallacy of *post hoc, ergo propter hoc.*

8.3.6   Remuneration Issues[17]

Even before the current crisis there has been growing investor dissatisfaction with remuneration levels, particularly in the financial sector, and the lack of correlation between pay and performance.

APRA released its prudential requirements on the remuneration for authorized deposit-taking institutions and general and life insurance companies on 30 November 2009. The revised governance standards came into effect between April and July 2010. APRA required that a Capital Board Remuneration Committee with appropriate composition and charter be established and a suitable remuneration policy be in place. APRA's requirements take as their starting point the Financial Stability Board's 'Principles for sound compensation practices' of April 2009. These principles have been endorsed by the G20 leaders.

The Basel Committee on Banking Supervision Consultative Document, 'Principles for Enhancing Corporate Governance', March 2010, Principle 11 provides:

> An employee's compensation should be effectively aligned with prudent risk taking: compensation should be adjusted for all types of risk; compensation outcomes should be symmetric with risk outcomes; compensation payout schedules should be sensitive to the time horizon of risks; and the mix of cash, equity and other forms of compensation should be consistent with risk alignment.

The UK review recommended that the remuneration committee of a financial institution should have a remit extended to all aspects of a remuneration policy, with particular emphasis on risk. The report makes detailed recommendations in respect of disclosure and provision for the deferral of incentive payments to align rewards with sustainable performance. There should be a dialogue between the remuneration committee and the board risk management committee on an arm's length basis on specific risk adjustments applied to incentive packages. It also recommends that if the non-binding resolution on a remuneration committee report attracts less than 75 per cent of the total votes cast, the chair of the committee should stand for re-election in the following year.

The matter has received some general attention by the recent report of the Australian Productivity Commission. It recommends that the matter should remain with boards and does not favour capping pay or introducing a binding shareholder vote. Instead it favours independent remuneration committees and improved processes for using outside consultants. It favours enhanced disclosure and strengthening the consequences for boards that are unresponsive to shareholder views. These are much tamer recommendations than the UK report and APRA's new standards.

In the United States and United Kingdom, there are controversial moves to tax bonuses, which are politically justifiable but may drive business away. There is resistance for this to be applied to some member countries of the G20 group.

8.4   REDEFINING THE REGULATORY STATE[18]

An important question in respect of governance in general is the changing role of the state in the present global financial crisis. In British Commonwealth systems, we have an archaic concept of the state in the form of the Crown, but the reality of the modern state is multifunctional and complex. Historically the state in Australia and New Zealand provided a major source of development capital in the early history of the colonies. The state has been regulator of the financial sector and now it is thrust into the position of equity investor in the United States and United Kingdom. This has required new classes of shares to be taken up by the state in what was intended to be a temporary measure. There is the role of Reserve Banks as lenders of last resort.

In addition to a possible changing role of the state there has been increased emphasis on the international dimension and international approaches to the problems. There has been a need for closer international cooperation. Attention has been focused on the G20 countries and this has led to a reconstitution of the Financial Stability Board and increased action by the Basel Committee on Banking Supervision, the International Organization of Securities Commissions (IOSCO) and other global standards-setting bodies.

The crisis is not over, and the debate continues about a new system of regulation, one to be designed by the G20 group. There will be a temptation to over-regulate the sector, and one needs to remember that the regulators themselves cannot escape some responsibility for the crisis, and need themselves to be monitored. Some argue that we are undergoing a paradigm shift. This is probably an exaggeration and in any event when one is living through a period of crisis and change it is difficult to detect whether the paradigm is shifted. As regards corporate governance itself in Australia, we have the toughest but most obscure company and financial services law and superannuation regulation, as well as detailed self-regulation. The problem is to make it work well without impeding innovation and corporate performance.

The United States has passed the Dodd–Frank Wall Street Reform and the Consumer Protection Act 2010, which is a complex piece of federal legislation that still leaves the United States with an over-complex regulatory system.

The new Coalition Government in the United Kingdom has subsumed the Financial Services Authority into the Bank of England as well as setting up the Prudential Regulatory Authority and Consumer Protection and Markets Authority. This is still a work in progress.

Australia has a combination of the Reserve Bank, the Australian

Prudential Regulation Authority and the Australian Securities and Investments Commission, which seem to have weathered the storm better than some overseas systems.

New Zealand is in the process of setting up the Financial Markets Authority which will absorb the Securities Commission. This will coexist with the Reserve Bank, which will retain its prudential regulatory role.

8.5   THE NEW REGULATORY OBJECTIVES

The US Congressional Oversight Panel's 'Special report on regulatory reform' identified the following as the new regulatory objectives:

1. The identification and regulation of financial institutions which pose systemic risk;
2. limit to excessive leverage;
3. increased supervision of the shadow financial system;
4. creation of executive pay structures that discourage excessive risk-taking;
5. reform of the credit rating system;
6. making a global financial regulatory floor a diplomatic priority; and
7. Planning for the next crisis.

8.6   CONCLUSION

Banks have long had a complex relationship with the state. In the late seventeenth century they financed the state. Now the state is having to bail out the banks at high cost. There is general scepticism about the wisdom of the deregulation of the last 30 years and the efficacy of systems of self regulation. This has led to a resurgence of legal regulation and the power of the nation state. At the same time there is greater need for international cooperation. International cooperation is a work in progress and there is a natural tendency, like the Old English War Office, to be busy planning for the previous war. We need to assess the impact of the Global Financial Crisis on our ideas of globalization. Was this the end of the beginning or the beginning of the end for a globalized world?

NOTES

1. See R. Baxt, A. Black and P. Hanrahan, *Securities and Financial Services Law* 6th edn, Chapter 1, Lexis Nexis Butterworths, Chatswood, 2003; Gail Pearson, *Financial Services Law and Compliance in Australia*, 2.2, Cambridge University Press, Melbourne, 2009.
2. 'Rebuilding the banks', *The Economist*, 16 May 2009, A Special Report on International Banking, p. 3. Australia and Canada were spared catastrophe because of the commodity boom in both countries.
3. See R. Garnaut, *The Great Crash of 2008*, Melbourne University Press, Carlton, 2009.
4. See J.H. Farrar, *Corporate Governance: Theories, Principles and Practice*, Oxford University Press, 2008, p. 415.6.
5. Stijn Claessens, World Bank, 'Corporate governance of banks: why it is important, how it is special and what it implies', OECD World Bank Meeting on Corporate Governance, Hanoi, 6–7 December, 2004. See also Laura Ard and Alexander Berg, 'Bank governance – lessons from the financial crisis', Crisis Response, March 2010, Note Number 13, The World Bank Group.
6. See J.H. Farrar, 'The global financial crisis and the governance of financial institutions', *Australian Journal of Corporate Law* 2010, **24**, 227.
7. Farrar, ibid., pp. 232–4.
8. Farrar, ibid., pp. 234.
9. *Law of Corporations*, Callaghan, Chicago, rev. edn, 1946, para. 63a.
10. See ALI, *Principles of Corporate Governance: Analysis and Recommendations*, p. 211. See also *Atherton v FDIC* 519 US 213 (1997).
11. *The General Theory of Employment, Interest and Money*, Macmillan St Martins Press, London, 1936, p. 155.
12. Jonathan Macey and Maureen O'Hara, 'The corporate governance of banks', *FRBNY Economic Policy Review*, April 2003, p. 91.
13. Farrar (2010), p. 237 et seq.
14. See Gail Pearson, *Financial Services Law and Compliance in Australia*, Cambridge University Press, Melbourne, 2009, sections 2.3.2.4.
15. H.Paulson Jr, *On the Brink – Inside the Race to Stop the Collapse of the Global Financial System*, Business Plus, New York, 2010, p. 46.
16. 'Risk management in banking – a prudential perspective', 59 International Banking Summer School, Melbourne, 6 September 2006. See also IMF, Financial Sector Assessment Program, Australia, 'Detailed assessment of observance of standards and codes', October 2006, 26, 27; APRA, 'Implementation of the Basel II capital framework supervisory review process', 21 December 2007; Basel Committee on Banking Supervision, 'Principles for sound liquidity risk management and supervision', September 2008; Consultative Document, 'Principles for enhancing corporate governance, Principles 6–8. See Gail Pearson, *Financial Services Law and Compliance in Australia*, Cambridge University Press, Melbourne 2009, sections 2.3.24 and 7.5.
17. Farrar, 2010, pp. 239–40.
18. Farrar, 2010, pp. 242–3.

9. The work of IOSCO and the financial regulatory framework

Jane Diplock

9.1 INTRODUCTION

The topic of this chapter – the work of IOSCO and the financial regulatory framework – matters a great deal to the contributors to this volume, but its ramifications go so much wider.

The results of the crisis touch those still unaware that financial markets matter to them and their lives, as well as those who believed so until recently – when they discovered that what happens in the markets can send out shock waves that engulf them and their families, their homes and their livelihoods.

As a regulator, these people are one of my key concerns. We need them to invest in securities markets, and their confidence in the markets is key to the making of the market. We need to head market participants towards greater transparency, reduced conflicts of interest, and more focus on the interests of investors.

It is not enough to insist only on compliance with the law. We also work to promote high standards of market conduct on the part of all participants. Only high standards will allow the woman on Sydney's Bondi tram and the man on the Clapham omnibus to be confident enough in the rules of the game to invest in the securities market.

Once upon a time, the game, and therefore the setting of its rules, was more or less confined to individual jurisdictions. That has changed forever. Financial markets are now global. Money moves across international borders with the click of a computer mouse.

The systemic implications of what happens in one market can be felt immediately in other markets around the world.

Before the global financial crisis, few investors in Europe or the UK would have imagined that the mis-selling of a mortgage product to an unemployed person in the suburbs of Chicago could have impacted on their economic future and the futures of those around them in ways that have evolved during this crisis.

From a regulatory point of view, therefore, merely minding the shop at home is no longer enough. The financial crisis has convinced most of us of the need for greater cooperation between international regulators, particularly in relation to enforcement and supervision.

The International Organization of Securities Commissions (IOSCO) has emerged as a major player in the global financial architecture, and it is this organization's work that this chapter focuses on, because it does indeed promise a way forward.

The chapter proceeds by outlining IOSCO's structure, its perspective on regulation, and several of its important post-crisis projects. In section 9.2, the reader is introduced to the IOSCO as an international regulator. How systemic risk ought to be viewed is explained in section 9.3. The regulatory standards required in accounting standards setting are discussed in section 9.4 before making concluding comments in section 9.5.

9.2   ABOUT IOSCO

IOSCO promotes global financial stability, particularly stability in markets, and its members agree on, and apply, consistent international standards for those financial markets. Where standards are not met, IOSCO enables effective enforcement across jurisdictions.

IOSCO's members regulate more than 100 jurisdictions making up more than 90 per cent of the world's securities markets. Most are independently constituted government regulators. Each member retains the sovereign capacity to set and regulate standards within its own jurisdiction, but the consensus reached through IOSCO on what these standards should be puts the organization in a unique position. It is one of the very few international organizations with a truly global reach.

The twentieth century was the century of structural solutions. By the end of it, some of those post-World War II constructs were appearing outdated. The twenty-first century is likely to be that of networked solutions. The Internet and the possibilities it has presented for greater global integration is an apt metaphor for the way in which twentieth-century solutions are likely to be progressed.

IOSCO's strength lies in its understanding and practice of such solutions.

9.2.1   IOSCO's Perspective

IOSCO sees sound regulation of securities markets as vital to global financial stability. It also sees the prudential regulation of institutions as equally crucial. Together they promote the global financial stability essential for sustainable economic growth.

Accordingly, IOSCO works closely with prudential regulators: the Basel Committee on Banking Supervision and the International Association of Insurance Supervisors. IOSCO is also a founding member of, and has two seats on, the Financial Stability Board (FSB).

We believe good corporate governance is the key to capital market integrity and stability. We also believe that the overwhelming reliance on traditional, centuries-old standards of conduct by unregulated market forces was a major precipitant of the crisis.

We have all discovered the hard way that markets will not always correct themselves. Business ethics can no longer be perceived as a luxury. They are a necessity, if history is not to repeat itself.

9.2.2 IOSCO Principles

In 1998, the organization endorsed principles that recognize three objectives for securities regulation: protecting investors; ensuring markets are fair, efficient and transparent; and reducing systemic risk.

Based on these principles, each jurisdiction can assess and, if necessary, align its laws consistent with its own priorities, traditions, market developments and legal frameworks. The principles are not an attempt to create a single international body of rules and regulations, but a global benchmark.

The G20 nations recognized this when they included the IOSCO principles among the standards and codes they are committed to seeing implemented and peer-reviewed through the Financial Sector Assessment Programme (FSAP). This is no mere formality: it entails rigorous processes with detailed assessments by experts.

The G20 has recommended all members undertake an FSAP assessment and that other countries either engage in a self-assessment or an FSAP using the IOSCO principles.

9.2.3 IOSCO Multilateral Memorandum of Understanding (MMOU)

In 2002 IOSCO adopted an MMOU designed to facilitate cross-border enforcement and the exchange of information between national securities regulators. Three years later it endorsed the MMOU as the benchmark for this international cooperation, and notified all 109 members to sign up by end 2010. As at end 2011, all but five have done so.

The MMOU ushered in a new era. It has reshaped cross-border securities-market enforcement and made it easier to track transgressors across markets and political borders. It is a cornerstone of the new post-crisis financial world order.

9.3   IDENTIFYING SYSTEMIC RISK

IOSCO's post-crisis work has focused on market stability and on identifying the causes of systemic risk. It has analysed the underlying causes of the crisis and initiated work to address crucial aspects of market conduct.

It is also developing its own strategic direction currently to take the reforms onwards, and will emphasize the need for greater vigilance on systemic risks. It is monitoring the unregulated boundaries of otherwise well-regulated jurisdictions, where destabilizing products and market practices may well appear.

IOSCO is currently developing a new principle on systemic risks in markets. Below are outlined a number of IOSCO reports produced as a result of its initial work on the sub-prime crisis. Several of these focus on securities market activity currently lying on or beyond the borders of current regulation. These too need to be transparent since they deal with parties working within regulated markets.

9.3.1   Private Equity Conflicts of Interest, November 2009

Private equity firms are one such area. This report draws up principles for mitigating the potential conflicts of interest between a manager and third-party investors that can arise from a firm's obligations to multiple funds. These conflicts pose a risk to fund investors and efficient market functioning.

Private equity firms should manage any conflicts in the best interests of their fund(s), and the overall best interests of fund investors. They should draw up written policies and procedures for application across their whole business, and make sure these are always available to fund investors.

Firms should opt for the most effective mitigation techniques and those yielding most investor clarity. They should implement a well-documented process for consulting investors on conflict-of-interest matters, and they should promptly inform all affected investors on what emerges from investor consultation plus any actions taken.

Finally, private equity firms should ensure all investor disclosure is clear, complete, fair and not misleading.

9.3.2 Joint Forum Report on Special Purpose Entities, September 2009

Special purpose entities (SPEs) can be useful to institutions and investors. Their defining feature is bankruptcy remoteness. Poor understanding of SPE risk by management and investors, though, can lead to
failures.

The report recommends that supervisors ensure market participants
assess all SPE economic risks and business purposes throughout the life
of a transaction. Assessment should be ongoing, and management should
understand the risks.

If at any point financial firm support is evident or likely, SPE activities
should be aggregated with the institution's for supervisory assessment and
risk-management purposes.

SPE supervisors should support more standardization of definitions,
documentation, and disclosure requirement, and report any divergent
material to investors. They should also oversee and monitor SPE activity,
and assess its implications for regulated firms.

IOSCO will continue to monitor developments in off-balance sheet
financings, including unconsolidated SPEs.

9.3.3 International Regulatory Standards on Hedge Fund Related Issues, September 2009

This report was prompted by retail investors' increasing involvement in
hedge funds through funds of hedge funds. It aims to give investors better
information in this largely unregulated area.

The report recommends that managers determine if fund-of-hedge-fund
liquidity is consistent with that of the underlying hedge funds. Managers
should also consider whether conflicts of interest might arise between any
underlying hedge fund and other parties.

Funds of hedge funds' managers should monitor and analyse several
aspects of due diligence, the appropriateness of the legal regime and
service providers, and the transparency, valuation and reporting arrangements of a specific hedge fund.

The organizational structure, resources and procedures must be capable
of taking action on any anomalies identified by due diligence. Managers
should regularly assess whether selection procedures for eligible underlying hedge funds have been properly followed, and explain any deviations.

If any aspect of due diligence is outsourced, a fund of hedge funds'
manager should ensure conflicts of interest are addressed. They should
also see that outsourcing is consistent with the IOSCO 'Principles on outsourcing of financial services for market intermediaries'.

9.3.4 Non-professional Ownership Structures for Audit Firms, September 2009

Securities regulators and investors rely on audited financial statements. Quality audit-services availability is therefore critical. The EU, Japan and the US all restrict audit firm ownership, and securities regulators have long been concerned that the loss of just one of the big four firms – Deloitte Touche Tohmatsu, Ernst & Young, KPMG, PricewaterhouseCoopers – could disrupt the entire market for independent auditing of large companies.

In this report, IOSCO explores the barriers preventing more firms from competing in the market. At the same time it is of course keen to preserve auditor objectivity, independence, professionalism and competence, and thus, audit quality.

The report suggests that modifying rules for audit firm ownership would give public companies greater choice of audit firm services without compromising the quality of those services.

9.3.5 Periodic Disclosure by Listed Entities (Periodic Disclosure Principles), July 2009

This amounts to a guide for companies with securities listed or admitted to trading on a regulated market in which retail investors participate. Periodic reporting is the lynchpin of both investor protection and transparent operation of financial markets.

Information in periodic reports should be relevant, and include independently audited financial statements covering the entire previous financial year. These must be regular, clear, concise and understandable, and should identify who was responsible for producing them.

Financial reporting should be regularly reviewed internally to ensure assets are safeguarded from unauthorized or improper use, and transactions are properly recorded.

9.3.6 IOSCO Good Practices in Relation to Investment Managers' due Diligence, July 2009

The due diligence practices this report recommends are designed to help industry and regulators understand and monitor investments in structured finance instruments (SFIs) on behalf of collected investment schemes (CISs). SFIs carry different risks from more traditional instruments, thus calling for tailored due diligence.

The report also deals with using third parties to carry out due diligence.

Investment managers should understand the third party's methodology and parameters, and understand the basis of that third-party opinion.

9.3.7   Hedge Funds Oversight, June 2009

Hedge funds can provide liquidity, price efficiency and risk distribution, and contribute to global integration of financial markets and offer diversification benefits.

The global financial crisis was not a hedge fund crisis. However, hedge fund activities did amplify its consequences because of their need to unwind positions quickly.

This report suggests that regulation of hedge fund activity would mitigate its risks. Hedge funds and/or their managers or advisers should be registered and subject to regulatory requirements.

Conflicts of interest and other conduct rules should be established. Investors should be entitled to disclosure, and prudential regulation should be mandatory. Prime brokers and banks that fund hedge funds should also be registered, regulated and supervised.

Hedge fund managers/advisers and prime brokers should inform regulators about systemic risk, and regulators should encourage the implementation and convergence of industry good practices. Regulators should also have the authority to cooperate and share information with other regulators to mitigate cross-border risks.

9.4   POST-CRISIS ACCOUNTING ISSUES

The crisis increased the urgency of calls for globally convergent accounting standards to better serve investors in globalized capital markets, and IOSCO has a keen interest in global standard-setting for accounting.

International Financial Reporting Standards (IFRS) are used in more than 100 countries. The US, however, relies on the Financial Accounting Standards Board (FASB). Convergence of these two sets of accounting standards is critical.

The existence of two standards obscures market transparency. It makes it difficult to compare entities that use separate standards, especially those engaged in cross-border activity. It poses an ever-present risk of significant facts being lost in translation.

IOSCO has been closely involved in initiatives to improve transparency through better quality disclosures, and enhancements of international accounting standard-setting governance. This has included formation of the Monitoring Board of the International Accounting Standards Board (IASB).

9.5 CONCLUSION

The global financial crisis was a shocking reminder of how important corporate governance is to global financial stability. Since then, global financial leaders have become more aware of the need for effective market regulation as the virtuous twin of prudential regulation.

The way forward must be sustainable global growth, and this will only occur in conditions of global financial stability. The structure of financial entities and the interaction among them and the markets must be well regulated.

The new post-crisis global financial architecture may still be under construction, but promising characteristics are already emerging. Standards are likely to be more convergent, and greater enforcement cooperation across jurisdictions will leave transgressors with fewer places to hide.

The purpose of such standards is affecting the drivers of behaviour of market players, to encourage them towards greater transparency, reduction of conflicts of interest, and a focus on the interests of investors. IOSCO's work is directed towards ensuring that the drivers of behaviour of those who manage parties in global markets are congruent with the interests of investors in those markets. In other words, IOSCO aims to get markets to recognize that good governance is now good business.

10. Balancing national and international interests

Wayne Byres

10.1 INTRODUCTION

Readers may be familiar with the work of Ross Gittins, who writes on matters of economic interest for the *Sydney Morning Herald*. The following is quoted from one of Ross's articles on the subject of prudential supervision:

> To everyone but the supervisors and the supervised, it's a dull subject. That's because, in 19 years out of 20, nothing of interest happens. We don't give a second thought to the stability of the financial system because we know it's stable; always has been, always will be . . . But you can see where this story is leading: this is the one year in 20.[1]

What's notable about this statement is that it is quite prophetic: the quote comes from an article he wrote in 1990, the last time financial system problems put prudential supervision in the public spotlight. Twenty years later and, as predicted, once again prudential supervision is the talk of the town.

This chapter will discuss the case for reform, some of the more important items on the reform agenda for banks, and the Australian Prudential Regulation Authority (APRA)'s perspectives and approach to dealing with them in an Australian context. Our objective is straightforward: to get the reforms *just right* – not too much, not too little. But that, we explain later, is not an easy task. The case for a reform is found in section 10.2, followed by the agenda for reform described in section 10.3. Consensus-building challenge is the theme of section 10.4 on national versus international reforms. Before making some bold comments in the concluding Section 10.6, we address in section 10.5 the likely balance of reform packages that would emerge in international rule-setting.

10.2   THE CASE FOR REFORM IN AUSTRALIA

In Australia, there has been debate about the merits of the international reform agenda, and whether such reform is necessary, given the relative resilience of the Australian financial system. Maybe, some have suggested, we should have our own Australian versions of the international rules, or even perhaps not implement some aspects of the reform proposals at all?

Most people are familiar with the story of King Canute. Heaped with praise by those around him, and attributed with great powers, Canute attempted to stop the tides. He knew he would fail, but his purpose was to demonstrate to those around him that while he might appear powerful, there were forces in the world far more powerful than he.

In many respects, the Australian regulatory system at present has a number of parallels with King Canute. Over the past couple of years people have lauded its strengths, and it has been lavished with praise by many, but those of us within it are far more humble about our abilities. In practice, regulators like APRA played their part before and during the financial crisis, but as we will see later, it has also needed extraordinary interventions by the various arms of government, and a certain amount of luck, to enable us to safely negotiate the past couple of years. One should not think anyone should conclude that, by itself, our regulatory system could hold back the heavy seas that were battering our shore during the Global Financial Crisis.

That said, the resilience of the Australian financial system throughout the crisis is something that we should all be proud of, and thankful for. Our regulated institutions were, on the whole, well managed in the years leading up to the crisis. Our largest and most important institutions have maintained very strong credit ratings. Our regulatory regime, after some scrutiny and soul-searching early in the decade, was substantially strengthened and therefore was much better equipped to handle a period of extreme stress when the crisis emerged.

But reflecting the global nature of the financial system, we were not immune from some of the trends that occurred throughout the world. As was the case elsewhere, to remain competitive and improve their returns to shareholders our banks did increase their levels of leverage, until implementing a sharp reversal via substantial capital raisings beginning in late 2008. Business lines and transactions were pursued which, with the benefit of hindsight, some institutions now regret pursuing: thankfully, none of these were such that their folly seriously threatened the viability of any individual institution. And their liquidity planning was probably not as robust as first thought. These trends may have been less significant than in other countries, but they were evident here nonetheless.

And while there is no denying our system did prove *relatively* resilient to the global financial crisis, let us not forget that extraordinary support and intervention were necessary to ensure that the system was kept stable and the wheels of the economy kept turning:

- there was an unprecedented fiscal response – the stimulus package implemented by the Federal Government was, relative to GDP, one of the largest in the world;
- there was an unprecedented monetary response – the Reserve Bank of Australia (RBA) cut the official cash rate by 425 basis points in a little over six months;
- the RBA also substantially extended its market operations, expanding the list of repo-eligible collateral and lengthening the term for which it would provide funding;
- the Australian Securities Investment Commission (ASIC) imposed an eight-month ban on the short-selling of financial stocks; and
- at the height of the crisis, the Federal Government initiated a guarantee of retail deposits of up to A$1 million, and a facility for authorized deposit-taking institutions (ADIs) to purchase guarantees for larger deposits and wholesale funding for up to five years.

As a result of these initiatives – along with the underlying support from our favourable terms of trade, and the shock absorber provided by an exchange rate which fell from almost parity with the US$ to US60c (and has since 2010 rebounded most of the way back again) – the Australian economy has performed remarkably well. We have a banking system that has remained profitable throughout: the return on equity for the largest banks fell into the low teens from historical highs in the twenties before the crisis, but compared to the red ink elsewhere in the world, this is a very positive result.

However, it is impossible to argue that this outcome, or indeed anything like it, could have been achieved without substantial public sector support to both the broader economy and the banking system itself. Had we had to deal with six consecutive quarters of negative GDP (as occurred in the UK) or unemployment around 10 per cent (as has been the case in the US), the picture for our financial system would have obviously been far less attractive. Indeed, despite its evident strength, we are still dealing today with a banking system in which around one-third of its entire liabilities are subject to a Commonwealth government guarantee. If all that I have mentioned was needed to keep the system stable and operational, then it is difficult to argue that some further strengthening of the system is not justified.

APRA's position is that it is both pointless and unhelpful to try to stand against the tide of international reform. We are a small, open economy participating in a global financial system. Any attempt to declare independence from the rest of the world will inevitably be counter-productive. Whilst our banking system is so reliant on offshore funding, it is vital that we are seen to be playing by the international rules of the game. Whatever the merits of the Australian banking system and its regulatory framework, in the midst of the crisis the rest of the world did not distinguish a great deal between our banks and those elsewhere.

In late 2007, during the first wave of the crisis, the writer recalls one bank CFO telling him that 'it's quite scary when no one will lend to you for more than a few days'. The bank concerned was perfectly healthy, and without apparent problems. So we cannot be complacent. While we hope it is some time off before the next crisis emerges, we need to be better prepared. Our task was summed up quite nicely in another quote from the same Ross Gittins article referred to earlier:

> [Prudential supervisors] are like a student who faces one examination every 20 years, but doesn't know which year it will be. Now they – and we – are face-to-face with the occupational hazard of supervisors: how do you maintain your enthusiasm – your vigilance – for a job which everyone regards as an irrelevance (apart from the supervised who regard it as a pain in the neck).[2]

10.3   THE REFORM AGENDA

So, before prudential supervisors become an irrelevance again, let us now examine the key components of the reform agenda itself. The key objectives of the proposals are to:

- strengthen both *the quantum and quality of bank capital*;
- supplement this with a non-risk based measure designed to *limit absolute levels of leverage*;
- require banks to do *more self-insurance against a liquidity shock* (either specific to the bank itself, or the system as a whole);
- work with accounting standard setters to develop a more *forward-looking approach to provisioning*;
- develop additional *counter-cyclical prudential measures* to promote a longer-term perspective and some 'saving for a rainy day';
- consistent with this theme, promote *remunerations arrangements* which better align reward with risk over a longer time horizon; and

- establish, notwithstanding all of the above, better mechanisms for *dealing with the risks from systemically-important institutions.*

Some of these will be discussed in more detail below, but we could start by saying what the reforms will not deliver: they will not replace the Basel II capital adequacy framework. There has been a lot of finger-pointing at Basel II as a contributor to the crisis. But Basel II was introduced in most countries around the world at the beginning of 2008, long after the seeds of destruction had been sown. The US – the epicentre of the crisis – is still to implement Basel II. Basel II has its shortcomings, but it was not a cause of the crisis. Furthermore, Basel II was all about making the measurement of a bank's risk profile more sensitive to its true risks. It is strange to suggest – as some have done – that it should be scrapped in favour of some less risk-sensitive measures. The need for better risk measurement by banks and their supervisors must surely be one of the important lessons of the crisis: indeed, the G20 leaders have urged its implementation for this very reason.[3]

That said, some criticism can justifiably be levelled at the Basel Framework more broadly.[4] Global banks had too little high quality capital. The Basel Framework, at its minimum, only required banks to have the equivalent of 2 per cent of risk-weighted assets in the form of shareholders' funds; or to put it another way, each dollar of equity could be geared 50 times. And even then, some of this equity could be potentially represented by intangible assets of limited value.

Clearly this will need to change, and the Basel committee has recently released a wide-ranging set of proposals to this effect. In Australia, of course, we have had considerably tougher rules on the composition of capital for some time. This has stood our banks in good stead, and means the impact of the reform proposals will be less material for our banks than for many others around the world. Australian banks, who have long been arguing for greater harmonization between APRA's rules and those of foreign regulators, will presumably also be pleased with this development.

Nonetheless, the clear message is that, as far as minimum capital requirements for banks are concerned, the only way is up (even from Australia's more conservative starting position). Capital requirements – and in particular, equity requirements – for banks will be higher in future (Basel is increasing them to 7.5 per cent). That will be achieved via a range of measures, including higher minimum requirements, tighter eligibility definitions, capital conservation measures and countercyclical capital adjustments. And, since the G20 leaders asked for it, we will also have a (non-risk-based) leverage ratio as part of the supervisory armoury.

It is a similar story on liquidity. Globally, the crisis showed up some weaknesses in bank liquidity and funding profiles, many of which were founded on an assumption that apparently deep and liquid markets would not close completely. Australian banks, for example, typically had contingency funding plans that assumed that if they had trouble obtaining funding, they could securitize assets – but, of course, the securitization market was one of the first to close and is yet to recover. So in the future there will be greater focus on the quality of liquid assets, establishing a longer survival horizon without the need for central bank support, and a greater emphasis on longer-term funding.

Since the introduction of International Financial Reporting Standards (IFRS), provisioning for loan losses has been the source of some angst between prudential supervisors and the accounting standard-setters. The incurred loss approach favoured under IFRS saw banks in Australia substantially run down their stock of provisions during the good times, only to need to substantially rebuild them over the past couple of years. The Basel committee is now working closely with the International Accounting Standards Board (IASB) to attempt to develop an approach to provisioning which meets the needs of the accounting standard-setters (current, consistent, objective) and the prudential supervisors (prudent, forward-looking). This will hopefully produce an accounting regime which eliminates some of the procyclicality inherent in the current accounting approach, which many countries, although not Australia, are obliged to adopt within their prudential framework.

Remuneration is also a topic of great regulatory interest at present. The financial crisis highlighted clear deficiencies in remuneration practices within the financial sector. Some incentive structures have delivered substantial riches to managers that have not reflected returns to shareholders. In some cases, the disconnect have been so great that taxpayers are finding themselves footing the bill. As a result, almost the first regulatory cab off the rank from the G20 leaders reform plan has been new standards on remuneration. The Financial Stability Board (FSB) has produced its 'Principles for sound compensation practices' to guide the debate internationally. APRA was quite heavily involved in drafting the principles, and as a result our own standard follows them quite closely.[5]

Both the FSB and APRA have tried very hard to make sure we are focused on the principles of pay *structures* rather than pay *levels*. But do not see this as indicating any lack of desire amongst the regulatory world to enforce change. There is considerable regulatory momentum in this area, and it will continue to be an area of intense scrutiny for the foreseeable future.

Finally, one of the greatest conundrums facing policy-makers around the globe at present is what to do about the too big to fail problem. Recent actions by governments around the world, although entirely justified and appropriate for the circumstances, have solidified the perception that the largest and most important financial institutions (and even some non-financial institutions) will not be allowed to fail. This has created major incentive problems.

It is difficult to see where this debate will go from here, other than that the *status quo* is unlikely to remain. Commentators agree that the most likely long-term outcome will be an expectation that, as banks grow in both size and interconnectedness (Lehman was not actually that large in terms of total assets relative to the world's financial giants), tougher prudential standards will have to be imposed.

In the past, regulators have always given some credit for the stability and diversity that scale can bring to an institution. Under the Basel Framework, for example, the lowest capital requirements were always expected to apply to well-diversified, internationally-operating banks; others would generally need to meet higher requirements. That may no longer be the case. In this new way of thinking, once scale becomes sufficiently large as to be seen as a threat to the stability of the system as a whole, it will increasingly be viewed as a negative rather than a positive, and that brings additional regulatory burdens and oversight. In other words, disincentives to scale may be introduced. Compared to taxes and forced break-ups, that might seem relatively modest, but it will mark a fundamental change in regulatory thinking.

10.4   ADDING NATIONAL PERSPECTIVES TO INTERNATIONAL REFORMS

When faced with the global reform agenda, some Australian stakeholders have asked 'do we need all this?' (and in some cases 'do we need *any* of this?'). In essence, they are questioning whether we have the capacity to stand apart from the rest of the world: can we indeed outdo King Canute?

As noted earlier, APRA does not see any case for implementing a framework which the rest of the world would judge to be weak or less robust than the international norms – this will involve considerable cost to the banking system and, through it, the Australian community. Australian banks cannot simultaneously rely more than many of their international peers on cross-border funding, as they do normally. Therefore they could not seek to be exempted from some or all of the regulatory reforms applicable to the rest of the world's banks. Our starting point is that our regulatory system needs to be seen to be at least as strong as the international standards provide for. And we expect that, even if we attempted to implement a weaker set of rules, international markets and counterparties would hold Australian banks to the international standards and measures in any event. So we see little value in trying to stand apart from the rest of the world, claiming we know better.

Another concern raised by the banking industry has the possibility of uneven application of the reforms in different countries. If Australia rigorously implements and enforces the reforms, while others pay them only lip service, there will be an uneven playing field. This is a problem with any set of rules, be they remuneration, capital, liquidity or any other. But another of the initiatives to emerge from the G20 leaders is a greater commitment by countries to submit themselves to peer review.[6] This is designed to make sure that, as much as possible, a level playing field exists between jurisdictions, to provide additional incentives to countries to implement international standards. In the current environment, it is doubtful any country would want to be reported as having a weak regulatory framework or to be operating outside internationally accepted norms.

So our first objective is to see effective international standards developed that we can sensibly implement in Australia. We are actively engaged in the Basel committee's hectic work programme.[7] Our objective is to add our insights and ideas into the policy development process, and to influence global standards in such a way as to ensure they do not unfairly hinder Australian institutions.

But regardless of the success of that influence, we also acknowledge that no international framework is likely to be perfectly suitable to every single country to which it will apply. History tells us that, whatever the final form of the agreed reforms, some tailoring will inevitably be necessary around the globe. So it is worth saying some words about how APRA might go about applying any national discretion in Australia.

In addressing this issue, there are three types of national discretion available to policy-makers:

- The first is common in international standards: a choice, usually on narrow technical issues, that the standard-setting body deliberately and explicitly leaves to the national authority. In these cases, each national authority makes whatever decision it thinks best for its circumstances and, regardless of the decision taken and the options chosen, the country concerned will be seen to be in compliance with the international standard;
- A second form of national discretion is where a national authority seeks to strengthen an international standard to reflect its specific needs.[8] Typically, this might be where additional requirements are added to the *baseline* international standard, designed to take account of local circumstances. Provided that these do not water

down the spirit or intent of the global agreement, and that they are intended to strengthen it, the country concerned should still be seen to be in compliance with the international standard; and

- The third form of national discretion needs to be used with much more caution. This is where a country deliberately modifies an international standard in a manner which is not clearly superior (and may possibly be weaker). For a country such as Australia, such an approach is one we use rarely, as we consider the cost to Australia of being seen to be materially non-compliant with international standards to be significant.

APRA has in the past utilized all three types of national discretion:

- Most obviously, the Basel II framework contained more than 80 explicit national discretions, which APRA had to take a view on as it worked through the domestic implementation phase in Australia. After consultation with industry, APRA decided which of the available choices made sense in an Australian context and implemented them accordingly.
- APRA have also sought to strengthen international standards. APRA has elected, over time, to take a tougher stance on the definition of regulatory capital than the *baseline* Basel Committee requirement implemented in many other jurisdictions, recognizing it to be just as important to pay attention to the quality of capital as to the quantity. Pleasingly, this is a stance the international standard-setters are now adopting too; and
- And, occasionally, we have also diverged from international standards. For example, in our remuneration requirements, we have elected not to adopt some of the more prescriptive limits and caps that have been recommended by the FSB, sticking instead to a principles-based approach.

In all these cases, the decision process involves the same basic question: what makes most sense for Australia, given the costs and benefits involved?

10.5   WHERE MIGHT THE BALANCE BE HARDEST TO FIND?

Within the current round of reforms, where do regulators see the biggest challenges in making sure that what is proposed internationally works in Australia?

Broadly, APRA is supportive of the objectives of the initiatives, but can see plenty of challenges:

- In the area of capital adequacy, many of the changes being proposed to improve the quality of capital are consistent with the philosophy already adopted in Australia, so the impact will be relatively less here than in many other parts of the world. Higher minimum levels of equity capital are inevitable, but we already have a profitable banking system which is operating with strong capital levels. We therefore expect the new rules will reduce banks' reported capital ratios, but at this point we do not expect the Australian banking system to be found to be short of capital under the new risk-based measures;

- The leverage ratio will be an interesting development for Australian banks. Our banks tend to operate with relatively high levels of leverage, but this is mitigated by the relatively low-risk profile of their balance sheets (driven by large mortgage portfolios). We see limited benefit from a leverage ratio if the risk-based ratio is correctly implemented and policed. Nonetheless, if it is to be introduced, we will need to work with our international counterparts to calibrate the minimum leverage ratio so that it does not act as the binding constraint on normal banks in normal times;

- In the area of liquidity, there are a number of challenges. It will be difficult to both raise the size of the liquid asset buffer and simultaneously require that buffer to be comprised of the most reliably liquid assets (for example sovereign bonds), when those assets are less abundant in Australia than in most other jurisdictions. And the proposed structural funding measure may be more difficult to meet for banks which hold customer assets on their balance sheet rather than originating assets for onward distribution to non-bank financial agents;

- In the area of remuneration, Australia has not adopted the prescription evident in some parts of the FSB's guidelines. We are confident that we can achieve sensible outcomes without this level of prescription, although there is a considerable amount of work to do to bed down the new requirements, and some institutions will need some time to revise their practices.

- The regulators are watching with interest the international work on dealing with systemically important institutions. APRA's supervisory framework[9] may be ahead of the game here, as it already directs its greatest intensity to the largest and most complex institutions, by factoring scale into its risk assessment and supervisory response processes. But at this stage we do not have mechanical formulas or prescriptive rules which dictate how increasing systemic importance should be dealt with, allowing instead the exercise of supervisory judgement.

Finally, the biggest challenge of all will be to assess all of the proposals as a single package, to understand the interlinkages between the various components, and to assess the overall impact. This challenge cannot be underestimated, given the complexity of what is proposed. Inevitably, a large amount of judgement will be necessary to try to get the reforms *just right*.

10.6   CONCLUDING REMARKS

We conclude this chapter by returning once more to the Ross Gittins article quoted from earlier: 'Taking an interest in prudential supervision is like watching paint dry. The only audience it gets is the people who take ten minutes to realise that they're in the wrong room.'[10]

Readers of this volume probably reflect something else: a strong interest in the global reform agenda, and an understanding of the impact that it may have on the Australian financial sector, and through it the community as a whole.

The reform agenda set by the G20 leaders is substantial. From the perspective of the banking industry, APRA and the RBA are at the table of the Basel Committee seeking to influence these reforms and to make sure they address issues of importance to this country. Inevitably, however, there will be aspects of the international standards that are not what we would have created if the task of producing the reforms was left entirely to us. This difference between national and international rules are a cost of doing business in a global system, but there are also costs to a country like Australia if it decides it does not want to play by those international rules.

The latest round of international reforms, given their breadth, will undoubtedly throw up many difficult challenges for APRA and other regulators in balancing international initiatives with domestic perspectives. Ultimately Australia will need to balance up the pros and cons, and decide what we think is in Australia's best interests. No doubt we will get lots of helpful advice along the way. But like King Canute, we know we cannot stand against the tide, even if we wished to do so.

158 *Regulatory failure and the global financial crisis*

NOTES

1. Gittins, Ross (1990), 'Was the Reserve awake while the rest of us were asleep?', *Sydney Morning Herald*, 25 August.
2. Ibid.
3. The G20 leaders statement, issued at the conclusion of the Pittsburgh Summit in September 2009, included a statement that 'All major G20 financial centers commit to have adopted the Basel II Capital Framework by 2011'.
4. In its simplest form, there are three components to the Basel Framework: a measure of capital, a measure of risk, and a minimum ratio of the former to the latter. The Basel II reforms which came into force in Australia at the beginning of 2008 dealt essentially with the measure of risk.
5. Although, as will be explained in a later part of the chapter, APRA has not followed them blindly, and there are some areas where we diverge from the international principles.
6. This will build additional external review mechanisms on top of that already provided by the Financial Sector Assessment Program, conducted jointly by the International Monetary Fund and the World Bank.
7. APRA is represented on the Basel Committee's Policy Development Group, the Accounting Task Force, the Definition of Capital Group, the Working Group on Liquidity and the Top-Down Calibration Group, amongst others.
8. In some jurisdictions, this would be referred to as 'gold-plating', or adopting a standard that is 'super-equivalent'.
9. See APRA's explanation of its Supervisory Oversight and Response System, available at http://www.apra.gov.au/PAIRS/upload/SOARS_Final_May_2008_External_Version.pdf.
10. Gittins (op. cit).

PART IV

Lessons from the crisis

11. Executive remuneration in Australia

Allan Fels

11.1 INTRODUCTION

How much did executive pay practices contribute to the global financial crisis? Opinions have tended to be starkly polarized. Some argue that the use of the wrong types of incentives led executives to be blinded by greed and to engage in wholesale irresponsibility, especially in the finance sector. Others argue that volatility is just part of the normal behaviour of markets and that there is no need to throw out market-based rewards. We can still trust self-interest, they say, because at least you know it is trying.

Even though some time has elapsed since the worst of the crisis, opinions are still divided. There is a widespread perception that executives have been rewarded for failure or good luck. They received rewards for rises in the share price that had little to do with their contribution to company performance, and instead reflected excesses in asset markets.

The criticisms are not unreasonable. If executives are to take the credit on the way up, then they should assume responsibility on the way down. Executives of public companies expect that of their employees, so why should it not be the same for them? For the most part executives are employees, not owners.

But answering the criticisms is neither simple nor straightforward. Just because there are good reasons to scrutinize executive rewards does not mean the answers are easy to locate. To assess whether executives are *worth* the amount of money they are paid requires a leap in the dark. Logically, the only reliable way is to compare the remuneration approach with what would have happened had it not been used. Because this is impossible, there is always an element of speculation. It is perfectly conceivable that other types of pay arrangements might have led to worse outcomes. It certainly does not necessarily follow that the removal of incentives would have made performance substantially better.

In this chapter, the reader is introduced to the regulatory service provider, the productivity commission: section 11.2. The findings on this important governance challenge are summarised in section 11.3. The inherent conflict of interest at the helm of the institution is discussed in section 11.4 before the chapter conclusion in section 11.5.

11.2   THE ROLE OF THE PRODUCTIVITY COMMISSION

The Productivity Commission's inquiry aimed at unravelling the complexities of executive pay in order to establish the facts about executive remuneration. That would help to establish the reasons why executive remuneration was on the rise. It was also aimed at presenting a more nuanced view about the changes occurring to executive pay, corporate governance and shareholder accountability.

What did we find? On any measure, remuneration for executives of larger companies has grown strongly since the early 1990s. In the 50 to 100 largest companies, it increased, between 1993 and 2007, by 300 per cent in real terms.

It sounds a lot, but it is comparatively modest when compared with international trends. Australian company chief executive pay is less than half that of chief executives in the United States who perform comparable roles. It is also below the level of pay of the major European countries. The strengthening Australian dollar has brought local pay close to the European average, but it remains well below the extremes seen in the United States.

The rise in executive pay in Australia is far from surprising. The liberalization of the Australian economy, exposure to global competition and the increased size of companies, plus the shift to incentive pay structures have profoundly changed the way executive pay has been determined. It has likewise altered corporate governance in relation to pay, sometimes for the better but also, in a concerning number of cases, considerably for the worse.

Predictable it may have been, but Australia has not escaped excess in executive pay. The Productivity Commission concluded that there have been periods of widespread extremes, particularly in the 1990s, when chief executive pay grew by 13 per cent a year in real terms for the top 100 companies, and 16 per cent for the ASX Top 50. Between 2000 and 2007 annual real growth moderated to a more modest 6 per cent for the top 100 companies, but this still led to a 50 per cent increase overall. Since 2007, from the onset of the Global Financial Crisis, the trend has been reversed to some extent, pay returning to 2004–05 levels.

11.3   FINDINGS

The picture is not uniform. There have been some instances of excess with individuals. Executive pay varies greatly across Australia's public listed 200 companies. For the top 20 chief executives, it averaged A$7.2 million, compared with about A$250 000 for the smallest listed companies.

Nearly all the growth in reported chief executive pay for the top 300 companies was attributable to increases in incentive pay, especially long-term incentives. These tripled between 2004 and 2007. This has represented a dramatic change in how the motivation and performance of chief executives is understood. The global financial crisis has underlined that aligning the interests of companies and managers – what is called the *agency problem* – is not simple.

What the Productivity Commission also found is that there is a strong correlation between company size and executive remuneration. Size, it seems, matters. A 10 per cent increase in company size equates with about a 4 per cent increase in chief executive pay. Success for a chief executive seems to be defined almost entirely by size. This is true at the individual company level, and in aggregate. It raises questions about why other measures, such as profitability or return on assets, are not similarly important. An examination of executive pay in relation to other operational metrics, such as earnings or revenue growth, reveals no clear pattern.

It is tempting to conclude that the pursuit of size has led to too much risk-taking, especially given the poor track record of many mergers and acquisitions. A large pay packet looks proportionately smaller when the company is very big. But the relationship between corporate performance and executive pay is subject to multiple influences, whose effects can be difficult to trace. Just as there is no simple solution to aligning incentives with company performance so there is no simple way to analyse the many types of incentives in use. Companies adopt a variety of hurdles and their efficacy has to be understood according to the company's unique strategic approach.

Virtually everyone agrees that it is important to get executive pay right in order to make sure that the interests of shareholders, boards, executives (employees) and the community are consistent. There is a peculiar, double-barrelled principal–agent relationship in public companies. We have executives and boards on one side, and boards and shareholders on the other. This is not reflected in the way remuneration is decided. A chief executive answers only to the board that hires, rewards and sometimes removes him or her.

But this lop-sided relationship is not going to change. The principal–agent problem cannot be eliminated without also removing the public company structure, or for that matter the joint stock corporation. We are left with boards as the only practicable means by which the many shareholders, with their diverse interests and varying investment strategies can be provided with a mechanism for having their interests protected. There is no substitute for boards exercising sound judgement.

Australian boards have some strong features. There are few instances of the chairman also being the chief executive as is commonly the case in America. There is a high proportion of non-executive directors, about three-quarters of total board numbers. There is no strong evidence of unhealthy hiring practices with internal candidates. There does not seem to be any evidence that boards are reluctant to fire because the boards have been captured by executives.

Still, the suspicion remains that there is a directors' and executives' *club*. This is hard to pin down, but three areas are definitely a problem.

1.   One is the practice of boards declaring that the maximum number of directors is the number of directors presently on the board. It is usually employed when shareholders nominate a candidate. The Productivity Commission recommends that if there are elections of directors at a general meeting, and if the board seeks to declare no vacancies, and the number of directors is less than the constitutional maximum, then approval should be sought from shareholders. This would improve board accountability;
2.   Secondly, there is little doubt that boards are a male club. This has to change. In 2003 Norway mandated that 40 per cent of board members be women. Such soft quotas may be a step too far, but a useful first step would be the introduction of targets that would be determined by companies according to their particular circumstances, to be reported on an *if not, why not* basis. This would promote greater board diversity in a way that could be expected to enhance company performance, and which would create few downside risks;
3.   Thirdly, there is clear evidence that corporate regulators are a club. Corporate law making until now has largely been the province of a narrow set of interests, mainly big business and corporate law experts. Greater diversity is required.

Remuneration has been made fairly transparent in public documents, but this is not necessarily a panacea, or even a positive development. Improved disclosure may well have led to a Lake Wobegon effect (a mythical place where all children are above average). Chief executives and boards may have looked on the pay of other executives and started a pay spiral. No one wishes to be hired at below average levels, and boards tend to want to pay their executives well as evidence that they have hired a strong candidate. There is no doubt that executives have been demanding more, and this may be one reason why.

11.4 CONFLICTS OF INTEREST

There are some clear areas of conflicts of interest that can be improved. The Commission is recommending a strengthening of the requirement to establish a remuneration committee whose membership is independent. Remuneration consultants should also be required to report directly to the board or remuneration committee, as well as consulting with management. There should also be disclosure in company reports of the use of remuneration consultants.

Brevity and clarity in remuneration reports should be improved. They are often unduly lengthy and complex, and routinely have crucial omissions. Plain English presentations would promote a better investor understanding.

It is important to report on actual pay. The remuneration report should be confined to key management personnel, with more detailed reporting limited to the chief executive and other executives on the board. There is widespread concern about whether long-term incentives are long-term enough, whether too much of the remuneration is at risk, encouraging too much of a risk-taking mentality, and whether there is a tendency to reward average rather than superior performance. Once again, the answers are not always clear, despite appearances. Proffering carrots may in some cases prove less costly to the firm than imposing penalties. But this must be made clear to shareholders.

It is necessary to encourage greater shareholder engagement. The world did not end when a non-binding vote on the remuneration report was introduced – despite the ominous warnings from the business community. Instead, communication mostly improved. The Commission is recommending going to the next level and giving shareholders a *real say on pay*. The recommendation is that if there are two successive negative votes on board remuneration reports at annual general meetings by 25 per cent or more of shareholders, this should automatically immediately trigger a vote on whether there should be a spill of all board positions within three months. Such a resolution must be carried by 50 per cent of those voting.

This proposal would target boards that ignored shareholder concerns. It is also likely to generate more care by boards in setting executive pay, while making sure that boards are responsible for setting pay rather than having it handed over to shareholders or governments. It is a way of giving shareholders more leverage over the minority of boards that are not *listening*, without supplanting the boards' role in setting pay.

It should be added that the final recommendation differs from the draft recommendation published by the Productivity Commission in its interim report in September, 2010. The draft recommendation had proposed that if there were two successive 'no' votes there would be an automatic re-election of membership. However, it became apparent that if a second significant 'no' vote on the remuneration report resulted directly in a board re-election, many institutional investors would become reluctant to cast such a 'no' vote because of the destabilizing effect it might have on the company, which may well affect the share price. This would somewhat defeat the purpose. Accordingly, the recommendation was reformulated so that shareholders can express their opinion about the company's remuneration policies in the knowledge that a second 'no' vote above 25 per cent would trigger a separate (majority) resolution to re-elect the board, but not a re-election itself.

There are some further areas where conflict of interest can occur which should be addressed. Directors and company executives identified as key management personnel should be prohibited from voting their shares on remuneration reports. Key management personnel should also be prevented from voting undirected proxies on remuneration reports. Institutional investors, particularly superannuation funds, should disclose, at least on an annual basis, how they voted on remuneration reports and other remuneration-related issues. Initially this should be on a voluntary basis.

Electronic voting should be made legally permissible without the need for constitutional amendments. The taxation of incentive payments should change. Equity-based payments should be taxed at the point at which the executive assumes effective ownership (or at seven years, if that comes earlier).

In the post-industrial capital markets of the twenty-first century, ensuring that there is an effective principal–agent relationship between shareholders and managers has become more problematic. Shareholders who trade in and out of companies or institutional shareholders who buy shares on behalf of their unit holders are not direct, long-term owners of those companies in the way conceived when the joint stock corporation was first devised. The principal–agent problem is becoming progressively more complex.

The financial aims are clear enough. Company, shareholder and wider community interests are thought to be best served by maximizing the net present value of a company's future profit streams (after taking any external social costs into account). But how this translates into specifics will vary considerably. Witness Macquarie Group, which had a 225 per cent turnover in its share registry in a year, and Origin Energy, which had a 92 per cent turnover in a year. Shareholders are at best owners of a company in a collective, average sense over time. While it is desirable to increase shareholder influence over executives, it should not be seen as the sole imperative, or indeed necessarily the best and only way to protect the long-term sustainability of the corporation or, for that matter, the health of the overall economy.

11.5 CONCLUSION

The global financial crisis has, at the very least, given us a warning that corporate governance should continually change to meet new challenges. There was clearly something wrong with the existing structures, and while it is probably too simplistic to blame executive greed, there is little doubt that poor corporate governance and poor remuneration practices were a factor in the collapse.

But a heavy legalistic response could be counterproductive. Improving corporate governance and enhancing shareholder power is greatly to be preferred to direct regulation, whose consequences are often unpredictable. Sensible, balanced measures are needed to restrict further unwarranted increases in executive pay. An evolutionary approach – a *nudge* rather than heavy regulation – is preferable. This is what has been outlined in the Productivity Commission's report.

12. Regulatory lessons from the global financial crisis[1]

Jeffrey Carmichael

12.1 INTRODUCTION

The global financial crisis of 2008 (the crisis) was one of the most dramatic events of this century in that it took the global financial and economic systems to the brink of disaster. Without extensive intervention by major governments, it is likely that the rippling effects of bank failures could have frozen financial markets completely. The lessons from this period, which will be debated for decades, range from public policy issues, to the role of financial institutions, to the appropriate role of regulation.

This chapter focuses on the last of these and, indeed, on just two regulatory issues: first, the importance of regulatory architecture in avoiding crises in section 12.2; and second, the need for reforms in the tools and methods of prudential regulation in section 12.3. Thereafter, sections 12.4 and 12.5 address the lessons for reform actions. Section 12.6 explores the special cases of the Basel Committee and Australia before concluding this chapter in section 12.7.

12.2 LESSONS ABOUT REGULATORY ARCHITECTURE

The term 'regulatory architecture' refers to the number of agencies with regulatory responsibilities and the allocation of responsibilities among them.[2] Whereas there was little discussion about architecture as recently as 20 years ago, the past two decades have seen it become one of the more hotly debated topics in the field of regulation. The same period has seen a marked trend towards amalgamation of regulatory agencies in many countries. According to the World Bank the dominant architecture has shifted in this period from an industry-based architecture (in which each industry segment has its own regulator) to an integrated architecture in which most or all financial institutions are regulated by a single agency.[3]

While regulatory architecture is important, it is not an end in itself. A *good* regulatory architecture does not guarantee good regulation; that requires strong laws, experienced regulators, *and* the will to enforce efficiently and effectively. A poor architecture can nevertheless make effective regulation almost impossible. This can occur if the architecture impedes effective oversight (for example, if different agencies regulate different members of a financial conglomerate), encourages regulatory arbitrage, for example, if different regulators impose very different regulatory burdens on the same products offered by different institutions, or weakens the balance of power between the regulator and the industry.

12.2.1 Lessons from the United States

All of these flaws were evident in the US regulatory architecture leading into the crisis. Notwithstanding the overall international trend towards amalgamation, the US remained at the other end of the spectrum in having not only an industry-based architecture, but one in which multiple regulators operated in the same industries. If the state-based regulators of community banks, insurance companies, and non-bank financial intermediaries are all included, the US had (and still has) several hundred State and Federal regulatory agencies.

There were two particular characteristics of the US architecture that stand out in the context of the crisis.

First, the heavily fragmented and competitive regulatory architecture in the US had many gaps in regulatory coverage that resulted from the need to ring-fence regulators in order to minimize turf battles. Under this architecture a largely-unregulated *shadow* banking sector emerged in the US as a direct and lower-cost alternative to the regulated banking system. In particular, the powerful Wall Street investment banks were regulated by the Securities and Exchange Commission, rather than by any of the many banking regulators, and were regulated to a much lower standard of prudence than banks. Similarly, insurance companies, which were regulated under a fragmented state-based system, were regulated to a lower level of prudence than banks. Under this structure many of the complex products that contributed to the crisis fell outside the scope of the mainstream regulatory agencies. Critical parts of the mortgage lending process, for example, were completely unregulated.

Second, the US architecture provided, at best, a fragmented and ineffective framework for regulating financial conglomerates. For example, while the US Federal Reserve Bank regulated bank holding companies, it regulated neither banks nor any of the other financial institutions that operate under bank holding companies. Thus, in regulating conglomerates, the

Federal Reserve was completely reliant on the quality of regulation implemented by other agencies. Non-bank financial groups were even less tightly regulated. As a direct result of this weak framework for conglomerate regulation, banks were able to shift risky assets off balance sheet into unregulated or under-regulated local and off-shore affiliates; regulatory arbitrage enabled financial institutions to choose the regulator that best suited their appetite for risk;[4] and there was insufficient systemic oversight of the financial sector as a whole; when each regulator is assigned a small stand of trees it is hardly surprising that none has a good view of the forest.

It is difficult to reach any conclusion other than that the regulatory architecture in the US contributed to both the emergence of the crisis and its severity.

12.2.2 Lessons from the United Kingdom

Because the crisis affected the UK financial system as much as it did that of the United States, some have argued that the unified architecture model under the UK Financial Services Authority (FSA) also failed the test of the crisis. While this will be debated for years to come, in my view the failures in the UK lay not so much in its regulatory architecture as in the execution of its regulatory responsibilities. For example, the FSA's own Internal Audit Report on Northern Rock identifies a number of shortcomings in the way in which Northern Rock was supervised, including:

- contrary to FSA procedures, formal records of key meetings were not kept;
- there was no analysis by the FSA of the (flawed) business model employed by Northern Rock;
- the supervisory review period was increased from 24 months to 36 months;
- the FSA supervisory team appeared not to fully understand the requirements of the risk rating placed on Northern Rock, nor did they adequately identify and pursue risks arising in the firm as a whole;
- there was a shortage of supervisory expertise within the FSA in some critical areas, most notably in prudential banking and financial data analysis;
- related to this, there was an over-emphasis by the FSA on conduct issues and an under-emphasis on prudential issues.

This latter point is probably the most relevant. In the period leading up to the crisis there was intense focus by the UK public and politicians on market conduct issues. As a result, the FSA, which had responsibility for both prudence and conduct, focused its energies and resources where the public demands were greatest – in enforcement of conduct issues, at the expense of prudential issues.

A second factor in the UK experience was the pressure exerted by the City of London on the FSA to *keep London competitive* by ensuring that UK financial institutions were not overly regulated relative to their foreign, especially US counterparts.

These pressures were unrelated to the UK's regulatory architecture and are a good reminder that a sound architecture by itself is a necessary rather than a sufficient condition for effective regulation. Given the different contributions of architecture to the crises in the US and UK, it is ironic that the architecture in the US has survived largely intact, notwithstanding the voluminous reforms in the Dodd–Frank Act, while the UK moved swiftly to incorporate the FSA as part of the Bank of England, the industry preferred the previous arrangement of the softer regulatory stance of the FSA.[5] The failure of the US reforms to deliver changes to a grossly flawed architecture derives much less from a failure to recognize the problems than from the difficulty of gaining support for genuine institutional reform under the US political system.

12.2.3 Lessons from Cross-Border Arrangements

A third area in which regulatory architecture was found wanting by the crisis was in the area of international cooperation. Under the framework for banking supervision implemented by the Basel Committee on Banking Supervision (BCBS) international cooperation is implemented through a *home–host* model. Under this model the home regulator (the country in which the parent bank is domiciled) takes the lead responsibility, while the host regulator (the country in which the branch or subsidiary operates) plays a secondary role. The lynchpin of the model is the level of cooperation assumed between the two agencies.

Experience during the crisis with cooperation between home and host regulators left much to be desired. In many cases host regulators have noted that they were simply cut out of the communication loop. More importantly, as highlighted by the experience with Icelandic banks, the open branching model of the European Union was found to create unacceptable risks for host economies and regulators. A third disappointing feature of the crisis was the level of panic that emerged in the system related to uncertainty surrounding how the failure of Lehman Brothers would be handled across international borders. The level of uncertainty may have been disappointing, but it was entirely justified by past experience with cross-border failures (such as that by BCCI) and also by the intensely nationalistic legal responses that followed Lehman Brothers' failure.

On the positive side, the BCBS and Financial Stability Board have responded strongly to these challenges. Home and host regulators are being brought closer to each other by the establishment of 'colleges' of regulators. At the same time, establishing a simpler and more effective resolution process for failed banks has been a top priority of both the BCBS (though living wills) and Financial Stability Board (seeking to simplify cross-border resolution mechanisms).

12.3   LESSONS ABOUT REGULATORY TOOLS AND TECHNIQUES

The crisis exposed many weaknesses in the tools and techniques of financial regulation. Regulatory capital was both inadequate in many countries, and of insufficient quality to absorb losses. In particular, there was significant international inconsistency in both the definition of and level of capital required by different regulators. Despite the superficial appearance of a worldwide commitment to a common capital framework, the reality was that the rules set by the BCBS included many *discretions* that enabled some countries to lower the level and quality of regulatory capital. In the United Kingdom, for example, the pressure from the City of London and the British Government to keep the UK competitive resulted in the FSA setting one of the weakest capital standards in the world. It is no surprise that the two countries that had the toughest capital standards, Australia and Canada, survived the crisis better than those (such as the US, the UK, and many of the continental European countries) with weaker standards.

One of the discretions that had a material impact on the quality of capital was that which permitted banks to hold part of their Tier 1 Capital in the form of hybrid equity. This allowance drove a wedge between Tier 1 Capital and the amount of common equity held by many banks. The divergence was most marked in countries that took advantage of further discretions to increase the limit on hybrid capital. This included the US, which permitted Trust Preferred Shares to be included without limit as part of Tier 1 and in the UK, where Trust Preferred Shares were included subject to a limit, but in which the calculation of Net Tier 1 Capital was distorted in a way that enabled hybrid capital to fully fund all Tier 1 deductions (as distinct from most countries where it was not permitted to fund any such deductions).

A second weakness in the Basel capital framework exposed by the crisis was the fact that the amount of regulatory capital required for market risk was considerably lower than the comparable amount required for credit risk.[6] The disparity between the capital requirements for market risk and credit risk was amplified by a loophole in the Basel Capital Accord that imposed a market risk capital requirement on a bank's *trading book* but *not* a credit risk capital requirement – and the reverse on a bank's *banking book*.[7] With market risk requirements lower than credit risk requirements, and considerable flexibility offered to banks in the way they classified assets, some banks exploited this loophole to switch assets from their banking books to their trading books, thereby lowering the overall amount of capital they needed to hold. It is noteworthy that, between 2000 and 2007, the percentage of trading book assets held by major global banks increased from around 20 per cent of total assets to around 40 per cent. Not only did this transfer reduce the amount of equity that banks were required to hold (that is, increase their leverage), the general asset market boom throughout the run-up to the crisis meant that these banks booked mark-to-market trading gains that inflated their measured capital bases.

A further weakness in the market risk capital framework, exposed by the crisis, was the focus of the computation. Under the Basel model, value-at-risk is calculated in terms of a set number of standard deviations of the measured statistical distribution for movements in asset prices. This computation focuses on the centre of the statistical distribution, a computation that makes sense only if price movements are relatively small and predictable on the basis of past history. The experience in the crisis exposed the limitations of these assumptions and suggested that market risk calculations should focus more on the risk in the tails of the distribution than on its centre.

The second major regulatory tool that was found wanting by the crisis was the management of liquidity risk. In the decades prior to the crisis the importance of liquidity risk had been progressively downgraded by both industry and regulators. The experience in 2008 put liquidity risk back on the front burner.

Other areas of regulatory weakness exposed by the crisis include:

- Risk concentration – both banks and regulators failed to understand that risk concentration extends far beyond related parties of borrowers. The failure of the sub-prime market in the US created a systemic risk of global proportions because the market had taken a single risk class and spread it like a virus into products that were then marketed globally;
- Conglomerate regulation – as noted earlier, the crisis exposed a weakness in the way financial conglomerates are regulated.

The biggest failing in this respect was the scope that weak consolidated regulation gave to financial groups to shift risks within
a group to those points in which the regulatory requirements were
lowest;

- Pro-cyclicality in regulatory and accounting rules – the crisis provided a dramatic illustration of the dangers of basing regulatory
and accounting rules on current market valuations of assets and
liabilities when markets are in turmoil. While it is difficult to argue
with the market value approach in normal times, distressed markets
produce prices that do not accurately reflect rational decision-
making; and

- Importance of supervision – while the terms 'regulation' and 'supervision' are generally used interchangeably in this chapter, there is
an important distinction between them; one that was highlighted by
the crisis. Regulation refers to the rules and laws that are imposed
on regulated institutions. Supervision refers to the process of
implementing and enforcing these rules and regulations. One of the
flaws exposed by the crisis was the tendency for some regulators
to rely excessively on the rules and insufficiently on their enforcement. Indeed, it could easily be argued that the Basel II framework
established by the BCBS (including discretionary intervention under
Pillar 2) provided more than enough flexibility for regulatory agencies to avoid the crisis. What was missing in many cases was an
adequate understanding of the danger signals that were in evidence
and/or the will to enforce the rules that were available. Either way,
what is clear is that those countries that put more emphasis on
supervision performed relatively better than those that put more
emphasis on regulation.

12.4   REFORM PROPOSALS

There is no question that, in the aftermath of the crisis, banks will be
expected to hold more capital, more liquidity, and to act more prudently.
The question is not whether regulatory demands will be more onerous,
but how much *more onerous* they will be. It would be absurd to argue that
regulation should not be tougher; it must be. At the same time, as the ava-
lanche of proposed changes grows, it is important to recognize that banks
cannot be made stronger without incurring considerable cost; a cost that
will be borne largely by the community. In such a context it is prudent to
assess the impact of each change and to ensure that the benefits of each
proposal outweigh its costs.

There is a risk in the current, highly-politicized environment that the race to toughen regulations is not being accompanied by the usual level of healthy debate, hard-edged logical analysis, and cost–benefit alignment that characterized past BCBS policy changes. There is currently a strong push for *more of everything* in many of the current Basel proposals. This push to be tougher in the level of regulation has distracted the focus from one of the biggest failures of the crisis; namely, the need to regulate smarter. Ironically, the charge for *more of everything* appears to be being led by those countries that fared worst during the crisis, with insufficient reflection on the experiences of those countries (such as Australia and Canada) that weathered the storm more comfortably.

The Basel proposals (known in the industry as Basel III) are contained in three documents released in 2009.[8] While these are only a sub-set of the many proposals currently under consideration, their endorsement by the BCBS and G20 countries makes their implementation highly likely. The proposals include the following main elements:

1. Liquidity: BCBS has emphasized that they are seeking an internationally consistent approach based on two standards:
   - a liquidity coverage ratio (LCR) designed to cover an acute short-term (30-day) stress scenario; and
   - a net stable funding ratio (NSFR) designed to ensure that banks hold more long-term stable funds than they are likely to need in the coming year.
2. Capital: the BSCB has emphasized that it is seeking to increase the quality, consistency and transparency of banks' capital bases. The proposals include several components:
   - existing discretions in the measurement of capital will be removed to ensure that Tier 1 capital consists predominantly of shareholders' funds;
   - existing rules for the deduction of certain items (e.g. investments in subsidiaries) from capital are being tightened, with the result that most deductions will now be taken against shareholders' funds;
   - the capital requirements for counterparty credit risk, market risk, securitization, and other off-balance sheet assets will all be increased materially;
   - the BCBS will introduce a simple leverage ratio in addition to the existing risk-based ratio;
   - the BCBS will introduce a series of measures to promote the build-up of capital buffers in good times so that they can be drawn on in periods of stress (including the right of the

regulator to dictate whether banks can or cannot pay dividends depending on where they are in the buffer range); and
● the BCBS is considering introducing an additional capital charge for systemically significant banks.

While some of these are unobjectionable, others are of more questionable value and logic. More importantly, the combined impact of the changes as a group is likely to be of an order of magnitude not previously experienced. Notwithstanding the BCBS's promises of a transition period and some grandfathering, the net cost of these changes needs close attention before they are implemented. The following are some comments on individual aspects of the proposals.

12.4.1   Liquidity

In my view, the BCBS proposals on liquidity contain some questionable logic. To begin with, the BCBS has proposed a primary liquidity ratio (LCR) based on the assumption that a bank must be able to survive for up to 30 days on its own, by selling down prime *liquid* assets. In reality few banks could hope to survive a liquidity run in this way for such a long period.

As any central bank that has dealt with a *single name* liquidity crisis knows, a bank that sells large quantities of liquid assets into the market effectively announces to the world that it has a liquidity problem, thereby exacerbating the problem of confidence and worsening the situation. For this reason, liquidity runs are almost always met in the first instance by emergency support from the central bank. In the event that the central bank decides to let the distressed bank fail, this decision would normally be made long before 30 days have passed. Thus, the 30-day horizon proposed by the BCBS appears to be out of line with reality.

The challenge for the BCBS is to establish a standard that is relevant. The crisis certainly exposed weaknesses in liquidity management, but these were in the context of a complete seizing up of a global multi-trillion dollar market. It is doubtful that any liquidity standard, no matter how stringent, could deal with such a situation. Nor, for that matter, would it make any sense to set such a standard for day-to-day liquidity operations. After all, in the 40 or more years preceding the crisis there were very few liquidity events and these were generally handled without much fuss.

The 30-day standard proposed by the BCBS appears to be setting the bar at a level that is appropriate to neither the crisis nor the business-as-usual context of international banking.

The composition of admissible liquid assets proposed by the BCBS is even more unrealistic. While making the obligatory noises about central bank eligibility, and liquidity depending on market-related characteristics, the Committee inevitably followed its rule-based tradition of specifying a menu of assets that will qualify for the standard. These include (all in local currency): cash; central bank assets; and marketable securities issued by governments, semi-government agencies, and international agencies. The BCBS is also considering (subject to a substantial haircut) certain corporate bonds and covered bonds.

The inappropriateness of such a definition for a country like Australia is highlighted by the fact that the entire stock of eligible securities is likely to be less than the total amount required under the LCR – and by a large margin (at least if the 30-day fiction is maintained). The same will be true for any country that has a history of fiscal responsibility and which survived the crisis without having to bail out its banking system. Ironically, in Australia, even if banks could commandeer the entire stock of eligible securities, they would become illiquid in the process.

The basic flaw in the BCBS argument is the assumption that liquidity should be regulated under a prescriptive, one-size-fits-all standard. This statement may seem at odds with the clear need for a one-size-fits-all approach to capital – or at least for a much greater level of harmonization than existed prior to the crisis. The reality, however, is that capital and liquidity are very different. Unlike capital, which is a *global* concept, liquidity is a *local* concept. Equity has the same meaning in any market around the world and banks can effectively access capital in any market around the world. The same is not true for liquidity. Liquidity is a characteristic conferred by a combination of the currency in which an asset is denominated and the nature of the market in which it is traded. An asset that is highly liquid in one country may be totally illiquid in another. This can be true for government securities every bit as much as for private securities.

Importantly, liquidity needs to be considered against the availability of central bank emergency liquidity support. As noted above, the reality is that a bank facing a liquidity run is likely to either fail quickly or receive liquidity support directly from the central bank, rather than from selling assets into the market and signalling its distress. There are many assets that are acceptable to a central bank as collateral for emergency support that are not included in the BCBS list. Indeed, those central banks that are also responsible for banking supervision must feel a little schizophrenic reading the BCBS proposal; as a banking supervisor they are being instructed that they can only accept certain assets as liquid while, as a central bank, they have a different set of assets against which they will provide liquidity support when it is needed. A strange state indeed.

The solution to these flaws is reasonably simple. The LCR needs to be set at a realistic level (albeit higher than banks' current holdings of liquidity) while the composition of acceptable assets should be determined by the local regulator, taking into account local market conditions and local central bank practices. One-size-fits-all simply does not work for liquidity and has the potential to create some bizarre anomalies for fiscally-responsible countries such as Australia. A flexible approach runs the risk of being *gamed* by some countries; but that risk is a small price to pay for avoiding a meaningless and costly uniform approach.

The net stable funding ratio also involves some questionable logic. The intention of promoting more medium- and long-term funding for banks is unobjectionable. As with the LCR, the devil is in the detail and the BCBS's enthusiasm to fall back on rules rather than giving local regulators flexibility to align the definitions with local realities.

In its simplest form, the NSFR requires the available amount of stable funding to exceed the required amount of stable funding. The concept of a stable funding ratio is not new, although some of the definitions have been broadened from those used by banks in setting their own internal liquidity benchmarks. The BCBS methodology defines required stable funding to include all illiquid assets (for example loans and advances) plus all securities held. Available stable funding consists of a menu of funding sources, each subject to a weighting factor. Thus, term deposits (provided they cannot be redeemed early) with a maturity greater than a year receive a 100 per cent weight, *stable* retail demand deposits (those subject to conditions such as being covered by deposit insurance) receive a weight of 85 per cent, *less stable* deposits a weight of 70 per cent and so on.

The difficulty with this framework is its arbitrary requirement that this ratio be greater than 1 (as a point of reference, the major Australian banks appear to have NSFR ratios around 0.7). While 1 may be an attractive number for a range of irrelevant reasons, it is far from clear that there is any science in the requirement that this ratio be greater than 1 in the context of banks. The arbitrariness of the requirement is amplified by the arbitrariness of the weights assigned to various categories of liabilities.[9] More fundamentally, banks are in the business of liquidity transformation. From the time that banks first emerged, a central part of their business has been turning liquid deposits into illiquid loans. Thus banks start from a position where this ratio should naturally be less than 1 as a result of the business they are in. If banks are forced out of the liquidity transformation business by arbitrary regulations, the question is whether other, less-heavily regulated institutions will start providing this service – and whether that will strengthen the financial system or weaken it. The logic here requires further work.

12.4.2 Capital

While less objectionable than the liquidity proposals, a number of the capital proposals also contain logical anomalies that require further thought. That said, it is hard to argue with the central proposition that banks need to carry more capital than they did prior to the crisis, and that the capital held should be of higher quality. It is also hard to argue against the need for a uniform approach across international boundaries (unlike the case with liquidity); Australian banks are likely to endorse this aspect very strongly. There are nevertheless elements which, while neutral between banks, are likely to be far from neutral in their potential impact on consumers and the economy.

Issues requiring further discussion in the area oi capital requirements include:

- Deductions for unconsolidated subsidiaries: prior to the introduction of Basel II, investments in unconsolidated subsidiaries (for example. insurance subsidiaries) were deducted from Tier 2 capital. Under Basel II this deduction was adjusted to come 50 per cent from Tier 1 and 50 per cent from Tier 2. Under the new proposals the deduction will come entirely from Tier 1. The idea that an insurance subsidiary will have no value in the event of a bank failure is somewhat harsh and places a severe capital penalty on banks that hold insurance subsidiaries. One consequence of the proposal (perhaps not unintended) may be to force banks to sell their insurance subsidiaries in order to increase their capital and competitiveness. Another concern about the proposed changes to the deductions framework is the proposal that a number of deductions will be replaced by a 1250 per cent risk weighting. Under the original Basel model, *deduction* and a 1250 per cent *risk weight* were effectively equivalent, given the 8 per cent capital adequacy requirement. With the general upward drift in capital requirements, however, a 1250 per cent risk weight will have the odd impact of requiring some assets to have capital held against them that is greater than the value of the asset itself.
- Simple leverage ratio: the objective of preventing banks from becoming overly reliant on leverage is unobjectionable. While a few countries use a simple leverage ratio to supplement the risk-weighted Basel model, the country in which they are most widely applied, and which has been one of the champions of this proposal, is the United States. The failure of large US banks during the crisis, despite the existence of a simple leverage ratio, should give pause for thought to anyone who sees this as part of the solution to crisis-type

situations. Over-leveraging of banks, where it did occur, resulted primarily from design flaws in the BCBS capital framework, including from the discretions mentioned earlier, and from the banking book-trading book distortion. Provided these flaws are corrected (and the new proposals attempt to do so) a simple leverage ratio should not be needed to address over-leverage.

- Capital charge for systemically-important institutions: while there is something appealing in the idea that institutions that are seen as *too big to fail* should pay a premium for that advantage, the practicalities of how to impose such a fee in advance of any particular situation is daunting. The nub of the problem is that institutions that may appear unimportant at present may turn out to be systemically dangerous under circumstances that cannot be anticipated. Further, institutions have a way of evolving to avoid taxes. Imposing a *stability* tax on one set of institutions has the potential to shift the business to a parallel set of *untaxed* institutions. The result could be a less stable and less secure financial system overall.
- Countercyclical capital: again the concept has a theoretical appeal. The challenge is in how to apply it. On the one hand, the more mechanical the approach (for example. the Spanish approach to dynamic provisioning), the less the regulator will have to make difficult judgements. On the other hand, without flexibility, there is a danger that the regulator could be seen to be strangling an economic recovery, or even a period of benign steady growth, if provisioning and capital accumulation stifle bank lending. As with the systemic capital charge there is also the potential for lending and deposits to spill outside the banking sector into less regulated shadow banks. As outlined above for liquidity, any framework for countercyclical capital buffers must take account of local conditions: for example 5 per cent growth in Australia is not equivalent to 5 per cent growth in India.

12.5   MEASURING THE POTENTIAL COST OF THE BCBS PROPOSALS

Irrespective of whether one agrees or disagrees with the logic of the BCBS proposals, there is little doubt that their combined impact could have major implications for the cost and availability of loans to the community and, through them, for economic growth and employment. These are not changes to be taken lightly.

The BCBS has commissioned a quantitative impact survey (QIS) with results to be returned by 30 April 2011. It was revealed that the QIS was large and that there was a massive gap between the current state of the industry and the world envisaged by the proposals. Therefore it is likely that the QIS will have a significant impact on bank profitability and that modifications to the proposals are likely to follow. In the meantime, it is important to make at least some preliminary calculations to guide discussion.

The main channel through which the impact will be transmitted is interest rates.

12.5.1 Some Simple Arithmetic

Banks attract share capital by offering an acceptable return for the risk involved. Historically, for Australian banks (and most internationally-operating banks) this return on equity has ranged somewhere between 15 per cent and 20 per cent. Since banks typically earn a low return on assets employed (typically closer to 1 per cent) the yield on equity is generated by leverage. The return on leverage is generated, in turn, by the spread between borrowing and lending rates.

It is a simple matter of arithmetic that any regulatory imposition that lowers the return on equity (either by increasing the amount of capital that must be held against any given set of assets or by requiring banks to hold lower yielding assets for liquidity purposes) will lead to a rise in the spread between borrowing and lending rates. It is also a matter of arithmetic that any action (regulatory or otherwise) that increases the cost of funds will increase the cost of loans. In part these trends have already emerged, as banks have rebuilt their capital bases following the crisis. The cost of funding from wholesale markets has risen following the liquidity crisis, and as banks have generally increased their pricing of risk following the period of under-pricing leading up to the crisis.[10] The net impact on borrowing rates has nevertheless, to date, been mitigated somewhat by the global low-interest environment established by central banks fighting against recession.

The BCBS proposals, if implemented fully, would change that configuration quite dramatically.

The most comprehensive estimates to date of the initial impact of the BCBS proposals on the cost structure of banks have been made for international banks by the International Institute of Finance (IIF) and JP Morgan. Some stylized estimates have also been produced by UBS Global Equity Research. While their assumptions vary a little, their initial estimates are remarkably similar.

The Morgan study estimates that, *ceteris paribus*, the current proposals[11] would reduce the return on equity of global banks from 13.3 per cent to 5.4 per cent – a fall of around 60 per cent – with the biggest impact being felt in the UK. The smallest individual country reduction is around 40 per cent. Unfortunately, they do not include Australian banks in their sample. The JP Morgan study also concludes that required capital will increase by around 20 per cent under the proposals and, if banks are to maintain a 15 per cent return on equity (ROE) (which they assume will be needed to attract the additional capital), the pricing of bank products would need to increase by around 33 per cent on average, while on financial products it would be closer to 40 per cent.

Focusing just on the capital and liquidity changes outlined in this chapter, the UBS stylized model suggests that bank income would fall by around a third as a result of lower earning assets and higher funding costs. When the additional required capital is taken into consideration, UBS reaches the conclusion that the ROE would drop by around 60 per cent (in their example, from a little over 26 per cent to a little under 9 per cent).

The relevance of these estimates is not that banks are likely to become unprofitable. Banks will respond to these changes by repricing their products until they restore a return on equity that is acceptable to the market. The acceptable level need not be as high as the historical norm, especially if the regulatory measures are seen as making banks safer, but there can be no question that it will be higher than one third of historical levels. It is this repricing of deposit and lending rates that will impact on the community.

The IIF study is broader ranging in that it is an attempt to gather information on multiple countries and to integrate the banking analysis into a simple model of the financial sector and the economy. In this way the IIF study attempts to follow through the repricing impact of the changes. Their results are furthest progressed for the United States. Their estimated impact on bank profitability and ROE is considerably lower than those of the Morgan and UBS studies (in the order of a 20 per cent reduction in ROE at the peak in around five years' time). This lower estimate is not unexpected given that the IIF analysis attempts to take into account the general equilibrium impact on the economy as well. Thus, the high impact effects calculated by JP Morgan and UBS are partly offset in the IIF study by the response of banks, borrowers, competitors, and the economy.

12.5.2 From Bank Profitability to Economic Activity

Transmission from regulatory changes to the economy begins with the initial impact on bank balance sheets, followed by the reaction of banks as they try to restore profitability and an acceptable return on capital. These decisions, on pricing and underwriting standards, flow through into the markets for borrowing and lending, consumption and savings, and finally to production and employment, as the economy finds a new equilibrium.

Estimating the impact is complicated greatly by the need to know how banks will implement the changes (e.g. by simply raising lending rates or by tightening underwriting standards to *crowd out* higher-risk borrowers, thereby absorbing part of the pressure by lowering risk premia); how borrowers will respond (e.g. if the demand for loans is highly elastic, a small increase in lending rates will reduce lending significantly, thereby absorbing the pressure more in the quantity of lending than in the price); and how non-bank competitors will respond (e.g. the impact on the economy will be greatly reduced if there is a ready supply of non-bank lenders able to fill the gap if banks cut back on lending).

Unfortunately, there are no readily available numerical or statistical models to help guide us in assessing these interactions and calibrating the outcomes. In the first place there is a paucity of statistical analyses of the financial sector. This has long been a weakness in academic assessments of the macroeconomy, both in Australia and elsewhere. Second, even if there were statistical studies that could be used, the parameters estimated by such studies would be based on marginal changes – and the changes proposed by the BCBS are not marginal but substantive.

The scale of the changes can be understood by considering the impact of just one of the two elements of the liquidity proposals on Australian banks. Australian banks currently hold around A$260 billion in liquid assets. Under the proposed LCR this would roughly double. Under the proposed liquid asset definition banks would have to increase their holdings of eligible assets by around A$400 billion or more.[12] Since banks' balance sheets must balance, they would need to either raise additional funding or reduce lending, or some combination of the two. Against total bank assets of around A$2 trillion, a change of this magnitude is anything but marginal.

Notwithstanding the arbitrariness of some of the assumptions that need to be made, some guidance can be taken from work that has been done by the IIF.[13]

12.5.3 Higher Costs for Banks will Slow the Economy

The IIF model is relatively simple. The regulatory changes impact bank profitability by lowering the return on assets and increasing the cost of funding. Banks respond to this by raising both deposit and lending rates. The spread between these rates must also increase. The extent to which the impact of the changes falls on the quantity of lending rather than on the price of lending depends on the demand elasticity for bank lending and the supply elasticity of non-bank lending. In the case of the US, where the banking system is small relative to the total financial system, the availability of non-bank lending is relatively elastic. The net reduction in private sector credit growth is thus smaller than it might otherwise be (the impact peaks after four years at a reduction in growth of around 3 percentage points, from 7.3 to 3.8 per cent). The capacity for US non-bank finance to replace bank finance also softens the impact of the changes on real economic activity. Even so, the cumulative impact of the changes on real GDP growth is around 2 percentage points over a 4–5-year time frame.

12.6   HOW MIGHT AUSTRALIA FARE UNDER THE CHANGES?

It will be some time before detailed estimates can be made for the impact of the proposed changes on Australia. Further, assessing the impact will be difficult until APRA makes its position clear on all the issues. Also, ahead of the QIS results it is difficult to compare impacts across countries because the *starting gaps* may be very different. There are nevertheless a number of factors that suggest that the overall impact in Australia could be at, or above, the upper end of the estimates currently available for the US and Europe:

1. First, at least with respect to liquidity, the sizes of the regulatory gaps to be closed in the case of Australian banks appear likely to be larger than the equivalent gaps facing banks in other countries:
    *   US banks currently hold a high level of liquidity, including a large share of assets that have been included in the BCBS definition of eligible liquid securities. Australian banks currently hold a much smaller fraction of eligible assets. Thus the size of the gap to be closed by Australian banks in order to meet the LCR will be much greater than that facing US banks.
    *   Similarly, based on the UBS estimates, European banks have an NSFR of around 0.8, compared with a ratio for Australian banks of around 0.7. Again this suggests that Australian banks may face a bigger gap in their NSFR than European banks.
2. Second, closing the liquidity gaps will be much more difficult for Australian banks than it will be in many other countries. For example, there is ample supply of, and liquidity in, the market for US government securities and in those European countries that bailed out their banking systems. In contrast, the scramble that could ensue if Australian banks are forced to acquire and hold government securities would lead to a bigger fall in interest earnings for Australian banks.

3. Third, there is little historical evidence of a high demand elasticity for retail deposits in Australia, and wholesale markets are showing strong rationing tendencies since the crisis. Thus Australian banks are unlikely to find much additional funding by offering higher deposit rates in either retail or wholesale markets.
4. Fourth, the Australian non-bank financial sector is neither as well developed as in the US nor as competitive as an alternative source of funding.
5. Finally, as a general point, the capital requirements should not impact Australian banks any harder than others, given that Australian banks have traditionally been more strongly capitalized than most, and with a higher reliance on shareholders' funds. While the positive gap between Australian banks and banks in many other jurisdictions has been closed to some extent as international banks have recapitalized following the crisis, Australian banks remain generally strong in their capital positions. The proposals will nevertheless hit Australian banks in particular areas, including the additional capital they will be required to hold for unconsolidated subsidiaries and, depending on their final forms, the simple leverage ratio, the cyclical capital buffer, and the capital charge for systemically significant institutions.

While it is too early to offer reliable estimates, the studies cited and the factors listed above suggest that the impact of the proposed changes on Australian banks is likely to be pervasive. Prior to strategic responses by the banks, the reduction in earnings and ROE is likely to be at least as great as the estimates for international banks provided by the Morgan and UBS studies; namely, earnings are likely to decrease by around 30 per cent and ROE by around 60 per cent. The net impact on lending rates by banks is likely to be at least the 3 percentage points predicted by the Morgan study, and most probably higher. The big unknown in this equation is how Australia might resolve the conundrum posed by a supply of eligible liquid assets that is smaller than the BCBS requirement. Unless this is resolved satisfactorily, the impact on interest rates will be amplified.

As these changes work their way through the financial sector and the economy, the impact is likely to fall much more heavily on reduced lending (a tightening of underwriting standards) and higher pricing of loans, than was simulated for the US by the IIF study. This follows from the lower demand elasticity for deposits and the more limited availability of bank substitutes in supplying loans to the private sector. On balance, the cumulative reduction in growth of 2 per cent estimated for the US economy is likely to be a material understatement of the impact that will be felt in Australia.

12.7 CONCLUDING THOUGHTS

There have been many important lessons from the crisis. It is still early days; there has been enormous political pressure to implement reforms that are seen to be tough and that address weaknesses in the regulatory framework exposed by the crisis.

Unfortunately, the reform proposals put forward to date appear to be as flawed as the framework they are attempting to patch. In broad terms, regulators are addressing the easy problems rather than the important ones. In particular:

- there has been virtually no change in the flawed US regulatory architecture;
- the Basel III framework proposed by the BCBS contains some useful reforms but, overall, focuses too much on regulation and too little on supervision; and
- the BCBS proposals also suffer from an over-zealous attempt to impose a one-size-fits-all model for liquidity risk.

Most importantly, the sheer scale of the proposed changes is likely to have a material impact on both the cost and availability of finance. Unless there are significant modifications to the BCBS proposals in the wake of the QIS, there is a real risk that the global recovery may be short-lived.

NOTES

1. The comments in this chapter about regulatory proposals (for example, by the Basel Committee) refer to proposals as at the date of the Symposium (9 April 2010). A number of these proposals have been altered since that time, including several that have responded to issues such as those raised in this chapter.
2. In the financial world these agencies are typically referred to as supervisors, rather than regulators, in order to draw a distinction between the setting of regulations (largely a legislative process) and their implementation and enforcement (largely an oversight process). In practice the distinction between regulation and supervision is quite blurred, with supervisory agencies often having extensive regulatory powers as well. In this chapter, as in much of the literature on financial regulation, the terms 'regulator' and 'supervisor' will, for the most part, be used interchangeably.
3. See Fleming, Alex, David Llewellyn, Silvina Vatnick and Diego Sourouille (2006), 'Updated international survey of integrated financial supervisors', *Workshop on Aligning Supervisory Structures with Country Needs*, World Bank, Washington, DC, June.
4. One of the great anomalies to emerge from the crisis was the fact that AIG Financial Holding Company, the parent company of the world's largest insurance company, AIG, was regulated on a consolidated basis by the Office of Thrift Supervision (a renamed version of the agency that had presided over the Savings and Loan failures of the early 1980s).

5.   The Dodd–Frank Act offered only a modest gesture in the direction of architectural reform by abolishing the Office of Thrift Supervision. At the same time, several new regulatory layers were added: the Fed will gain responsibility for consumer protection and for regulating systemically significant institutions; and a new Council of Supervisors will be formed to oversee systemic stability issues.

6.   The market risk requirement was three times the 10-day value-at-risk position calculated by banks using their internal models of market risk.

7.   A bank's trading book is defined to include those assets held for short-run trading purposes (including most derivative and complex products), whereas the banking book is defined to include longer-terms loans and advances.

8.   The relevant documents are: 'Enhancements to the Basel II framework and revisions to the Basel II market risk framework' (July 2009); 'International framework for liquidity risk measurement, standards and monitoring' (December 2009); and 'Strengthening the resilience of the banking sector' (December 2009).

9.   For example, the requirement for retail deposits to be guaranteed in order to attract the 'concessional' weight of 80 per cent creates a clear bias against countries that do not have explicit deposit insurance, while making no adjustment for the nature of the insurance scheme involved. While Australia now has a deposit insurance scheme, it did not have one historically (relying instead on legislated depositor preference), and yet it has had one of the most stable retail deposit bases anywhere in the world.

10.   UK banks, for example, have increased the spread on mortgage loans above the Bank of England base rate from effectively zero before the crisis to between 300 and 350 basis points post-crisis.

11.   The Morgan study includes a broader range of proposals than those contained in the recent Basel proposals.

12.   This leaves aside the 'small' problem that the total stock of assets defined as eligible under the BCBS proposal account for only about half of what will be required.

13.   While Australia is participating in the IIF work, the results of the analysis for Australia are not yet available.

13. Should we stop the IMF from doing what it should not do? A radical idea

Ross P. Buckley

13.1 INTRODUCTION

The International Monetary Fund (IMF) was established to facilitate the management of a global fixed exchange rate regime. That role largely disappeared in the 1970s. Since then the IMF has become the economic policy director of countries in crisis, a role it is ill-suited to serve, and which it has fulfilled poorly. This chapter reviews the IMF's performance in managing the debt crisis of the 1980s, the East Asian crisis of the late 1990s, Argentina's crisis of 2001, poverty in Africa generally, and its role in the recent global financial crisis. It considers how the IMF has served to promote and entrench the strong resistance of the global financial system to needed changes, and analyses the steps that need to be taken to reform the IMF, including removing the role of setting economic policy for developing nations in crisis.

The IMF was founded, along with the World Bank, in 1945. In the words of its website, 'It was established to promote international monetary cooperation, exchange stability, and orderly exchange arrangements; to foster economic growth and high levels of employment; and to provide temporary financial assistance to countries to help ease balance of payments adjustment.'[1]

This is a reasonable summary. But the website proceeds, 'Since the IMF was established its purposes have remained unchanged but its operations – which involve surveillance, financial assistance, and technical assistance – have developed to meet the changing needs of its member countries in an evolving world economy.'

At best, this is spin, for the IMF's purposes have changed. They changed in the 1970s when most developed countries moved away from fixed, to floating, exchange rates and the core function of the Fund, the maintenance of exchange stability, was ceded by governments to the market.

The IMF performed a useful function throughout the 1950s and 1960s advising on fixed exchange rate regimes and making short-term loans to assist governments in managing their exchange rates. The 1950s and 1960s were a period of sustained growth in much of the world. But by the end of the 1970s, the IMF was an organization with a much reduced mission. In the words of the former Chair of Citibank, Walter Wriston, 'The IMF was created to iron out the bumps in a fixed exchange rate system and like any bureaucracy, when its mission . . . became irrelevant when rates started floating, it had to reinvent itself and began making interim loans in Latin America.'[2] This lengthy chapter focuses on providing evidence for its radical proposal in ten sections with references to extensive literature.

13.2   THE DEBT CRISIS OF 1982

The debt crisis that engulfed Africa and Latin America in late 1982 gave the IMF a new lease of life – it reinvented itself as the manager of developing country crises. The IMF quickly came to discharge a critical role in the management of the debt crisis in the 1980s: directing the debtor nations' economic policies. Debtors needed new money, not least to service interest. Creditors, understandably, wanted some assurance that the debtors' economic policies that had contributed to the crisis had been changed. The commercial banks had firm views on the need for economic austerity by countries whose debt they were rescheduling. Yet considerations of national sovereignty made direct commercial bank involvement in the setting of local economic policies a political impossibility. The IMF was ideally placed, as an apparently independent international financial institution, to determine and monitor the economic policies of the debtor nations.[3]

The IMF fashioned this role for itself by conditioning its loans upon domestic economic policy reform. Then the foreign commercial banks, in turn, conditioned their loans upon debtor nations, securing the approval of the IMF for their economic policies. Thus was born cross-conditionality – the practice by which foreign commercial banks would only extend new loans to debtor nations upon the new policies of those nations receiving the IMF's stamp of approval.[4] This practice 'strengthened creditor solidarity and created close ties between the IMF and the commercial banks'.[5] This entire process, and the policies it imposed on the debtor nations, became known as 'structural adjustment', a 'stunningly bland name'[6] for policies with a stunningly high human cost.[7]

As early as 1983 the banks were describing the IMF's role in these terms:[8] '[A] fruitful co-operation is emerging between the commercial

banks and the IMF . . . without IMF persuasion of the borrowing countries to undertake needed adjustment and in the absence of Fund monitoring of the progress, the banks would be unwilling to advance sufficient
additional credit.'[9]

This utterly overstated the strength of the banks' position. In 1983 the
major banks would have advanced sufficient additional credit, irrespective
of IMF involvement, as the consequence of not doing so was the debtors
defaulting on their loans.[10] The debtors simply had insufficient foreign
exchange to service the debts. Some banks had insufficient capital to
withstand the losses that would have to be taken onto their books should
there be a generalized default. Advancing additional credit was simply a
survival strategy for the major banks but, of course, their rhetoric never
disclosed this.

The focus of the IMF reform programmes was to permit the debtors
to generate sufficient foreign exchange resources to stay current on their
debts.[11] The policies imposed to achieve that goal typically included:

- reductions in the budget deficit to limit inflation, and the need for
  foreign borrowing;
- limits on domestic credit expansion to control inflation;
- exchange rate devaluations to discourage imports and encourage
  exports; and
- generally a much reduced role for government and a much increased
  role for markets.[12]

Other structural adjustment policies imposed on debtors, at times,
included: (i) higher income and sales taxes; (ii) higher charges for state-
produced goods and services such as electricity and water; (iii) privatization of state-owned companies; (iv) deregulation of the labour market;
and (v) reform of tariffs and import quota regimes.[13] These policies have
been criticized for their adverse effect on economic growth[14] and their
devastating effect upon the living standard of the local people, particularly
the poor.[15]

Another explicit aim, and effect, of the IMF's policies was to reduce
protectionism in the Latin American countries. The Washington consensus was that economic growth is promoted through unilateral tariff
cuts and reductions in import restrictions. Once again, this policy flies in
the face of the experience of OECD countries. Britain in the nineteenth
century, and the United States in the twentieth century, promoted free
trade 'because they were the most efficient producers of the highest value-
added goods. They did not become so through free trade; they protected
themselves for decades in order to achieve that end.'[16]

John Kenneth Galbraith wrote of this nineteenth-century protectionism in these terms:

> For Britain, the industrially most advanced of countries, free trade was of obvious advantage, and like laissez-faire, it acquired a strong theological aura. In Germany and the United States, on the other hand, economic interest was better served by tariffs. Accordingly, the most respected economists in those countries . . . spoke vigorously for protection for their national 'infant industries' . . . from the products of the British colossus.[17]

Free trade and laissez-faire economics do indeed attract a theological aura; as do the economic theories of the IMF.[18] Ultimately, like all matters religious, one embraces the theology of the IMF by a leap of faith, not logical reasoning. The consequences of this theology since 1982 were literally a matter of life or death for millions of people.

The IMF policy prescriptions for Africa and Latin America meant that the 1980s were a lost decade. A decade in which net capital flows from these nations were North bound. A decade in which infrastructure crumbled, a decade, in sub-Saharan Africa, in which life expectancy at the decade's end was shorter than at the beginning.[19] As Hal Scott has put it so simply, 'there is little evidence that IMF conditions, usually requiring contractionary fiscal and monetary policies, have worked.'[20]

In the early years of the debt crisis the IMF severely underestimated its magnitude[21] and the Fund's policies did little to alleviate the crisis. The debt crisis was eventually relieved for the banks by the Brady Restructurings of the early 1990s in which the loans were converted into tradable bonds, with security for the repayment of principal and 12 to 18 months of interest repayments, and upon which some debt relief was granted. The Brady process did less for the debtor nations than for the banks, but brought some modest relief and encouraged genuinely new capital inflows into the region.[22] Of particular importance in terms of the contribution of the IMF, is that the Brady Plan was devised initially in Sao Paulo and Mexico City and given the imprimatur and support of the US Treasury.[23] The fingerprints of the IMF were nowhere to be found on the only creative measure brought to bear on the worst international economic crisis since World War II.

13.3 THE EAST ASIAN CRISIS OF 1997

In mid to late 1997 a succession of East Asian countries ran out of foreign exchange reserves with which to defend the value of their currencies in the markets. The currencies of Thailand, Indonesia, Malaysia and finally

Korea, collapsed, and foreign capital fled from the region. Asia's was a fundamentally different crisis from the debt crisis of 1982 or Mexico's peso crisis of 1994–95 in that the great majority of the troublesome indebtedness was of the private, not the public or quasi-public sector and it was not a crisis of over-consumption. The Latin American nations had been borrowing, in part, to fund general government budgets. The East Asian governments had not been similarly seduced. Their fiscal policies were prudent. In the words of Laurence Meyer, a member of the Board of Governors of the US Federal Reserve System, 'By conventional standards, the monetary and fiscal policies of the developing Asian economies prior to the crisis were largely disciplined and appropriate. . . . consumer price inflation . . . was relatively subdued [and] fiscal policy also appears to have been disciplined.'[24]

Furthermore, Asia's crisis occurred within a benign international environment with low interest rates and solid growth in output and exports.[25] Asia's crisis was primarily a crisis of inadequate local prudential regulation and inadequate confidence in the region by global capital.[26] It was a contractionary crisis in which the largest problems were that the exodus of global capital and loss of confidence in the region meant a steep decline in economic activity.

Notwithstanding all of these differences, the IMF ventured into Asia dispensing the policy prescriptions it believed had worked in Latin America in the 1980s and Mexico in 1995 – prescriptions of budgetary tightening and austerity. Austerity is always bad policy for a contractionary crisis. It is utterly ineffective in encouraging contracting economies to expand.

At the time the Nobel laureate, Joseph Stiglitz, was the Chief Economist of the World Bank and he spoke out repeatedly to highlight the fundamental error in the Fund's response to the Asian crisis.[27] The vast gulf separating Stiglitz's views from those of the IMF can be seen in two quotations. Stiglitz said that economic pain 'should contribute to strengthening the economy, not exacerbating economic downturns'. Michael Mussa, the IMF's economic counsellor, responded, 'Those who argue that monetary policy should have been eased rather than tightened in those economies are smoking something that is not entirely legal.'[28]

Stiglitz was proven right by later events, but when it mattered the most, the IMF disagreed with him. Subsequently the Reserve Bank of Australia approached the US Treasury to deliver essentially the same message: the fiscal policies of the Asian economies had been in the main conservative and prudent. This was a contractionary crisis, a crisis of confidence, and expansion was needed to stimulate these economies, not the higher interest rates and budget tightening being prescribed by the IMF.

The US Treasury took the message on board and managed to persuade the Fund that its diagnosis of the crisis was quite wrong. So about 15 months after the onset of the crisis, the IMF began to acquiesce to requests by national governments for more expansionary policy settings.[29] While the IMF eventually came around, the crisis was deepened by its initial misdiagnosis and considerable, otherwise avoidable, human suffering was the result. Furthermore, the IMF only altered its views to the extent of easing the austerity it had imposed. In the meantime, Malaysia had adopted more successful strategies that remain outside the Fund's kitbag of policy options.

13.4 MALAYSIA'S EXIT FROM THE ASIAN CRISIS

Malaysia refused IMF funding and advice in late 1997 and 1998 and chose to chart its own way out of the Asian crisis. The policies Malaysia eventually settled upon were in sharp contrast to the IMF's. Malaysia imposed capital outflow controls to keep foreign capital within the country, and pegged the ringgit to the US dollar.[30] Through these policies Malaysia was able to ease monetary policy and pursue expansionary fiscal policies, without being hampered by concerns about the impact on the exchange rate of capital outflows.[31] Suddenly Malaysia had created as close to a controlled laboratory experiment as one ever gets in economics. Thailand and Korea were seeking to exit the Asian Crisis using the Fund's policies, while Malaysia was charting an utterly different course. I leave Indonesia out of the analysis as its high debt levels means that the nature of its problems was quite different and proved to be of much longer duration.

All three economies recovered from the crisis, but Malaysia's recovery was more rapid, and its poor were harmed far less by its recovery policies than were the poor in countries following the IMF approach.[32] In the words of Kaplan and Rodrik, 'compared to IMF programs, we find that the Malaysian policies provided faster economic recovery . . . smaller declines in employment and real wages, and more rapid turn around in the stock market.'[33] Yet the IMF's mistakes in East Asia, so clearly highlighted by Malaysia's taking the road less travelled, paled in comparison to its more egregious errors in Argentina.

13.5 THE ARGENTINE CRISIS

To put Argentina's collapse in 2001 into perspective, we need to go back a decade. In 1991 Argentina was emerging from the aftermath of the debt crisis and fresh capital was flowing into the country. The years from 1991 to 1998 were prosperous. Argentina's economy performed strongly. GDP per capita increased 44 per cent in these eight years.[34] Inflation was completely under control.[35] Finally it seemed Argentina's time had come. It has always had a strong base for an economy: high literacy rates, the best educational system in Latin America and rich natural resources.[36] Now Argentina significantly improved its banking system, more than doubled its exports, privatized a broad range of industries, experienced significant growth in oil and mineral production and achieved record levels of agricultural and industrial output.[37] Argentina in the 1990s was a darling of the IMF and global financial markets. It was toasted as 'the best case of responsible leadership in the developing world'.[38]

Nonetheless at the end of 1998 Argentina entered a severe recession. The timing was dictated in part by external factors, in particular the 1997 Asian economic crisis and the August 1998 Russian crisis, which together severely limited capital flows to emerging markets economies. Argentina accordingly had very limited access to new capital to finance budget deficits and service its debt.[39] However, as with the debt crisis of 1982, external factors influenced the timing of the crisis, but were not its cause.[40] The causes were excessive borrowing to support general government expenditure, the peg of the peso to the US dollar, and Argentina's widespread and apparently endemic corruption.[41]

The recession was magnified by massive levels of capital flight, so much so that the government had to impose harsh caps on withdrawals from bank accounts, and eventually had to close the banks. Still the crisis deepened in late 2001 when the IMF refused to extend further credit to the nation, believing its economic programmes to be unsustainable. As commercial lenders followed this lead, Argentina was denied access to capital and defaulted on its external debt of some US$132 billion. In the year from March 2001 to March 2002, total domestic Argentine financial assets shrunk from US$126.8 billion to US$41.5 billion, according to Business Monitor International.[42] Nonetheless, Argentina was exceptionally resolute in its negotiations with its external creditors and refused to accept conventional levels of debt relief. President Kirchner maintained his refusal to service the debt from the 'suffering and hunger of the people'.[43] He had good grounds: Argentina's poverty rate, 27 per cent in 1999, had doubled by 2003 to 54.7 per cent; per capita GDP, US$7800 in 1999, had fallen by more than half by 2004 to $3800; and debt that represented 47.4 per cent of GDP in 1999, was 140 per cent of GDP in 2004.[44]

In the words of an article in *The Financial Times,* 'Argentina gambled, and the gamble paid off'.[45] In March 2005, 76 per cent of Argentina's creditors accepted its offer to exchange its debt for bonds at the unprecedented discount of some 66 per cent on a net present value basis. Argentina emerged from its default on the most advantageous terms ever secured by a middle-income country in a debt restructuring. The IMF emerged from Argentina's collapse with its credibility in tatters. Never before had a country that had so faithfully followed the Fund's policies collapsed so severely. Never before had the IMF's image been so badly damaged by a sovereign default.

In addition to these very public and profound policy errors of the IMF, there are more subtle practices and policy stances that, over decades, have severely damaged debtor nations in general and the poor in such nations in particular. Together, these practices and policies fall under the rubric of the socialization of private sector debt.

13.6 THE SOCIALIZATION OF PRIVATE SECTOR DEBT

One of the depressingly consistent themes of the aftermath of each of the three financial crises that have been considered here is the way that the common people of the debtor nations have in the end repaid substantial portions of the debt incurred by private corporations – a consequence which the IMF either engineered or to which it acquiesced. After the debt crisis broke in 1982 the creditors persuaded each nation to represent all debtors within its borders in the rescheduling negotiations and to do so by bringing all the debts of those debtors under its sovereign guarantee. The first step was necessary. The second was not.

Bringing all debts under the sovereign guarantee improved the security of the creditors – particularly of the creditors who had made most of the loans to private sector corporations – and these just happened to be the major lenders who were sitting on the creditor steering committees and orchestrating the process.[46] Bringing corporate debts under the sovereign guarantee also represented an utterly unjustifiable charge on the common people of these countries – these loans have been serviced by decades of higher taxes and lower social services.

Fifteen years later in Asia the nature of the crisis was quite different, but the resolution of it was the same – the poor in the debtor countries were shafted – this time by a process engineered by the IMF. The IMF organized bailouts of Indonesia, Thailand and Korea. While described as IMF bailouts of the countries, they were in fact long-term loans made on condition they be used to repay creditors.[47] These loans thus became debts of the nation and the bailouts were of the creditors, not the debtor nations at all.[48] It took four years before bailouts were generally understood to be a welfare system for Wall Street[49] as the funds flowed directly through to creditors.

To make matters worse the creditors with debts due typically held short-term bonds – and short-term debt is particularly destabilizing for developing countries. So the IMF bailouts encouraged precisely the type of debt that a stable system would discourage. The idea was that the nations would again take responsibility for the indebtedness of corporations incorporated in the nation, use the loans obtained in the bailout to pay off the foreign creditors, and later recover the debts from the corporate debtors. On average, the Indonesian government recovered some 28 per cent of the value of the loans it incurred on behalf of the banking sector.[50] The other 72 per cent became a charge on the Indonesian people. And these are large sums of money. The amount of the IMF bailout now represents some 29 per cent of the total sovereign indebtedness of Indonesia.[51]

After Argentina's economic implosion, the international financial community, with the assistance of a compliant Argentine government and the IMF, found two ways to socialize private indebtedness. The first is the familiar IMF bailout, in this case a massive US$40 billion loan to Argentina in late 2000, which was required to be used to repay a mix of public and corporate debt.[52] The second was a new way to achieve an old end: having the people repay corporate debts. This technique was known as 'pesofication'. Under pesofication, dollar-denominated bank loans and deposits were redenominated in pesos. Banks were required to convert their assets (such as loans) into pesos at a one-for-one rate and their liabilities (such as deposits) into pesos at a rate of 1.4 to 1. This generated huge losses for the banks for which the government sought to compensate them by a massive issue of government bonds of necessarily doubtful value.[53]

Thus the circle was completed in the usual way in such crises – the ultimate burden fell on the public purse. In the words of Pedro Pou, President of the Central Bank of Argentina until mid-2001, 'The government has transferred about 40% of private debt to workers . . . We are experiencing a mega-redistribution of wealth and income unprecedented in the history of the capitalist world.'[54]

To require the common people to repay private corporate debts, through increased taxes and reduced government services, is immoral. It is a massive interference with the market system that the IMF professes to support. In each of these crises, the market, through the mechanism of bankruptcy, would have allocated the costs of the poor lending and borrowing decisions upon the lenders and borrowers. The IMF, either as architect, or complicit partner, in each case allocated the costs of these poor credit decisions to parties who had nothing to do with them: the common people of the debtor nations.[55]

Given the failures of the IMF are manifold, whether the IMF should be allowed to continue depends upon whether it can reform itself sufficiently to become a positive force in the development of poor nations. In short, does the IMF have a track record of listening and responding constructively to criticism from within and without?

13.7   THE IMF'S ABILITY TO REINVENT ITSELF

Criticisms of the Fund's policy prescriptions have been sustained, fierce and unrelenting from the left ever since the early to mid 1980s, principally for the impact of its policies on the poor and because the Fund is seen, by the left, to be the handmaiden of the G7 nations in implementing their policies and those of their banking sectors. More recently, for the past 15 years or so, commentators from the right have joined battle in criticizing the Fund for having lost its mission, purpose and relevance. Commentators from both sides of politics and from developed and developing nations have argued for the Fund's fundamental re-conceptualization or closure.[56]

The Fund has done much to appear to respond to these criticisms. In 1999 it replaced the economic policies which it had been imposing upon developing nations in crisis, the so-called Structural Adjustment Policies (SAPs), with Poverty Reduction Strategy Papers (PRSP). PRSPs were to be a new tool for poverty reduction, debt relief, and access to funding from donors. According to the IMF, 'PRSPs are prepared by the member countries through a participatory process involving domestic stakeholders as well as external development partners, including the World Bank and the International Monetary Fund.'[57] PRSPs outline the economic, social and structural programmes to be used to reduce poverty.[58] Instead of focusing on macroeconomic stability and growth like SAPs, PRSPs, as their name suggests, were to put poverty reduction at the core of the nation's economic policies. Once approved, the PRSP forms the basis for future funding.[59] Potential recipients of debt relief under the Heavily Indebted Poor Country (HIPC) Initiative and the IMF's Poverty Reduction and Growth Facility (PRGF) are required to produce a PRSP to be eligible.[60]

However, the change from SAPs to PRSPs was more an effort to rescue the IMF from its crisis of legitimacy[61] than to respond to the needs of the poor in poor countries.[62] If programmes were truly national creatures, tailored to each individual nation's needs, one would expect some PRSPs to exhibit strategies that differ from the standard policy prescriptions of the past. But this is not the case – the PRSPs of virtually all countries are strikingly similar. The macroeconomic policies under PRSPs have essentially been a continuation of the policies under SAPs[63] and PRSPs don't contemplate alternative approaches to poverty reduction such as resource redistribution.[64]

In short, there has been a marked gap between IMF rhetoric and policies.[65] The clearest example of this is to be found in the IMF's policies in Africa.

13.8   THE IMPACT ON POVERTY OF IMF POLICIES IN AFRICA

In 2000, Michel Camdessus, the Fund's Managing Director said:

> [T]he greatest concern of our time is poverty . . . it is the ultimate systemic threat facing humanity. . . . If the poor are left hopeless, poverty will undermine the fabric of our societies through confrontation, violence, and civil disorder. We cannot afford to ignore poverty, wherever it exists, whether in the advanced countries, emerging economies, or the least developed nations. But it is in the poorest countries that extreme poverty can no longer be tolerated; it is our duty to work together to relieve suffering.[66]

The IMF has its own internal evaluation division, the Independent Evaluation Office (IEO), and in March 2007, it released an evaluation report, 'The IMF and Aid to Sub-Saharan Africa'.[67] The report concluded that there were different views among the Executive Board of the IMF about the IMF's role and policies in poor countries, and that 'lacking clarity on what they should do on the mobilization of aid . . . and the application of poverty and social impact analysis, IMF staff tended to focus on macroeconomic stability, in line with the institution's core mandate and their deeply ingrained professional culture.'[68]

In other words, some seven years after the Managing Director's speech cited above, seven years after the replacement of SAPs with PRSPs, seven years after the establishment of the Poverty Reduction and Growth Facility, IMF staff were unclear on the priority to be given to poverty reduction and how to achieve it, and so sought to attain that which they knew how to attain, macroeconomic stability. In the first year or two of the introduction of new priorities and programmes this would be understandable, though regrettable. After seven years this is ridiculous. For an institution that is the subject of unremitting criticism for the impact of its programmes and policies on poverty, and which has been maintaining steadfastly in all its press releases and public pronouncements since 2000 that poverty reduction is its highest priority, to still be trying to bed down new initiatives and priorities on poverty reduction over seven years after their introduction is utterly unacceptable. In most corporate or government settings, one would expect such non-performance to result in the sacking of senior staff.

The report also found that the IMF's policies have accommodated increased aid in countries whose recent policies have led to high stocks of reserves and low inflation, but in other countries additional aid was programmed to be saved to increase reserves or to retire domestic debt.[69] Yet virtually no sub-Saharan African countries have strong foreign exchange reserves and low inflation rates. So extra aid was routinely being channelled by the IMF into foreign exchange reserves or into the repayment of debt in most poor African countries. This is a perfect illustration of the damage that overly restrictive policy settings on inflation rates can do in developing countries. The obsession with the macroeconomic profile of the country denies much-needed resources to the poor. Such an approach has two flaws:

> It diverts extra aid away from healthcare, education or other social welfare expenditures;
> It risks being a 'self-fulfilling prophecy' as diverting aid flows into reserves and debt reduction is likely to dissuade donors from giving more aid.[70] Most donors want to give aid to assist suffering people directly, not to improve the macroeconomic profile of the nation in which they live.

This profound inability to implement its own priorities and policies gives rise to the question of whether the IMF can reform itself. When Malaysia was charting its own course out of the Asian crisis and imposing capital outflow controls, Michel Camdessus was Malaysia's sternest critic. In speech after speech around the world he admonished Malaysia in terms such as: 'investor confidence has been damaged by the capital controls, and some official sources of external finance have dried up. Neither source is likely to recover until the overall stance policies is modified.'[71]

The extraordinary feature of this episode is not that Camdessus was wrong; there has been nothing unusual about that at all in IMF's performance in the past 25 years. The extraordinary and laudable feature is that as quickly as 12 months after the Fund's Managing Director was delivering withering attacks on Malaysia's use of capital controls, members of the Fund's staff felt able to write a balanced and generally positive assessment of Malaysia's use of capital controls and to conclude that 'preliminary evidence suggests that the controls have been effective in realizing their intended objective of reducing the ringgit's internationalization and helping to contain capital outflows'.[72]

Furthermore, in the IMF's review of Malaysia's policies between 1997 and 2000, other staff members wrote that: 'Market assessment turned more positive, however, as it became clear that Malaysia's macroeconomic policies were not out of line, that the undervalued pegged exchange rate was contributing to the rapid recovery of exports and output, and that financial sector reforms were being vigorously pursued.'[73] And in yet another publication, the staff noted that the 'successful experience of the 1998 controls so far is largely due to the appropriate macroeconomic policy mix that prevailed at that time'[74] and that the controls were effective because they 'were wide ranging, effectively implemented, and generally supported by the business community'.[75]

So the IMF, through the work of its research department, has a proven capacity to be self-critical, a fundamental requirement for an organization's ability to learn from experience, change and adapt. The Fund enhanced this capacity in 2001 by establishing the Independent Evaluation Office. The IEO states that it is 'fully independent from the Management of the IMF and operates at arm's length from the Board of Executive Directors, representing the 185 member countries of the IMF.'[76] In its own words:

> The IEO's overarching mission is to improve the IMF's effectiveness by:
>
> - Enhancing the learning culture of the IMF and enabling it to better absorb lessons for improvements in its future work;
> - Helping build the IMF's external credibility by undertaking objective evaluations in a transparent manner;
> - Providing independent feedback to the Executive Board in its governance and oversight responsibilities over the IMF; and
> - Promoting greater understanding of the work of the IMF.[77]

Since its inception, the IEO has issued 25 evaluation reports.[78] Each has been an extensive, detailed, reasoned document, some more forthright and direct than others, but most tending to be relatively clear and critical in their findings. For example, the 'Summary of major findings, lessons and recommendations of the report on the evaluation of poverty reduction strategy papers and the poverty reduction growth facility', 6 July 2004,[79] states, *inter alia*, that:

> most PRSPs fall short of providing a strategic road map for policymaking, especially in the area of macroeconomic and related structural policies, [o]n balance, joint staff assessments do not perform adequately the many tasks expected of them, and [s]uccess in embedding the PGRF in the overall strategy for growth and poverty reduction has been limited in most cases – partly reflecting shortcomings in the strategies themselves.[80]

These are not the words of bureaucrats seeking to be coy or to obfuscate. These are honest assessments of the Fund's policies and achievements. The

IMF is able to accommodate within its research staff, and its IEO, officers who are sharply critical of its policies and performance, and yet somehow not modify its policies substantively in response to such criticisms. These honest and frank assessments have had almost no impact on altering the policies and culture of the IMF.

13.9 IMF ENTRENCHING RESISTANCE TO CHANGE IN THE INTERNATIONAL FINANCIAL SYSTEM

The anaemic regulatory responses to the global financial crisis (GFC) have proven the remarkable resistance of the global financial system to real change. Resistance to needed change is known in systems science as negative resilience. Resilience is the capacity of a system to withstand external shocks and regain its essential characteristics, its identity. Negative resilience is the capacity of a system to do this, even when the external shocks are because the system needs to reorganize itself and adopt a more functional identity. The global financial system is somewhat functional from the perspective of OECD nations and the international commercial banks, and quite dysfunctional from the perspective of developing countries. Yet it displays considerable negative resilience, in the sense of being highly resistant to required change.

The GFC has so far led to higher capital requirements particularly for trading, tighter liquidity controls, closer supervision and restrictions on bankers' bonuses, but none of these changes are fundamental. If one considers how profoundly different the global financial system is today from what it was 30 or 40 years ago, these changes are merely cosmetic. Even the macro-prudential regulatory function in which systemic risk across the financial system is to be assessed and monitored, which is to be carried out by institutions such as the new European Systemic Risk Board, is but a belated example of regulation beginning to catch up with market changes that are decades old.

The major change to the system as a result of the GFC has been the handover of economic coordinating authority from the G7 to the G20 nations. Comprising 19 nations and the European Union, the G20 represents 85 per cent of global GDP, 80 per cent of world trade, and two-thirds of the world's people. In addition to the G7 nations, it includes Brazil, China, India, Indonesia, Turkey, Australia, South Africa and others. This is an important change. Brazil, China and India not having a voice in economic policy coordination was becoming increasingly ridiculous.

So why is a system that for so many of its participants is deeply dysfunctional, so resilient? The answer lies in who the current system serves, and the general paucity of knowledge, outside those it serves, about how it works and its consequences. Resilience science teaches us that strongly resilient systems have strong feedback loops. This concept of feedback loops, developed in analysing systems, explains much of the resilience of our global financial system. The feedback loops in global financial governance are that the system tends to reward the international commercial banks and the elites in developing countries, at the expense of the common people in the debtor countries, and the IMF is central to engineering these outcomes. A few examples will suffice.

After the 1982 debt crisis, bringing all the debts incurred by entities in a nation, both public and private, under the sovereign guarantee, benefited the foreign commercial banks at the expense of the local people who paid for decades in higher taxes and reduced services so that the foreign banks could receive a free credit upgrade on most of their assets. Likewise in 1998 the IMF and foreign banks insisted Indonesia assume the obligations of the local banks to foreign lenders, and then recover the funds from the local banks. Yet there was no reason for Indonesia to assume responsibility for these loans. The market mechanism, if left to work, would have seen many of these Indonesian banks placed into bankruptcy by their Western creditors who would have received a proportion of their claims in the bankruptcy proceedings. Instead insolvent local banks were put into bankruptcy by Indonesia, the creditors were repaid in full, and the Indonesian people bore most of the cost of that repayment.

The funds to repay the creditors came from the long-term loans organized by the IMF and invariably described as bailouts of the debtor nations. Yet these loans were required to be used to repay outstanding indebtedness so the bailouts were of the foreign banks. In short, in Indonesia the IMF coordinated a restructuring that socialized massive amounts of private sector debt, and without the role of the IMF it is difficult to envisage how this could have been done, or at least, done without attracting the immediate opprobrium of civil society.[81]

Similarly, the centrepiece of the G20 response to the GFC in April 2009 was a US$500 billion additional credit facility for debtor nations. However, the conditions required to be eligible for these loans exclude virtually all African and most Latin American nations. While it is not apparent on the face of the conditions, they are carefully crafted so that most of these loans will go to their intended destination, East European countries. The German banks are heavily over-exposed to these countries. So this additional credit facility, in large measure, is designed to bail out the German banks.

The funds lent come from the G20 nations, which know they will be repaid. Official credit always is. The loss will fall on the people of these Eastern European nations who will labour under massive debt burdens for decades to come. Once again normal market processes, which in Eastern Europe would have led to German banks incurring large losses on their ill-judged, excessive lending to the region, are abrogated to prefer foreign banks at the direct expense of the people of the poorer nations.

The entire practice of IMF-organized bailouts is problematic. Consider the rescue package put in place in 2010 for Greece which will allow Greece to repay debts due to commercial banks. The net effect of this arrangement has been to replace Greek sovereign debt owed to commercial banks with a Greek sovereign loan owed to the IMF, Germany, France and other nations. When the debt was owed to commercial banks, defaulting on it was a real option, and for this risk the commercial banks had received higher interest rates reflecting Greece's creditworthiness. Now that the debt is owed to official creditors, defaulting on it will have far more serious ramifications for Greece, and is a far less palatable option. The Greek bailout therefore greatly benefited the banks of the creditor nations, principally Germany and France.

If the IMF really believes in the efficiency of markets, it could have insisted the Greek rescue package be structured in a way that did not create moral hazard and that actually would have offered a real prospect to Greece to work its way out of its current problems. (In my view, the severe austerity measures imposed on Greece as part of the rescue package severely imperil its long-term solvency). The correct way to structure the rescue package, given that it is in essence a rescue of the commercial bank lenders to Greece, would have been to make the package available provided the lenders agreed to take a certain haircut on the debt owing to them, such discount to be calculated by reference to Greece's realistic longer-term capacity to service its debt. So, for instance, and plucking figures from the ether, the IMF could have said to the banks – we will lend the funds to Greece and require they use them to discharge their debts to you, provided you reduce those debts by 40 per cent. If you will accept 60 per cent of the face value in full satisfaction, your loans will be repaid. If you won't, then the funding won't be forthcoming, and you can take your chances with Greece and its capacity to service the loans you made to it.

Of course this was not done because the political reason for the package was more to rescue the euro than Greece, and this approach would have put at risk the continued viability of the euro, or at the least the participation of Greece, Spain and Portugal in the eurozone. The benefits of our system of global financial governance to the commercial banks are thus manifestly clear. The market is given full rein when yielding large profits to the banks, but is interfered with when it would yield large losses. The benefits to the elites in developing countries are far less obvious, but are often very substantial, and are the reason that voices well placed to argue against the current system are rarely raised against it.

An example is in the restructuring of Indonesia's indebtedness after the Asian crisis. When the assets of the insolvent local banks were sold, who was best placed to bid for those assets? Who knew everything about the assets and precisely what they were worth? The families that had owned them, and that had been the principal shareholders of the banks, that is who. So in effect, these families were able to regain control of the assets they had owned before the crisis, with their foreign debts discharged by their government, all for an average cost of 28 per cent. Who would speak out against such extraordinary largesse? Would you if, somehow, you could repay your home mortgage for a quarter of the debt owing? Our system of financial governance neatly transferred the real cost of the crisis, which should have been borne by borrowers and lenders that had engaged in imprudent borrowing and lending, onto the people of the debtor nations, who had done nothing.

As Professor Luis Carlos Bresser Pereria, former Finance Minister of Brazil, testified before a US House Committee in the aftermath of the debt crisis, the elites in the debtor nations often profited from that crisis.[82] Periods of great volatility and forced asset sales offer huge opportunities to those with access to better information, power, and financial resources. Overall the system of global financial governance has displayed a quite remarkable degree of resilience. When one analyses who it serves, this is unsurprising. Any system that rewards the powerful at the expense of the powerless is likely to prosper and the IMF stands at the centre of this system.

The IMF performed the new role it took on in the 1980s poorly, which is unsurprising, as it was neither staffed nor resourced for the role. Yet it has continued to fulfil the function, with substantially unchanged policies, for nearly three decades. Over time, as its litany of policy failures began to mount, the Fund attracted sustained, unrelenting criticism from both sides of politics in the US and from developing countries, and it was allowed to shrink in size from a total staff approaching 3000 to about 1700.[83]

Yet, again, in 2009, another crisis rescued the Fund. The GFC meant the G20 needed an organization through which it could channel most of its US$1.1 trillion funding package, a bill the IMF fitted. And so, today, the credibility of the IMF has been somewhat restored by having a new role, and its staffing levels are again climbing. So why do the normal checks and balances of democratic systems not rein in and redirect the system of global financial governance if it so often implements ends that serve the rich at the expense of the poor? Part of the answer is that voters in rich countries cannot understand how international finance works, and care far less about the problems of people in poor countries than they do about their own backyards. This lack of understanding is promoted by the media, which does a poor job of covering global financial governance. The media typically focuses on the most recent development, and reports it, shorn of context. Its coverage is often inaccurate, promoted by the closeness with which information is guarded in this sector. The poverty of the media coverage means the powerful can continue to use the system in ways that suit them free from countervailing pressures from civil society and democratic voters.

So if the system exhibits such strong negative resilience, how might that resilience be lessened so that needed changes come about? The need for reform of the governance of the IMF through reforming the voting right entitlements of its members has long been widely recognized, and was acted upon in 2010 at the behest of the G20. The IMF's Board of Executive Directors approved the transfer of over 6 per cent of quotas from advanced economies to emerging and developing countries. The BRICs (Brazil, Russia, India and China) now have 14.17 per cent, close to the 15 per cent needed to exercise a veto. Europe's shares dropped. The voting power of Belgium, Britain, France, the Netherlands and Switzerland declined, while the US share fell marginally from 17.67 per cent to 17.41 per cent.[84] These reforms are better than nothing, yet the critical issue is that the US retains its veto and remains the country with the greatest power in the IMF, and the BRICs fall marginally short, even acting in concert, of being able to exercise the same veto power.

So these small changes would not shift the fundamental balance of power in the IMF. The principal clients of these institutions need a real voice in their governance. The European nations, in particular, remain overrepresented on the IMF and World Bank, as they are in the G20. A full-quarter of the seats on the G20 go to Europe: those of Britain, France, Germany, Italy and the EU. This is ridiculous. Europe desperately needs to provide real leadership on these issues.

Yet in the absence of transformative leadership on voting rights, the issue becomes how to reform the culture and belief system of the Fund. This is a major challenge as organizational cultures are formed over long periods of time, and are often resistant to change. The initial step that needs to be taken is to return the IMF to its original mandate, or what is left of its original mandate. The IMF is the wrong organization to set economic policy for nations in crisis and it should be removed from this role. If an international financial institution is required to play this role, a new one, with the right skills set, attitudes and culture needs to be established. This change would limit the IMF to data collection, technical surveillance and advice-giving roles.

The second step is to reduce negative resilience, or resistance to change, by diminishing the strength of the current feedback loops. The best way to do this is to make the system more fair and balanced, and to do this we also need to take the IMF out of its policy prescription role. History tells us nothing less than this will suffice. The strength of the feedback loops arises because of the degree to which the system currently favour the powerful among banks and within developing nations, and the IMF is invariably the instrument through which those preferences are effected.

13.10   CONCLUSION

Why, and how, could the IMF staff have been unsure throughout the last decade of the priority to be afforded to poverty reduction in Africa, when poverty reduction was at the centre of the Fund's policies and rhetoric? Why did the staff revert to structural adjustment because it was what they knew best? Why is an organization unable to learn and adapt when its staff have sufficient intellectual freedom to adopt positions in direct opposition to those recently taken by their Managing Director and its internal evaluation office regularly critiques its performance in honest, unflattering terms? In short, how can this organization be so unable to reform itself?

The reason the IMF cannot reinvent itself is that it is a fundamentalist organization. At core it is no different, really, from a fundamentalist church of any faith. Officers who subscribe to its dogma are promoted; those that question the prevailing faith are not. This explains why in Africa the IMF could promote the privatization of healthcare provision, and impose salary caps upon expenditure by government on healthcare, because the IMF officers involved really believe that the private sector will deliver better healthcare than the public sector. This is notwithstanding that all the evidence indicates that privatization of healthcare in poor countries results in good, albeit expensive, care for middle class urban residents, and virtually no care for the urban poor and for people in rural or remote communities.

This explains why the IMF could divert foreign aid designated for healthcare or education in Africa into foreign exchange reserves or debt reduction, because the officers involved genuinely believed that an improved macroeconomic profile would mean more to the poor, in the medium term, than healthcare or education for their children. This explains why the IMF could agree with Argentina maintaining the rigid peg of the peso to the dollar when there was no way the Argentine economy could remain as competitive as that of the US over time, because the officers genuinely believed inflation was the number one enemy to be fought.

Fund officers who subscribe to this worldview get promoted, those who do not languish in minor roles. The leadership of the Fund hires in its own image and promotes in its own image, as do most organizations. In this case, however, the core belief of the organization is fundamentalist and disconnected from reality.

None of this would matter so much if the Fund's role was continuing to shrink, as it did for much of 2000 to 2008, when more and more developing countries simply refused to borrow from it and accept the policy prescriptions which accompanied the loans, and if the Fund's staff was continuing to shrink, as it did in those years. But the role of the Fund has been expanded greatly by the need to respond to the GFC, and its staffing numbers, which had fallen precipitately in the preceding decade, are now growing as strongly as before they declined.

The Fund's recent rhetoric has been that it has learned from its errors and has revised its policies so that there is now considerable scope for developing nations to adopt counter cyclical and expansionary policies. And it is true that at the height of the recent crisis some countries were permitted to run moderately expansionary policy settings – at the same time that most OECD nations were enacting aggressively expansionary stimulus packages. However, by 2010 the IMF's deeply ingrained beliefs were reasserting themselves and pro-cyclical contractionary policies were once again the norm. A study by scholars from the School of Oriental and African Studies (SOAS) in April 2010 found that in the 13 IMF agreements with poorer nations that they selected as a representative sample, in 2009 allowed fiscal expansion was on average 1.5 per cent of GDP, but for 2010 the average was a contraction of 0.5 per cent of GDP.[85] A study by Oxfam in July 2010 found that half of African countries and three-quarters of other developing nations with IMF programmes in place are being required to reduce spending in 2010, precisely when expansionary policy settings are needed to offset reduced export revenues due to the GFC.[86]

The new US$500 million Flexible Credit Line was promoted as if it would provide the funding to allow developing nations to pursue countercyclical expansionary policy settings in response to the GFC. However, to be eligible for this credit countries must fulfil a number of harsh IMF criteria that in effect disqualify virtually all of the poorer nations from using it. As at late 2010 only three nations had drawn upon this line of credit, Colombia, Mexico and Poland, hardly among the poorer of the poor. In light of this restricted take-up, and at the urging of the G20 2010 co-chair, South Korea, in September 2010 the Fund reduced the severity of the entry conditions for access to the credit, but not profoundly.

In summary, the IMF's policy stance has remained essentially unchanged throughout the GFC, and its belief in markets appears undimmed by the largest financial crisis in 80 years. So the job of changing the animating beliefs of the Fund remains before us. The recent reforms to the voting and membership shares in the Fund in favour of developing countries are a small step in the right direction but are too minor to have a substantial effect.

One of the Fund's essential difficulties lies in the narrow backgrounds of its staff. The World Bank, to fulfil its remit, employs economists and finance professionals, but it also employs engineers and scientists of all kinds, and experts in social policy, development and many other fields. This diverse mix of people gives rise to strong debates within the Bank which have assisted in the Bank reassessing its roles and how it might best fulfil them in any given situation. The Fund, on the other hand, draws its staff from essentially two sources: national central banks and PhD programmes in macroeconomics (and even then the graduates of certain faculties are much preferred over those from other, more liberal, faculties). Yet the skill set and attitudes required to be successful in a central bank are utterly different from those required to redirect and turn around the economy of a failing nation. In the corporate world, technocrats who are effective in highly structured corporations rarely, if ever, have the entrepreneurial zeal and instincts that characterize corporate turnaround merchants, those people who make careers out of rescuing failing companies. Why should we expect this to be any different at all at the sovereign level?

As long ago as the 1990s, Walter Wriston, the former Chair of Citibank, said, 'If [the IMF] weren't around, countries would be better off because once the IMF got into the business of advising governments on policy it created more trouble than it cured.'[87] This is unsurprising, as the IMF was never intended to advise governments on policy generally. Its original remit was exchange rate policy. Its staffing profile made perfect sense given its original role. Yet its role has changed, utterly, while its staff profile, and even more importantly, the prevailing mindset and perspectives of the organization, remain unchanged. This is the core challenge in reforming the IMF and it is going to require visionary and strong leadership, over a sustained period of time, if true reform is ever going to be achieved. Fundamentalist organizations are tremendously difficult to reform.

NOTES

1. IMF Website, available at <http://www.imf.org/external/about.htm>, accessed on 6 November 2009.

2. Walter Wriston, quoted in 'The day after default', available at <http://www.bradynet.com/bbs/bradybonds/100110-0.html>, accessed on 6 November 2009.
3. But only at the cost of resentment from within the debtor nations: remarks of Lee C. Buchheit, 'Comity, act of state, and the international debt crisis: is there an emerging legal equivalent of bankruptcy protection for nations?', *Proceedings*, Seventy-Ninth Annual Meeting, The American Society of International Law, 126, p. 135.
4. Duncan Green, *Silent Revolution – The Rise of Market Economics in Latin America* (London: Cassell, 1995) pp. 36–7; and Rory MacMillan, 'The next sovereign debt crisis', (1995) 31 *Stanford Journal of International Law*, **31**, pp. 320–21.
5. MacMillan, ibid., p. 320.
6. See Green, op. cit., p. 11.
7. See Susan George, *A Fate Worse than Debt* (London: Penguin Books Ltd, 1987); Susan George and Fabrizio Sabelli, *Faith and Credit: The World Bank's Secular Empire* (London: Penguin Books Ltd, 1994); and Walden Bello, *Dark Victory: The United States, Structural Adjustment and Global Poverty* (London: Pluto Press, 1994).
8. Statement by Rimmer de Vries, Senior Vice President, Morgan Guaranty Trust Company, before the Subcommittee on International Economic Policy of the Senate Foreign Relations Committee, Washington, DC, 19 January 1983 (reprinted in *World Financial Markets*, February 1983, p. 9).
9. The cooperation of debtors with the IMF was indeed fruitful, for the banks: Carlos Marichal, *A Century of Debt Crises in Latin America* (Princeton, NJ: Princeton University Press, 1989) p. 235. Adherence to IMF austerity programmes permitted continued servicing of the debt so that by the end of the decade, the banks were in a much stronger state than in 1983 and the debtor nations in a worse state.
10. Between 1982 and year-end 1988, the nine largest US commercial banks nearly doubled their capital from $29 billion in 1982 to $55.8 billion in 1988, with the result that the ratio of the exposure of these nine banks to Latin America to their capital decreased from 176.5 per cent to 83.6 per cent over the same period. See Atsushi Masuda, 'Mexico's debt reduction agreement and the new debt strategy', (July 1991) 11(1) *EXIM Review* 26, pp. 36–7. In 1983 and 1984 they were certainly in no position to stop advancing fresh funds to Latin American debtors, because their capital was less than their exposure to the region.
11. Hossein Askari, *Third World Debt and Financial Innovation: The Experiences of Chile and Mexico* (Paris: Development Centre of the OECD, 1991) p. 21; Esther W. Hannan and Edward L. Hudgins, 'A US strategy for Latin America's debts,' *The Backgrounder*, No. 502, 7 April 1986 (Washington, DC: The Heritage Foundation) p. 4.
12. Askari, op. cit., p. 22; and David Suratgar, 'The international financial system and the management of the international debt crisis', in Daniel D. Bradlow (ed.), Chapter 18 in *International Borrowing: Negotiating and Structuring International Debt Transactions* (Washington, DC: International Law Institute, 1986), p. 494.
13. Green, op. cit., pp. 45–6; and Hannon and Hudgins, op. cit., pp. 4–5.
14. Hannon and Hudgins, op. cit., pp. 4–5.
15. Bello, op. cit.; George, op. cit.; Green, op. cit., pp. 90–111 and 130–38 (Green entitled his chapter on the IMF and the World Bank, 'poverty brokers', pp. 32 et seq); and Wade Mansell, 'Legal aspects of international debt', (1991) 18(4) *Journal of Law and Society* 381 pp. 388–90.
16. Jorge G. Castenada, *Utopia Unarmed* (New York: Alfred A Knopf, 1993), p. 464.
17. John K. Galbraith, *The Culture of Contentment* (Boston: Houghton Mifflin, 1992), p. 46.
18. George, op. cit.
19. Eduard R. Bos (ed.), *Disease and Mortality in Sub-Saharan Africa* (2nd edn) (Herndon, VA, USA: The World Bank, 2006), p. 12.
20. Hal S. Scott, 'A bankruptcy procedure for sovereign debtors?', (2003) 37 *The International Lawyer* 103, p. 115.
21. Sebastian Edwards, 'The International Monetary Fund and the developing countries: a critical evaluation' (Working Paper No 2909, National Bureau of Economic Research, 1990).

22. Ross P. Buckley, 'Turning loans into bonds: lessons for East Asia from the Latin American Brady Plan', (2004) 1(1) *Journal of Restructuring Finance* 185.
23. Ibid.
24. Laurence H. Meyer, *Lessons from the Asian Crisis: A Central Banker's Perspective* (Working Paper No. 276, Levy Economics Institute, August 1999).
25. World Bank, *Global Development Finance 1998*, vol 1, pp. 4, 30.
26. With the exception of Indonesia which was overly indebted and experienced a more traditional debt crisis. For more on the Asian crisis, see Ross P. Buckley, 'An oft-ignored perspective on the Asian economic crisis: the role of creditors and investors', (2000) 15 *Banking and Finance Law Review* 431.
27. Peter Passell, 'Critics: the IMF is misguided. Skeptics: too much rot in Asia', *The New York Times*, 15 January 1998, p. D2; and 'World Bank's Stiglitz criticises IMF on S. Korea', *Reuters News*, 17 March 1998.
28. Eduardo Lachica, 'IMF- World Bank: rethinking the Global Financial System – oh, brother: World Bank, IMF jockey for position', *The Asian Wall Street Journal*, 5 October 1998, p. 13.
29. 'A new realism?', *The Straits Times*, 25 July 1998.
30. Ross P. Buckley and Sarala Fitzgerald, 'An assessment of Malaysia's response to the IMF during the Asian economic crisis', (2004) *Singapore Journal of Legal Studies* 96.
31. International Monetary Fund, *Malaysia: Recent Economic Developments* (1999), p. 16.
32. Buckley and Fitzgerald, op. cit.
33. Ethan Kaplan and Dani Rodrik, 'Did the Malaysian capital controls work?' (Working Paper No. 8142, National Bureau of Economic Research, 2001).
34. Miguel Kiguel, 'Structural reforms in Argentina: success or failure?', (Summer 2002) XLIV No. 2 *Comparative Economic Studies* 83, p. 84; percentage calculated from Figure 1. There was a brief hiatus in the growth during 1995 in response to the Tequila effect: the contagion from Mexico's crisis in late 1994 and early 1995: pp. 94–5.
35. Ibid.
36. Sophie Arie, 'Rich Argentina tastes hunger', *The Observer*, 19 May 2002. In the 1930s, on the back of strong beef and grain exports, per capita income in Argentina was on a par with that in France.
37. Kiguel, op. cit., pp. 100–101. This is not to suggest that many of the privatizations were not deeply problematic. It is always a profound challenge to realize appropriate prices for the privatization of major businesses and assets in emerging markets nations because the range of potential purchasers is not wide and because of the risk of very favourable prices for well-connected purchasers. The scrupulous and rigorous public accountability procedures that would mitigate against the latter risk are rarely present. There is much to suggest that many of the privatizations of the 1990s in Argentina were at a deep undervalue.
38. 'Chaos in Argentina', *The Nation*, 21 January 2002, 3; 'Argentina: a poster child for the failure of liberalized policies? Interview with Lance Taylor', *Challenge*, November–December 2001, p. 28.
39. Kiguel, op. cit.
40. Ross P. Buckley, *Emerging Markets Debt: an analysis of the secondary Market*, (London: Kluwer Law International, 1999), p. 21.
41. Ross P. Buckley, 'Do cry for the Argentines: an analysis of their crisis', (2003) 17 *Banking & Finance Law Review* 373.
42. Business Monitor International, *Economic Outlook, Argentina Quarterly Forecast Report, 2002*.
43. 'Argentina and the IMF: which is the victim?' *The Economist*, 4 March 2004, available at <http://www.economist.com.hk/displayStory.cfm?story_id=2482323>, accessed on 6 November 2009.
44. J.F. Hornbeck, *Argentina's Sovereign Debt Restructuring*, CRS Report for Congress, October 2004.

45. 'Argentina sets a dangerous precedent: The IMF should set tough conditions for further lending', *The Financial Times*, 7 March 2005, p. 20.
46. Buckley, op. cit, p. 43.
47. Jared Levinson, 'Living dangerously: Indonesia and the reality of the global economic system', (1998) 7 *Journal of International Law & Practice* 425, pp. 437–41, 446.
48. Charles W. Calomiris and Allan H. Meltzer, 'Fixing the IMF', (Summer 1999) 56 *The National Interest* 88.
49. In the words of a senior G7 official, quoted in Charlotte Denny, 'IMF sheds no tears for Argentina', *The Guardian*, 29 April 2002.
50. Asian Development Bank, *Asian Development Outlook 2004: II. Economic Trends and Prospects in Developing Asia: Southeast Asia*, available at <www.adb.org/Documents/books/ADO/2004/ino.asp>, accessed 6 November 2009.
51. Indonesia's total sovereign debt is estimated to be US$147.6 billion and the bailout was for US$43 billion: Central Intelligence Agency, *The World Factbook – Indonesia*, available at <https://www.cia.gov/library/publications/the-world-factbook/geos/id.html>, accessed 15 August 2008; and Tubagus Feridhanusetyawan, 'Escaping the debt trap', in *Governance in Indonesia: Challenges Facing the Megawati Presidency*, Hadi Soesastro, Anthony L. Smith and Han Mui Ling (eds) (Singapore: Institute of Southeast Asian Studies, 2003) p. 236.
52. Eric Hershberg, 'Why Argentina crashed – and is still crashing?', (July/August 2002) 36 *NACLA Report on the Americas* 30, p. 32.
53. Andres Gaudin, 'Thirteen days that shook Argentina – and now what?', (March/April, 2002) 35 *NACLA Report on the Americas* 6; and 'Latin banks: eyes on Brazil', (19 August 2002) 8(18) *Emerging Markets Monitor* 12.
54. As cited in Gaudin, id.
55. See generally Ross P. Buckley, 'The fatal flaw in international finance: the rich borrow and the poor repay', (Winter 2002/03) XIX (4) *World Policy Journal* 59–64.
56. Desmond Lachman, Allan Meltzer, Charles Calomiris, 'Is the IMF obsolete?', American Enterprise Institute for Public Policy Research, 18 May 2007, available at <http://www.aei.org/publications/filter.all,pubID.26202/pub_detail.asp>; Charles W. Calomiris, 'How to invent a new IMF', Hoover Institution Public Policy Inquiry, IMF Reform Proposals, available at <http://www.imfsite.org/reform/calomiris2.html>; George P. Schultz, William E. Simon and Walter B. Wriston, 'Who needs the IMF?' *The Wall Street Journal*, 3 February 1998; Alan Walters, *Do We Need the IMF and the World Bank?* (London: Institute of Economic Affairs, 1994); Steve H. Hanke, 'Abolish the IMF' *Forbes*, 13 April 2000; Anna J. Schwartz, 'Time to terminate the ESF and the IMF' (1998) 48 *Cato Foreign Policy Briefing*; George P. Shultz, 'Merge the IMF and World Bank', (1998) 12(1) *International Economy*, p. 14; James Burnham, 'The IMF and World Bank: time to merge', (1999) 22(2) *Washington Quarterly* 101; and Lindley H. Clark Jr., 'Speaking of business: let's merge the World Bank and the IMF', *The Wall Street Journal*, 4 January 1990, p. A12.
57. International Monetary Fund, *Poverty Reduction Strategy Papers* (2007), available at <http://www.imf.org/external/np/prsp/prsp.asp>, accessed 6 November 2009.
58. Frances Stewart and Michael Wang, 'Do PRSPs empower poor countries and disempower the World Bank, or is it the other way round?' (Working Paper No. 108, QEH, October 2003), p. 4.
59. Diana Sanchez and Katherine Cash, 'Reducing poverty or repeating mistakes? A civil society critique of poverty reduction strategy papers', (Church of Sweden Aid, Diakonia, Save the Children Sweden and the Swedish Jubilee Network, December 2003), p. 13.
60. Stewart and Wang, op. cit, p. 5.
61. George Dor, 'G8, Tony Blair's commission for Africa and debt' (7 July 2005) *Global Policy Forum*, p. 1.
62. Dr. Ebrahim M. Samba, 'African healthcare systems: what went wrong' *Healthcare News*, 8 December 2004, p. 3.

63. Ricardo Gottschalk, 'The macroeconomic policy content of the PRSPs: how much pro-growth, how much pro-poor?' (The Institute of Development Studies, University of Sussex, February 2004), p. 3.
64. Stewart and Wang, op. cit., p. 19.
65. In the context of aid to Africa, this gap was noted by the Independent Evaluation Office of the IMF in Independent Evaluation Office of the IMF, 'The IMF and aid to sub-Saharan Africa' (2007), available at <http://www.imf.org/external/np/ieo/2007/ssa/eng/pdf/report.pdf>, accessed 6 November 2009.
66. Michel Camdessus, address at the Tenth UN Conference on Trade and Development, Bangkok, Thailand, 13 February 2000.
67. Independent Evaluation Office of the IMF, op. cit.
68. Foreword by Thomas A. Bernes, Director, IEO, op. cit.
69. IEO, ibid., p. 32.
70. Eurodad, *PRS Watch: A Eurodad Newsletter*, 16 August 2007.
71. Michel Camdessus, 'Economic and financial situation in Asia: latest developments', paper delivered to the Asia Europe Finance Ministers Meeting, Frankfurt, Germany, 16 January 1999, available at <http://www.imf.org/external/np/speeches/1999/011699.htm>.
72. Akira Ariyoshi, Karl Habermeier, Bernard Laurens, InciOtker-Robe, Jorge Iván Canales-Kriljenko and Andrei Kirilenko, 'Country experiences with the use and liberalization of capital controls', (occasional paper No. 190, IMF, May 2000), Appendix III – 'Malaysia's experience with the use of capital controls', pp. 104–105, available at <http://www.imf.org/external/pubs/ft/op/op190/index.htm>.
73. Kanitta Meesook, Il Houng Lee, Olin Liu, Yougesh Khatri, Natalia Tamirisa, Michael Moore and Mark Krysl, 'Malaysia: from crisis to recovery' (occasional paper No. 207, IMF, August 2001), p. 3, available at <http://www.imf.org/external/pubs/nft/op/207/index.htm>.
74. Ibid., p. 6.
75. International Monetary Fund, 'Malaysia: selected issues' (Staff Country Report No. 99/86, IMF, August 1999), p. 18, available at <http://www.imf.org/external/pubs/ft/scr/1999/cr9986.pdf>, accessed 12 December 2010.
76. See homepage of the Independent Evaluation Office, available at <http://www.ieo-imf.org/about/>.
77. See IEO Mission and Values page, available at<http://www.ieo-imf.org/about/mission.html>.
78. See Independent Evaluation Office of the IMF, 'IEO publications', available at <http://www.imf.org/external/np/ieo/pap.asp#1>.
79. Available at <http://www.ieo-imf.org/eval/complete/eval_07062004.html>.
80. Available at <http://www.ieo-imf.org/eval/complete/pdf/0762004/summary.pdf>.
81. Buckley, op. cit.
82. Luiz Carlos Bresser Pereira, 'Solving the debt crisis: debt relief and adjustment', statement delivered before the House Committee on Banking, Finance and Urban Affairs hearings on the 'Lesser Developed Countries' Debt Crisis', 101st Congress First Session, Washington DC, 5 January 1989, available at <http://www.rep.org/br/pdf/38-10.pdf>, accessed 6 November 2009.
83. S. Vines and C. Gilbert, *The IMF and its Critics: Reform of Global Financial Architecture* (Cambridge: Cambridge University Press, 2004); Allan H. Meltzer, *Report of the International Financial Institution Advisory Commission*, United States House of Representatives, Washington DC, March 2000, available at <http://www.house.gov/jec/imf/meltzer.pdf>.
84. B.S. Klapper, 'IMF: China, India, emerging powers become "major players" with enhanced voting rights', *Associated Press*, 6 November 2010; Liu Lina, 'Roundup: IMF board approves historic reforms', *Xinhua News Agency*, 6 November 2010.
85. Elisa Van Waeyenberge, Hannah Bargawi and Terry McKinley, 'Standing in the way of development?: a critical survey of the IMF's crisis response in low income countries',

(A Eurodad and Third World Network Report in cooperation with the Heinrich Böll Foundation, April 2010), p. 6.
86. Katerina Kyrili and Matthew Martin, 'The impact of the global economic crisis on the budgets of low-income countries', (Research Report for Oxfam, July 2010), p. 4.
87. Walter Wriston, quoted in 'The day after default', available at <http://www.bradynet.com/bbs/bradybonds/100110-0.html>, accessed 6 November 2009.

14. When history is ignored, business black swans and the use and abuse of a notion

Graeme Dean and Frank Clarke

14.1 WHEN HISTORY IS IGNORED

Historical enquiry reveals how ideas mutate. This account of the ideas underpinning how fair value accounting (FVA) drifted into corporate financial reporting shows that a primary lesson of business history is that we ignore history at our peril. Frequently we encourage the recall of history for possibly the wrong reason – to supposedly 'learn lessons' regarding what we might or might not repeat. It might be more fruitful to use history to gain insight into the development of the ideas (good and bad) that delivered us to where we are today.

The case of fair value is shown to have drifted from the basis for a specific-purpose calculation into a general application in accounting statements of financial position and financial performance. The mark-to-market dispute during the current global financial crisis has nurtured further mutation of its FVA predecessor. What originally arose as an attempt to disclose a present financial state or condition, is being denied by many in the name of the alleged virtue of hiding it. Doing so contradicts what history tells us has been the focus from when fair value accidentally 'drifted' into the accounting for adaptive companies. Our analysis also highlights the theme of the historical enquiry, which shows aptly how accounting is conducive to politicization – an easy victim of interested parties' special pleading, corrupting its technology function primarily because it is inconvenient to have accounting data *tell it how it is*.

14.1.1 Business Black Swans and the Use and Abuse of a Notion

Through [this system's] workings during the last twenty years there has grown in this country a set of colossal corporations in which unmeasured success and continued immunity from punishment have bred an insolent disregard of the law, of common morality, and of the public and private right, together with a

214

grim determination to hold on to, at all hazards, the great possessions they have gulped or captured. It is the same system that has taken from millions of our people billions of dollars . . .

The above extract sounds like perceptions surrounding the rise and fall of Australia's One.Tel or HIH, Allco, Centro, Opes Prime. Perhaps it brings to mind ABC Learning, Timbercorp, Great Southern, too, all in Australia? Then again, it equally sounds as if it pertains to the US's Enron, or WorldCom, or Bernie Madoff's investment fraud, Bear Stearns' rise and fall, or Lehman Brothers before and after it cratered, or to the financial dilemmas at AIG. It could easily pass as a description of the aftermath of recent financial dilemmas at Northern Rock or HSBC in the UK, or of the banks in bankrupt Iceland, or the 2008 collapses of several German *Landesbanks*, or to Iceland's fall from prosperity.

But, it refers to none of them! A disgruntled Thomas Lawson penned it over a hundred years ago in his *Frenzied Finance* (1905) to describe the robber barons' alleged crime against his mining company, Amalgamated Copper. Therein lies the primary lesson of business history – that, in a broad sense, very little has really changed. The annals of finance across many countries are replete with perceptions by financial observers that poor financial management and misleading accounting have slain thousands of companies. We ignore this aspect of business history at our peril. But we frequently encourage its recall for possibly the wrong reason – to supposedly *learn lessons* regarding what we might or might not repeat, rather than to gain insight into how the ideas (good and bad) delivered us to where we are.

In this chapter, we provide a well-argued and evidenced-based discussion on the importance of consistent standards as a tool for good governance. This is done first by showing in sections 14.2 and 14.3 how historical lessons get ignored. In section 14.4 we discuss the adoption of the mark-to-market principle and how it distorts measurement. The difficult task of explaining what caused the crisis is attempted also in section 14.4.

14.2   WHEN BUSINESS HISTORY IS IGNORED

Niall Ferguson, in his *Ascent of Money* (2008), noted (p. 392) that, whereas the well-known academic 'quants' Myron Scholes and Robert Merton, whose reasoning it is claimed underpinned the 1990s operations of the infamous Long Term Capital Management (LTCM), knew a lot about mathematics, they recalled little of history.[1] Paul Krugman's (2008)

Return to Depression Economics and the Crisis of 2008 makes similar observations. The implication is that, had market participants been familiar with business history, they may have been less willing to bet on nothing swanning in, unexpectedly, to wreck their fun. Nassim Taleb's black swan imagery (in *The Black Swan: The Impact of the Highly Improbable*, 2007) aptly illustrates that whilst events are unique per se, they nonetheless occur with an annoying frequency. Unique events such as: the Russian currency default that scuttled LTCM's progress, or the 1995 Kobe earthquake that rocked Nick Leeson's possible rehabilitation of his otherwise wrecking of Barings Bank, the 2001 terrorist attack on the New York Twin Towers and its unforeseen impact on commerce generally, the surprise court decision ruling that asbestos disease victims were covered by ordinary industrial policies in the US, and the 'one in a million' late-1990s Newcastle (New South Wales, Australia) earthquake that brought Lloyds' syndicates to their knees, nonetheless occur frequently. Indeed, much too often for 'the unlikely' to be ignored, and not factored somehow into decision-making, assessments and evaluations. Taleb and Spitznagel (2009) reason that the US bailout packages likewise draw upon reasoning that ignores the inevitability of the otherwise thought to be highly improbable.

In that sense, it is critical to observe from business history that unexpected events *do* occur, and that though each is characteristically a *one off*, they occur with a disturbing frequency, and often have common features. For, just as the GFC liquidity tightening created the run on Bernie Madoff's fund in 2008, which exposed his fraud and brought him down, so did a similar liquidity crisis in 1932 bring the international 'Match King', Ivar Kreuger down.[2] And, whereas the crash of 1929, the following 1930s depression and the 2007–09 credit-turned-GFC have different origins, broad business historic commonalities created the circumstances that uncovered those two most notorious of twentieth-century business fraudsters, Ivar Kreuger and Bernie Madoff. There, the lesson of business history is that, whereas there is a distinct likelihood for contemporary events to parallel broadly what happened in the past, it is almost certain that there will be black swans hovering.

Unquestionably, reflection on past events provides insights. Sometimes they are *sobering* in so far as they enlighten regarding the possible consequences of the event in focus being perhaps more serious than first thought, sometimes *relieving* inasmuch as they reveal potentially less serious outcomes than feared. Frequently, previous successful and unsuccessful solutions, and more importantly, the reasoning underlying them, are exposed. No doubt that experience feeds the idea that historical research is a learning experience.

It is not surprising to us that in the current GFC there have been appeals to history, particularly to the events leading up to the 1930s Great Depression and recourse to the solutions presented in President Roosevelt's New Deal. Equally appealing is the recall of the circumstances and responses to the savings and loans crisis. Indeed, a possible upside of the GFC is the way in which it has created a setting in which past literature has resurfaced and new literature has emerged re-examining the circumstances of past events. For example, regarding the circumstances of previous crises, like the USA's *Panic of 1907* (Bruner and Carr, 2007), the origins of the Great Depression and Roosevelt's 'New Deal' solution in Powell's (2003) *FDR's Folly* and a more recent look in Parker's (2008) *The Great Crash*, analysis of their current counterparts in Ritholtz's (2009) *Bailout Nation*, the re-examination of mortgage business in the US through the 1980s savings and loans debacle to the sub-primes of the 2000s in Muolo and Padilla's (2008) *Chain of Blame*, focus on past and present bubbles in Baker's (2009) *Plunder and Blunder*, to the re-interest in Pecora's (1939) examination of 'banks behaving badly' in his *Wall Street Under Oath*.

These and their like have the potential to play an important part in the debate regarding both the causes of the past and present crises and the evaluations of remedies applied by past and present national governments.[3] Reflection on how that has been pursued is instructive. For, underpinning complaints that market participants and regulators have not learned much from history is the pervading idea that the function of history is to provide a template to resolve contemporary problems. Not perhaps so much because of perceived commonalities between the past and the present, as by virtue of the illustration in history of how things might better be thought through, problems *restated* and resolutions devised, rather than simply being recycled to recur some decades later.[4]

This focus indicates that as much as wanting the past to provide guides as to what to do in the present, examining the history of what are perceived to be similar events serves to expand our understanding of how their intermingling blurs both their likely causes and possible solutions. It also serves to provide a window during the excitement and confusions of the moment, on the complications long forgotten. That is, history provides a unique opportunity to *experience* insights into what we are otherwise denied. Historical enquiry is thus a privilege. Reconstructing the past is easier than predicting our present would have been for those preceding us. In this setting, historical enquiry becomes a motivating force in so far as it allows recall of matters that few had thought about for a long time and exposes facets of those events that had remained forgotten or hidden.[5]

Current historical enquiry thus facilitates insight into the business environment of the 1920s – it forces us to imagine the rampant investment-trust driven stock-jobbing environment of the time fuelling the 'conspicuous consumption' path (Veblen, 1899) and F. Scott Fitzgerald's 1925 *Great Gatsby* (describing the 1920s investment trust boom) to presage the momentous 1929 *Great Crash* and the 1930s Great Depression (Galbraith, 1967). Importantly, it has revived debate over whether Roosevelt's 'New Deal' pursued good or bad policies, and whether it exacerbated the situation and caused the 1930s depression to be so deep and so long. It has given new life to the debate between the respective economic policies of the Keynesians and (say) the Austrian School (Aspromourgos, 2009; Krugman, 2009).

In the mulling over, President Herbert Hoover has emerged as someone who, rather than 'doing nothing' is now accused of really being too interventionist (as indeed was alleged in Roosevelt's campaign material). There has also been renewed interest in fraudsters in the 1920s and 1930s flourishing in much the same economic environment. We are thrown into the bewilderment of the crash of Carlo Ponzi's money-making arbitraging with International Reply Coupons (Zuckoff, 2006); Kreuger's infamous international match combine's rise and fall and his financial innovations, possibly one of the forerunners of the derivative instruments surfacing in the GFC (Sparling, 1932, Shaplen, 1960, Partnoy, 2009); the crash of Samuel Insull's utility empire (McDonald, 1962; revisited by Wasik, 2006); President Hoover's belligerent attitude to commercial behaviour; Roosevelt's promise to invoke legislation – the Securities and the Securities Exchange Acts – to drive his New Deal remedies to inject 'truth in securities'; creation of the corporate regulatory fix-it, the Securities and Exchange Commission; Ferdinand Pecora's witch hunt on American bankers and his hounding of New York Stock Exchange chief Richard Whitney eventually into jail; and the US government's creation of Fannie Mae in 1938, and its conservatorship 70 years later.

14.3   HISTORY AND CAUSALITY

Debate over historical causation has a long pedigree. It may be that the above brief overview of those enquiring into matters like the GFC provides a window showing what has gone awry in the present climate by dissecting what went wrong more than 75 years ago. The idea no doubt is that whatever was the cause then might be similar to the cause now, and that *fixes* in the past might be appropriate therapies now.

More specifically, accounting generally provides an ideal laboratory setting to consider history and causality issues (see Walker and Edwards, 2009; Edwards et al., 2009). At a general level we can, for example, research and faithfully report when 'double entry' was first used, according to the available evidence; we can partially reconstruct the patterns of accounting practices 400 years ago by analysing the timing of variations in methods employed in the early Italian ledgers. We can form opinions as to when, for pricing and performance evaluation purposes, the practice of allocating common costs in particular ways seems to have emerged and when transfer pricing became a common practice. We can show whether a decision-making or accountability function underpinned double entry bookkeeping treatises around the time of and after the Renaissance. The details of those events and of others like them are an important element in obtaining an overall perspective of the development of accounting *practices* in general and of those noted in particular. But, changes in ideas precede deliberate changes in practice. If we are interested in the development of ideas, then the chronology of practices is a useful device for signalling approximately when changes in ideas may have occurred. Thus, the history of accounting practice also provides an insight into how business was conducted at various times.

It is critical to recognize that ideas are products of the settings in which they arise. Once firmly entrenched in the literature of a discipline, a mere chronology of ideas is insufficient to explain their persistence. Nor does a chronology facilitate insights into from where those ideas emerged. Descriptions of the contexts in which the ideas first arose and of those into which they subsequently have been transported are essential for a proper understanding of things. It is understandable that Roosevelt implemented essentially Keynesian remedies in 1933. It was the heyday of Keynes's promotion of his general theory (although the *General Theory* was not published until 1936). But, if the contexts (then and now) are different and the differences have not been detected, the propriety of current governmental intervention may properly be questioned.

In this regard we might well note that '*the* cause of an event is likely to be impossible to detect amongst the agglomeration of occurrences about the same time' (emphasis added, Clarke, 1980). If the *real cause* of an historical event was asked for, Walsh (1951) explained, 'the proper answer would be that there was no cause over and above the several causes given' (p. 197). At best, only numerous other events that may have contributed collectively to the one being examined can be identified. Though the idea of *accident* is not always embraced by historians – 'To the purist historian nothing is accidental' (Walsh, 1951, p.191), there is some cause for every occurrence. Accident has been used in discussions of the philosophy of history to describe events which 'represent a sequence of cause and effect interrupting . . . clashing with – the sequence with which the historian is primarily concerned' (Carr, 1964, p. 99). Nevertheless, so-called accidents, such as the shape of Cleopatra's nose, which is reputed to have infatuated Antony; the monkey bite that led to King Alexander's death; and the premature death of Lenin at 54, did influence the course of subsequent events and 'it is futile to spirit them away, or to pretend that in some way or other they had no effect' (Carr, 1964 p. 103). The meaning given to accidents here does not conflict with the one just noted. Accident is used here to describe the *combination* of elements implicated in particular events, their *pattern* and not the events themselves. It applies also to the patterns which created settings conducive to the development and the entrenchment of particular ideas in the accounting literature.

Curiously, at a time when the abovementioned Great Depression events were occurring, Oakeshott (1933) was observing that history should give 'a complete account of change . . . in history, *pour savoir les choses, il fait savoir le détail*' (p. 143), thereby restricting history to a narration of the facts. Later, in contrast, Melden (1952) asserted the opposite view that history written as 'a mere catalogue arranged in chronological order . . . would explain nothing because it included everything' (p. 24).

There is no need to further engage here in that dispute, except to observe that for the purpose of the following narrative, it serves us well to bear both in mind, for in relation to revisiting the Great Depression and the measures taken to root out its 'causes' and events contributing to them, both have their place. Knowledge of the facts, their time and place, is critical to understanding the vagaries of the time, their similarities and dissimilarities with those of the present. And, discriminating those that are the more important and the anecdotal insights into the now notorious actions of Ponzi, Insull, Kreuger and Pecora and Roosevelt's almost legendary willingness to jump at solutions, admittedly colours, but also informs, our appreciation of what we should look for in understanding the present.

14.4   THE CAUSE OF THE GFC

Recurring claims about, and examinations of, accounting's role in economic booms and busts have appeared over the past 75 years. Consider this extract from Gottfried Haberler's (1937) League of Nations commissioned work under the caption, 'Wrong accounting procedures'.

> There is also another factor which tends to increase the demand for consumer goods. Accounting is more or less based on the assumption of a constant value of money. Periods of higher inflation have shown that this tradition is very deep-rooted and that long and unpleasant periods are necessary to change habits. The effect is that durable production goods – like machinery and factory buildings – entered into cost accounting at their acquisition costs and are

depreciated on that basis. When prices rise this procedure is wrong. The higher replacement costs should be substituted for the acquisition costs. However, that does not take place, or only to an insufficient extent and only after other prices have risen considerably. That results in depreciation charges which are too low, *paper profits*[6] arise and the entrepreneur is tempted to increase his consumption. In such a case capital is treated as income. In other words: consumption exceeds current production. (emphasis added)

Again, most recently, several financial commentators have lamented accounting's lack of serviceability in calculating 'real profits'. But that concern has re-emerged in the context of 'fair value accounting', specifically that consequently banks having to 'mark-to-market' their financial assets is being perceived the cause of (or at least *a* major culprit in causing) the GFC. The mark-to-market requirement has emerged as the villain, allegedly responsible for the GFC, its associated *unexpected* collapses and governmental bailouts of financial institutions worldwide. This theme emerged initially at the height of the crisis in September and October 2008, then again in April 2009.[7] Mark-to-market required the banks and other financial intermediaries to write down their financial assets to their current market prices. As the prices fell even lower, reported prices increased the banks' reported losses and drove the prices down even further. In early 2009 the US banks were relieved of this requirement and allowed to ignore the implications of further reductions in the current market worths of their financial (toxic) assets.

The US Congress pressured the US corporate regulator, the Securities and Exchange Commission (SEC), to suspend the mark-to-market rule, rather than *tell it how it is*, declaring a form of historic cost information preferable. None have noted the irony that, in earlier periods of instability, it was historical cost accounting that was deemed the culprit.

Importantly, most of the arguments currently presented to apply strictly to mark-to-market were far older than those parading them. It is as if 'fair value accounting' was a recent device arising in a uniquely contemporary setting. If so, perhaps it could be viewed as the one incremental factor that was the cause of all things bad that began sometime in 2007 and continued throughout 2009. But such a suggestion is vacuous. As Haberler's quote suggests, the emerging debate lacks input from those who have studied similar crises and accounting's role over the last 75 years. But, the post-World War I hyper-inflation leading to the 1929 crash, the 1930s Depression era, the 1965–67 conglomerate boom/bust, Australia's 1967–70 mining boom and bust, the post-1980s savings and loans crisis period, and the UK's 1970s secondary banking property-related crisis were analogous economic settings; as also was the 1990s Japanese banking crisis with Japan's associated 'lost decade' of economic growth.

Those episodes reveal similarities to the present. And there are unquestionably dissimilarities – for instance, how the asset classes differed, such as real estate property, inventories, and even companies in the case of merger manias. Matters of similarity included: under-capitalization, excessive leverage, regulatory failures (sometimes due to deregulatory initiatives, whilst on other occasions to poorly considered regulatory interventions), greed, and so on. But, of course, the perennial similarity is that accounting is 'a' or 'the' problem. Yet, interestingly, the accepted or prescribed forms of accounting that applied at those times have differed. If today's fair value accounting is the problem – and, as Haberler and Schmidt's concerns imply that previously historical cost accounting was the problem – where do regulators and standards setters go next in their search for an ideal accounting? We have discussed this at some length in *Indecent Disclosure* (Clarke and Dean, 2007).

To better understand this we now examine in more detail the latest special pleading which has created outrage from some who regarded the independence of professional standards setters as being eroded.[8] But this concern proved ineffective. On 9 April 2009 the Financial Accounting Standards Board (FASB) 'caved-in' to pressure, issuing FAS Financial Staff Position (FSP) 157-4 ('Determining fair value when the volume and level of activity for the asset or liability have significantly decreased and identifying transactions that are not orderly'), after allowing only about a week for submissions. Most importantly, approximately 360 submissions were received and the decision to suspend mark-to-market accounting contrasted to what was proposed in more than half of them. One can only speculate on the implications for standards setters and users of this sorry saga considering accounting measurement matters within the ongoing accounting conceptual framework deliberations of the International Accounting Standards Board and the Financial Accounting Standards Board.

The April 2009 FSP changes to FASB 157, 'Fair value measurement', which provides greater flexibility to the banks regarding how they use internally generated mark-to-market models to determine the reported current worth of their toxic assets, are contestable on many grounds.[9] The changes have relieved banks of any semblance of serious, verifiable, compliance with the mark-to-market rule. They sanction further mischief in accounts – facilitating the ultimate in untrue and unfair disclosures. US banks now find it easier to leave non-marketable toxic financial assets in their balance sheets at considerably more than they could fetch in the market. And where a market does not exist, more-flexible guidelines were anticipated regarding the models with which to 'invent' a non-existing price. Greater flexibility is also predicted for classifying financial assets

– whether to be *held to maturity* or *available for sale*. It is the latter class that attracted the 'mark-to-market' valuations. But now they do so with greater flexibility regarding the models to invent a number where the market is 'thin' (so-called 'distressed'), or where no market exists.

To what extent misleading balance sheets can other than mislead the market further, is anyone's guess. As noted; it is true, the mark-to-market requirement has been a popular whipping-boy, the alleged cause of the present crisis. Having to mark down many assets is said to have sapped confidence in the market. Undeniably it has informed the market's view of those assets' declining worth. Without mark-to-market (MtM) valuations many financial assets were reported as being worth more than they could fetch in the market. Unadjusted book values would be far greater than the amounts the banks' assets could contribute toward discharging their financial obligations, keep them solvent, contribute to their incomes and the like. Roosevelt's cry in 1933 for 'truth in securities' has certainly been betrayed.

Being members of the Sydney School of accounting we support the *current exit price* (and not the mark-to-market model) version of the mark-to-market basis for asset valuation embodied in some professional standards. The objective of accounting (at least for those of the Sydney School) is to best *tell it as it is*, never mind what managers say today that they intend to do with particular assets in the future; more important is what they can do financially. For the public at large to be informed, companies need to disclose serviceable indications of their current financial positions.

There is something positive to emerge from the latest brouhaha. The ongoing mark-to-market deliberations give standards setters an opportunity to rile against political pressure. It is time that business special pleading is rejected – this suggestion is positively avowed by the profession in more recent discussion papers and as reported in a recent international report by the Financial Crisis Advisory Group (July, 2009) which noted: 'We have become increasingly concerned about the excessive pressure placed on the two boards [IASB, FASB in April 2009] to make rapid, piecemeal, uncoordinated and prescribed changes to standards outside of their normal due process procedures'.[10]

The GFC thus pointedly provides an opportunity to reconsider the need for accounting data to comply with the canons of measurement – codified in the profession's conceptual framework project on measurement. We do not suggest that the result of applying such canons will result in a *true*, unique profit figure. But it will result in an accounting technology attempting (at least) to measure things as rigorously as they are measured in the physical sciences. The end result undoubtedly will have its errors. But they will be errors in estimation. This contrasts with what some commentators are saying about the current figures – that they are at the discretion of management as the current MtM prescription is written – producing 'dodgy numbers, gimmicky figures'.[11]

14.4.1   Mark-to-market: A Misused Resurrection of a Past Debate

History has been a curious victim in the GFC. For, although the role that FVA accounting (in particular its mark-to-market form) has played in the financial fallout is a much debated issue (see above), the ample and readily accessible history of fair value accounting has been a notable absentee. Whereas the arguments for and against the mark-to-market technique mirror what was said in the past, virtually no recourse is made to past discourse. It is unclear whether that is because of ignorance of a vast body of literature, the circumstances in which it arose, evidence upon which it drew and the arguments and counter-arguments it paraded, or whether all that has been dismissed out of hand. Importantly, whatever the reason, a valuable resource has been passed by.

It is more than 110 years since the first definitive statement of the genesis of the notion of the 'financial fair value' of assets, namely in the 1898 *Smyth v. Ames* judgment. US utility prices were set periodically to ensure a pre-determined fair rate-of-return (RoR) on the fair value of the assets employed. Critical to that was agreement on the 'fair value rate base' denominator for the RoR calculation used to set utility prices. Once settled it was an easy matter then to determine unit prices by dividing the revenues (net of the agreed expenses) by the units to be produced.

Importantly, especially in the current GFC and for understanding better the role of accounting, *Smyth v. Ames* introduced the concept of fair value as a generic value to be used for a specific pricing purpose. Those historical circumstances are most important for any subsequent interpretation. For, as *Smyth v. Ames* was heard after a sustained period of falling prices (from the end of the 1860s – see Sweeney, 1936), the parties understandably contested in accord with tradition: the consumer bodies argued in favour of a rate base that mainly reflected lower prices (current costs) and the (mostly) privately owned utility (often monopoly) companies argued for it to be more dependent upon historical (higher) costs. The fair value rate base was offered as an indication that the fair value metric was to hit upon and include whatever monetary amount was 'fair and reasonable' to both operators and consumers according to the circumstances of the time. The court would be the adjudicator.

As price levels changed frequently, rate-base cases were numerous.

Most of the US accounting literature for the first three decades of the twentieth century addressed those rate-base calculations within what was described as the 'Appreciation' debates, especially relevant to the private sector where asset revaluations were rife (Fabricant, 1936). It was in this setting that the notion of fair value 'drifted' from its special-purpose non-adaptive utility company setting into the asset valuation debate for ordinary, adaptable private sector companies. Consistent with the trend for the utilities to argue in the prevailing inflationary setting that current replacement price and reproduction cost should dominate determination of the fair value rate base, replacement price and reproduction cost assumed the mantle of being synonyms. The distinction between the special circumstances of the non-adaptable utilities and the adaptable ordinary companies was subsumed (Clarke, 1982).[12]

Later the problems of accounting for price and price level changes re-emerged universally in the context of the increased prices during the 1950s, 1960s and the rampant inflation in the mid-1970s following the 1973 'oil spike' and the aftermath of the freeing up of currencies (no longer being pegged to the Gold Standard). Inflation was the focus; appropriate levels of taxes and appropriate costs for pricing purposes were to the fore. But the episode refocused attention on matters that had first arisen as a specific accounting focus during the period of the German hyperinflation and similar major spikes in price levels in many European countries following World War I.[13] Researchers sought a better understanding of the factors that had influenced the 1920s European business economists' accounting proposals in the light of the economic vicissitudes of the 1921–23 hyperinflation.[14] This was particularly so with the re-emergence of many of those proposals in the Anglo-American inflation accounting literature during the late 1960s to the mid-1980s. In a peculiar coincidence it brought leading scholars into contact and placed them on similar paths of enquiry to many in the 'Sydney School' (for example, Clarke, 1976; Mattessich, 1982, 1984; Tweedie and Whittington, 1984; Dean and Clarke, 1986; Clarke and Dean, 1989a). Thus, whereas it emerged as a consequence, not as a deliberate primary path of enquiry, accounting measurement emerged as a contiguous development.

In this literature, the research objective of many was to provide public policy inputs into lengthy private (and later public) sector debates on the accounting for price and price-level changes during the 1970s and 1980s. Inflation peaked in Anglo-American countries in the mid-1970s at around 25 per cent. Of course some countries experienced much higher levels (Israel, Brazil, Mexico, and so on). More generally, the historical inquiries were to glean a better understanding of the antecedents of alternative systems of accounting, particularly indexed historical cost accounting and current value accounting.[15]

Against that background, the mark-to-market debate on the current GFC and accounting is familiar territory: the financial sector post-2000 seemed quite happy to argue for fair value accounting when prices were rising, collateral securing lending was rising and hence the amount of borrowings could be justified. This was especially pertinent to securitization growth in the post-9/11 period. International standards setters were proposing market prices for those financial instruments, and the finance sector were going along for the ride. But after events started to sour in early 2007, and nosedived after July/August 2007, the special pleading of the financial sector (and from many of their industrial clients) changed. The argument emerged that the market is not to be trusted; the prevailing claim now is that mark-to-market exacerbates economic cycles and is an inappropriate measure when markets are illiquid. The pressure built and it was suspended in April 2009. The politicization of accounting is trumped as an unbiased technology; that is, a technology *to tell it as it is*, even if it hurts.

14.5   PERORATION: A VICTIM OF INCONVENIENCE

History reveals how fair value ideas 'drifted' over time from one setting to another – in the 1920s from the utility rate-base setting context to the accounting by non-utility public companies, later in the 1960s and 1970s from the private sector company setting to the public setting of accounting for inflation, and more recently into the accounting for financial assets held according to intended disposal criteria. Frequently this vacillation has been without proper regard for the idiosyncrasies of each setting, without proper reference to the detailed debate on the matter that has preceded it. Further, *that* history shows how this aspect of accounting became politicized – with interested parties' special pleading – undeterred by circumstances, producing pragmatism at the expense of logical and consistent reasoning. That background not only helps to inculcate an understanding of the origins of the mark-to-market (fair value) accounting dispute, but also how notions of such have been exploited by special interest groups using arguments that differ from one another (for the most part) only in respect of time and place.

The history of accounting's fair value concept illustrates how ideas mutate. In the case of fair value, this is from the basis for a specific purpose (utility rate regulation, then ordinary pricing, and later taxation) calculation into a general application in accounting statements of financial position and financial performance. The current GFC has nurtured further mutation in the discourse of the mark-to-market dispute. What originally arose in an attempt to disclose a present financial state is being denied by many in the name of the alleged virtue of hiding it. Doing so contradicts what history tells us has been the focus from when fair value accidentally 'drifted' into the accounting for adaptive companies.

The above discussion also highlights historical enquiry, aptly showing (especially in respect of this new adoption) how accounting has become politicized – the victim of interested parties' special pleading, corrupting accounting technology primarily because it is inconvenient to *tell it how it is*.

NOTES

1. In a postgraduate finance seminar at Munich University in November 2008 Robert Merton suggested there was little evidence that a better understanding of history (such as determining if there were any similarities to the 1986–95 savings and loans crisis) would assist in unravelling what had occurred in the 2007–08 credit crisis, morphing into the 2008–09 GFC.
2. Similar circumstances underpinned Australia's unexpected November 1960 government-imposed 'credit squeeze' which caused many in the white goods industry to fail, and a decade later, many Australian stockbrokers virtually overnight could not raise short-term funding, as the short-term money market had 'frozen'. The crisis was only aborted when John Gorton hastily convened a meeting in the Kirribilli House. That meeting of business leaders resulted in the government intervention of liquidity to the short-term money market. Such affairs again highlight that business history has many useful insights about supposedly unexpected events.
3. Whilst there are many references one could cite, Paul Krugman's *Return to Depression Economics and the Crisis of 2008* (2008) and George Cooper's *The Origin of Financial Crises* (2008) will suffice.
4. In the accounting literature a leading critic, Robert Sterling, has long argued this (1975, 1979).
5. Current students of business disciplines ought to 'count their blessings' that they are studying during the GFC for they have a unique opportunity to *experience* simultaneously the reliving and analysis of the 1930s Great Depression, its events and characters.
6. The footnote in Gottfried Haberler (1937, p. 55) notes: 'These paper or fictitious profits [*Scheingewinne*] are also capable of enhancing the cumulative power of the upswing because they encourage creditors and debtors to borrow and to lend more. They promote an optimistic mood which is predominant during the upswing and as a result credit expansion is likely to be accelerated. This phenomenon is exactly reversed in the downswing of the cycle.' See F. Schmidt (1927), who tried to build up a complete theory of business cycles on this factor.
7. Financial Crisis Advisory Group (2009).
8. Investors Technical Advisory Committee (2009); Herz (2009).
9. This subsection is based partly on an *Opinion* contribution by Graeme Dean and Frank Clarke in *The Australian Financial Review* (2009, p. 55).
10. Financial Crisis Advisory Group (2009), p. 15, which was also reported in F. Norris (2009, p. 18). Further, press headlines in many countries suggest the political pressure

persists – and it appears now that the pleading has begun from the manufacturers as well as from within the financial sector – see Kara Scannell (2009).

11. Such phrases appear in submissions to FASB FSP-157-e exposure draft (resulting in FAS FSP 157-4), primarily by users of accounting data (www.fasb.org.).

12. Utility companies usually were constrained as to what they could do: generally, they were formed with the privilege (often entailing a monopoly) for the limited express purpose to produce continuously the particular utility service (electricity, gas, water services, etc.) of a specified quality and regularity, within a regulated price regime that guaranteed a specified RoR on the assets employed. In those respects they differed considerably from the ordinary companies able to engage in virtually any business falling within the boundaries of usually wide descriptions of their purposes. The distinction between the ordinary companies and the utilities companies is aptly illustrated by the strict control over how the utilities were subjected to a rigid accounting using historical cost valuations and structured to conform to a specified chart of accounts.

13. Sweeney (1936) provides many instances of this.

14. Holtfrerich (1986) is a comprehensive account of the German hyperinflation peaking in November 1923.

15. This entailed numerous lengthy translations by the authors coupled to analyses of some early 1920s German and Dutch accounting literature. Specifically, original works of the leading German and Dutch authorities, Fritz Schmidt and Theodor Limperg, were examined. Many of those works had their first exposure in the Anglo-American accounting literature (see Clarke, 1976; 1982; Dean and Clarke, 1986; Clarke and Dean, 1989b; 1990; Clarke Dean and Graves, 1990; and Graves, Clarke and Dean, 1989). Such enquiry entailed the resurrection of the musings of earlier scholars, generally long-forgotten, exiled from the contemporary accounting literature. Schmidt and Limperg re-emerged as leading protagonists regarding how to account for price-level changes (see Clarke and Dean, 1992 and a chapter on the leading 1920s German *Betriebswirtschafstlehre* theorist, Fritz Schmidt in Dick Edwards' *Twentieth Century Accounting Thinkers*, 1994).

REFERENCES

Aspromourgos, T. (2009), 'Should Keynes have a seat at the G-20 table?', *Australian Financial Review*, 28–29 March.

Baker, D. (2009), *Plunder and Blunder: The Rise and Fall of the Bubble Economy*, Sausalito, CA: Poli Point Press.

Bruner, R.F. and S.D. Carr (2007), *The Panic of 1907: Lessons Learned from the Market's Perfect Storm*, Hoboken, NJ: John Wiley and Sons.

Carr, E.H. (1964), *What is History?*, London: Penguin.

Clarke, F. (1976), 'A closer look at Sweeney's stabilized accounting proposals', *Accounting and Business Research*, Autumn, pp. 264–75.

Clarke, F. (1980), 'Inflation accounting and the accidents of history', *Abacus*, 16(2), December, 79–99.

Clarke, F. (1982), *The Tangled Web of Price Variation Accounting*, New York: Garland Publishing Inc., 1982. revision of PhD thesis, 'Accounting and the price variation problem: an examination of the development of the ideas underlying the inflation accounting prescriptions issued by the professional accountancy bodies in Australia, Canada, New Zealand, South Africa, the United Kingdom and the United States; to 1980', The University of Sydney, pp. xiv + 444; reproduced in The University of Sydney, *Accounting Classics Series*, 2006.

Clarke, F. and G. Dean (1989a), 'Conjectures on the European influences on Sweeney's stabilized accounting', *Accounting and Business Research*, Autumn, pp. 291–304.

Clarke, F. and G. Dean (1989b), 'Graves on Mahlberg: whither Sweeney and Schmidt's *Tageswirtbilanz*', *The Accounting Historians Journal*, Summer, pp. 101–109.

Clarke, F. and G. Dean (1990), *Limperg and Schmidt: Bedrijfseconomie or Betriebswirtschaft?*, New York: Garland Publishing Inc.

Clarke, F. and G. Dean (1992), 'The views of Limperg and Schmidt discovering patterns and identifying differences from a chaotic literature: pattern, chaos and order', *International Journal of Accounting and Education*, **27**, 287–309.

Clarke, F. and G. Dean (2007), *Indecent Disclosure: Gilding the Corporate Lily*, Cambridge: Cambridge University Press.

Clarke, F. and G. Dean (2009), 'Ray Chambers and Ernest Weinwurm: scholars in unison: a nurturing of mutual convictions on measurement in accounting', *Working Paper*, April.

Clarke, F., G. Dean and F. Graves (1990), *Replacement Costs for Cost Accumulation and Pricing: Accounting Reform in Post World War I Germany*, New York: Garland Publishing Inc.

Cooper, G. (2008), *The Origin of Financial Crises*, New York: Vintage.

Dean, G. and F. Clarke (1986), 'Schmidt's *Betriebswirtschaft* Theory', *Abacus*, September, pp. 65–102.

Dean, G. and F. Clarke (2009), 'Toxic plan is nothing but humbug', *The Australian Financial Review*, 14 April, p. 55.

Edwards, R. J. (1994), *Twentieth Century Accounting Thinkers*, London: Routledge.

Edwards, R.J., F. Clarke and G. Dean (2009), 'Merchants' accounts, performance assessment and decision making in mercantilist Britain', *Accounting, Organizations and Society*, June, pp. 551–70.

Fabricant, S. (1936), 'Revaluations of fixed assets, 1925–1934', *Bulletin 62*, National Bureau of Economic Research.

Ferguson, N. (2008), *The Ascent of Money: A Financial History of the World*, London: Allen Lane.

Financial Crisis Advisory Group (2009), 'Report of the financial crisis advisory group', 28 July.

Galbraith, J.K. (1967), *The Great Crash*, London: Penguin.

Graves, F., F. Clarke and G. Dean (1989), *Schmalenbach's Dynamic Accounting*, New York: Garland Publishing Inc.

Haberler, G. (1937), *Prosperity and Depression*, Geneva: League of Nations.

Holtfrerich, C.-L. (1986), *The German Inflation 1914–1923*, Berlin and New York: Walter de Gruyter.

Herz, R. (2009), 'History doesn't repeat itself, people repeat history: front-line thoughts and observations on creating a sounder financial system', address to National Press Club, 26 June.

Investors Technical Advisory Committee (2009), Letter to Mr John J. Brennan, Chairman, *FASB*, 15 June.

Keynes, J.M. (1936), *The General Theory of Employment, Interest and Money*, London: Macmillan.

Krugman, P. (2008), *Return to Depression Economics and the Crisis of 2008*, London: Penguin.

Krugman (2009), *NY Times,* September.

Lawson, T. (1905), *Frenzied Finance: The Crime of Amalgamated*, The Rydgway Thayer Company.

Mattessich, R. (1982), 'On the evolution of inflation accounting: with a comparison of seven major models', *Economia Aziendale*.

Mattessich, R. (1984), 'Fritz Schmidt (1982–1950) and his pioneering work of current value accounting in comparison to Edwards and Bell's theory', *Proceedings of the Fourth International Congress of Accounting Historians*, Editrice, Pisa.

McDonald, F. (1962), *Insull*, Chicago: University of Chicago Press.

Melden, A.I. (1952), 'Historical objectivity, a "noble dream"', *Journal of General Education*, October.

Muolo, P. and M. Padilla (2008), *Chain of Blame*, Hoboken, NJ: John Wiley and Sons.

Norris, F. (2009), 'Too many cooks spoil the broth', *Australian Financial Review*, 29 July p. 18.

Oakeshott, M. (1933), *Experience and its Modes*, Cambridge: Cambridge University Press.

Parker, S. (2008), *The Great Crash: How the Stock Market Crash of 1929 Plunged the World into Depression*, Piatkus.

Partnoy, F. (2009), *The Match King: Ivar Krueger, the Financial Genius behind a Century of Wall Street Scandals*, New York: Public Affairs.

Pecora, F. (1939), *Wall Street Under Oath: The Story of our Modern Money Changers*, New York: The Crest Press.

Powell, J. (2003), *FDR's Folly*, New York: Random House.

Ritholtz, B. (2009), *Bailout Nation*, Hoboken, NJ: John Wiley and Sons.

Scannell, Kara (2009), 'Big companies go to Washington to fight regulators on fancy derivatives', *Wall Street Journal*, 10 July.

Schmidt, F. (1927), *Die Industriekonjunktur – ein Rechenfehler* [Business Cycles in Industry – A Miscalculation], Berlin and Vienna.

Shaplen, R. (1960), *Kreuger: Genius and Swindler*, New York: Alfred A. Knopf.

Sparling, E. (1932), *Kreuger's Billion Dollar Bubble*, New York: Greenberg.

Sterling, R. (1975), 'Relevant financial reporting in an age of price changes', *Journal of Accountancy*, February, pp. 42–51.

Sterling, R. (1979), *Toward a Science of Accounting*, Houston: Scholars Book.

Sweeney, H. (1936), *Stabilized Accounting*, New York: Harper & Brothers.

Taleb, N.N. (2007), *The Black Swan: The Impact of the Highly Improbable*, London: Penguin.

Taleb, N.N. and M. Spitznagel (2009), 'Time to tackle the real evil: too much debt', *Financial Times*, 13 July.

Tweedie, D. and G. Whittington (1984), *The Debate on Inflation Accounting*, Cambridge: Cambridge University Press.

Veblen, T. (1899), *The Theory of the Leisure Class: An Economic Study in the Evolution of Institutions*, Macmillan.

Walsh, W.H. (1951), *An Introduction to the Philosophy of History*, Hutchison of London.

Walker, S. and R.J. Edwards (2009), *Compendium on Accounting*, London: Routledge.

Wasik, J. (2006), *The Merchant of Power*, New York: Palgrave Macmillan.

Zuckoff, M. (2006), *Ponzi's Scheme: True Story of a Financial Legend*, London: Random House.

Index

Accounting issues 145
AIG 4, 27, 30
American Law Institute
    131
APRA 9, 132, 147, 157
Ariff, M., vii, 1, 5, 33
Asset 15
Asian Finance Group 89
Audit firms 144

Bailout 202–203
Ballantine, H. 131
Bank deposits 46, 56
Banking 21, 31
Barclays Bank 26
Basel 44, 45, 47, 56, 59, 134, 153, 154,
    157, 175
BCRS 4
Bear Stearns 4, 33–4
Bernanke, Ben 3, 33, 35
Big bang 132
Big banks 5
Bigness 53
BISTRO xii
Black Swans 214
BNP Paribas 4
Board of directors 29–31, 133
    Composition 130
    Electronic vote 166
    Market 113, 115
    Multinational 51
    Too-big-to-fail 53
Boeing 40
Bond, Melisa vii, 5, 67
Brown, Gordon 2
Breton Woods 11
Bubble 2, 5, 15, 31, 79, 105, 113, 115,
    217
Buchanan, James 89
Buckley, Ross vii, 188
Budget 113

Buffett, Warren 5
Bush, George, President 24
Byrnes, Wayne vii, 147

Cadbury Report 132
Callaghan, James 102
Calomiris, C.W. 18
Capital loss 5
Capital 33, 179–80
    Accord 47
    Adequacy requirement 57, 58, 61,
        133
    Bank 44, 45, 48, 54, 150
    Canadian banks 58
    Contingent 56
    Hybrid 172
    International flow of 95
    Provisioning 151
    Quality of 60–61
    Regulatory 155
    Requirement 51–53
Carmichael, J. viii, 168
Cassel 19
Cause 21, 230
CDO xii, 5, 15, 17, 21, 29, 30
Chase Manhattan 4
Chiang Mai Initiative 120
China-bashing 36
Chrysler 5
Clarke, F. vii, 10
Clinton, Bill, President 24
Commodity exports 107
Conflict of interest 165
Consensus-building 147
Contagion 2, 18, 31
Cost
    Consequences 104, 119
    Costs 5
    Economic 111
    Financial 115
    Losses 105

NPL 115
Output loss 111
Sub-prime 105
Credit 23, 29, 36
Credit splurge 17
Credit worthiness 101
Crisis
    Deepen 194
    Displacement 31
    Genesis 21
    Origin 5, 15, 30
    Panic 18, 32
    Post-crisis 5, 56
    Revulsion 31
    Timeline 1, 4, 15
Currency
    Appreciation 36
    Depreciation 39
    Float 40
    Manipulation 38
    Mismatch 37, 40
    Parity 149
    Undervalued 36
    Yuan–dollar 40–42

Davis, Kevin vii, 1, 5, 44
Dean, Graeme vii, 10
Debt 33
    Crisis and 191
    Public 93
Debtors and creditors 189
Depositors 26
Derivatives 21, 27, 54
Diplock, Jane vii, 10, 139
Disclosures 144
Dodd–Frank Wall Street Act 34, 136
Due diligence 144
Duty and standard of care 131
Dynamic provisioning 180

Economic integration 84
Emerging countries 107
Equity injection 56
Equity-to-asset ratio 52, 54
European Union 171
Evans, Bill 11
Excess 94

Fair value accounting 214, 222
Fannie Mae 4

Farrar, John ix, 1, 127
FASB 145
FDI 78
Fed, Federal Reserve 2, 19, 21, 169
Fels, Allan ix, 10, 161
Financial conglomerate 169
Financial liberalisation 2
Financial literacy 121
Financial system 25
Fiscal
    Policy 89
    Structure 89, 100
    Tax 89
    Turnaround 94
Fisher 19, 92
Flexible Credit Line 207
Fool's gold 27
Foreclosures 3, 23
Freddie Mac 4
Fry 2
FSA 170
FSB 54, 141, 152
FTSE 27
Fundamentals 19

G-10 nations 47
G-20 nations xii, 10, 35, 113, 135,
    205
Gaston, Noel ix, 5, 67
Geithner, Timothy 40
General Motors 5
Glass–Steagall Act 25
Global crisis 4
Global financial crisis x, 10–11, 27,
    44, 51, 67, 89, 108, 139, 148,
    162
Global impact of GFC 106
Globalisation matters 77
Globalised financial system 38
Governance 127
    And banks 129-31
    And board composition 129
    Corporate 127, 146
    Financial structure 127
    Industry 127
    Review 130
    UK review of 130
Gramm–Leach–Bliley Act 25
Great Recession 102
Greenspan, Alan 24, 27, 31, 52

Harrod–Domar 19
Hedge funds 143
   Overseas 145
Hicks 92
High returns 3, 24
History ignored 214, 226
Hoover, Herbert, President 130

IFRS 145
IMF 2, 17, 22, 34, 78, 99, 188–208
Incomplete contracts 19
International financial system 201
Investor vigilance 27
IOSCO 9, 140, 145

JP Morgan 35

Kaufman, George 46
Keynesian 40
   Delusion 101
   General Theory 91, 219
   Liquidity 131
   Problem with 91
Khalid, Ahmad x, 8, 33, 104
King 7
King Canute 148, 153, 157
KOF index 77
Kreuger, Ivar 216
Krugman, Paul 5, 20

Labour
   Adaptable market 90
   Casualisation of 67
   Debt and 79
   Exposure 75
   Fundamentals 68
   And global factors 69
   Market deregulation 67
   Market institution 81
   Market 67
   Productivity 82
   Unemployment in OECD 72, 105
   Unemployment 67, 71
   And US trade 69, 85
Lake Wobegon effect 164
Lehman Brothers 4, 20, 52, 171
Lending rates 116
Leverage ratio 57–58
   see also equity-to-asset ratio
Linked products 3

Liquidity 132
   Coverage ratio 175–9
Lobbyists xii, 2, 24

MacKinnon, Ron x, xii, 2, 8, 36, 89
Madoff, Bernie 216
Makin, Tony x, 1, 89
Mark-to-market 223
   Bank stock and 222-6
   Fallout 224
   Smyth vs Ames 224
   vs historical cost 223
Merrill Lynch 5
Minsky, Hyman 15
MMOU 141
Monetary vs fiscal 90

New Century Finance 4, 22
Nixon, Richard, President 24
Non-performing loans 30, 115, 117
Northern Rock 4

Obama, Barack, President 20, 89
Off-balance sheet 33, 48
Remittances 111

Panic 22–3
Payment system 5
Pension funds 41
People's Bank of China 36
P-I-I-I-G-S 73
Policy 8
Poverty reduction 198
Prescott, James 89
Productivity Commission 162
Protectionism 38
Prudential standards 133, 150

Rating, internal 47
Rating, voodoo science 27
RBA 149
Reagan, Ronald, President 24
Reform 1, 2, 9, 10, 35, 75, 120, 137,
      147–58, 168, 171, 174, 186, 188–
      90, 196, 200, 205, 206, 208
Regulation of financial sector 44
Regulation, light-touch 2
Regulatory architecture 168
Regulatory forgiveness 27
Regulatory framework xii

Regulatory tools 172
Regulatory weakening 27, 32
Remuneration 134, 161–7
  Committee 164
  Company size 163
  Incentives 135
  Report 165
  And shareholders 165
  Standards 135
  Structures 152
  UK review 125
Remuneration arrangement 150
Rescue 22
Reserve proposals 174–80
Reserve, statutory 25
Reverse convertible debentures 54
Risk 20, 21, 27, 31, 33, 34, 44, 51, 58,
  131, 134, 173
risk, systematic 142
Risk-adjusted 59
Risk-weighted capital 58, 59, 179
ROE 182, 185
Roosevelt, Franklin D., President 223

Schemer, Charles 38
Securitisation 27
Shareholder equity 47

Shaw 2
Signalling effect 44
Socialization of private debt 195
Squam Lake Group 53, 55
Stiglitz, J. 5
Stimulus 3, 8, 9, 15, 118
Stock market crash 4
SVC 26
Symbiotic 15, 27, 105
Systematically 151
Systematic risk 142

TARP 52
Trade surplus, balance 41, 42
Trading vs banking books 173
Tulip Mania 1637 17, 20

UBS 4, 182

VAR, value at risk 51, 57

Wall Street 5, 20, 21, 168, 169
Wells–Krugman 79
World Bank 57
WTO 25, 38

Z-scores 134